£6·00

A Practical Guide to
PRUNING

A PRACTICAL GUIDE TO
PRUNING

PETER McHOY

**Eagle
Editions**

A QUANTUM BOOK

Published by Eagle Editions Ltd
11 Heathfield
Royston
Hertfordshire SG8 5BW

Copyright ©MCMXCIII Quarto Publishing plc.

This edition printed 2001

ISBN 1-86160-397-5

QUMPRB

This book is produced by
Quantum Publishing
6 Blundell Street
London N7 9BH

Printed in Singapore by
Star Standard Industries (Pte) Ltd

CONTENTS

PRUNING ESSENTIALS

Good pruning brings substantial rewards in the form of bigger and better plants, higher fruit yields and well-shaped trees and hedges. Understanding the effect of pruning on plant growth is especially useful when you are trying to shape a plant or restrict its size. This chapter explains why pruning works and shows you how to put the theory into practice.

Suitable tools make pruning easier and give better results. If you intend to do a lot of pruning it is worth investing in good tools that are comfortable to use and will do the job efficiently. This chapter will help you to choose the most appropriate secateurs, pruners or saw for the jobs in your garden.

1

HOW TO USE
THIS BOOK

THIS BOOK will tell you how to prune the trees, shrubs, climbers, hedges and fruit that you are likely to grow in your garden. If you want to prune a particular tree, climber or shrub, look it up in the A – Z list of ornamental plants which will then guide you to the appropriate pruning technique as well as giving other handy tips and general advice. The A – Z list is arranged by Latin names so if you only have the common name, or can't find a Latin name listed, look in the Index for synonyms. If you are interested in general pruning for a shrub not in the book, turn to Chapter Two which will give you a step-by-step guide through all the basic pruning methods.

How the book is arranged
The first chapter – *Pruning Essentials* – explains why pruning works, and discusses the tools and equipment that you will find useful. Armed with this information, you will be able to tackle most pruning jobs with more confidence.

Basic Techniques (Chapter Two) explains how to prune, using the nine techniques that will cover most of the shrubs that you are likely to grow in your garden. This chapter also looks at how to deal with general problems.

The *A – Z of Ornamental Plants* (Chapter Three), is an extensive listing of popular trees, shrubs and climbers. This section will recommend one of the pruning techniques explained in Chapter Two, and give specific advice for individual plants. It also tells you when to prune according to season rather than months which is often

more helpful – see page 11. Where a technique is specific to one type of plant, such as clematis or roses, you will find the 'how-to' illustrations and instructions within the entry itself.

Broadleaved trees and conifers need little routine pruning once established (major work on a large tree is best done by a tree surgeon anyway), but early pruning and training can help prevent later problems. *Pruning and Training Trees* (Chapter Four) explains what you can do to get your trees off to a good start and how to deal with problems that may arise. It also explains how to train trees and shrubs on a wall.

Hedges need regular pruning or clipping to retain a good shape, and *Maintaining Hedges* (Chapter Five) will tell you the best time to do this, with hints and advice on cutting and shaping your hedge.

Pruning is often critical for fruit trees, and the size and quality of the crop may depend on it. *Pruning and Training Fruit* (Chapter Six) shows you how to make sense of the different methods of pruning and training for all the popular fruits. In this section specific months are given for pruning rather than seasons, as fruit pruning requires more exact timing for maximum yields.

Technical terms have been kept to a minimum, but if you come across a word that you do not understand you should find an explanation in the *Glossary* on page 232.

Over the next few pages we give a more detailed look at Chapters Two and Three to help you familiarise yourself with how the information is presented.

BASIC TECHNIQUES
(Chapter Two)

TECHNIQUE

1

CLIPPING TO SHAPE

IF YOU WANT to grow shrubs such as box (*Buxus sempervirens*) and *Berberis darwinii* perhaps in a lawn or container, they will look better if regularly clipped
  Plants listed on page 186 as suitable for formal hedges generally respond well to this kind of shaping.

Before pruning
Many evergreens can be clipped to a formal shape.

26

ABOUT THE TECHNIQUE
Which type of plant the technique is suitable for, and advice on when to prune. *But always check the A – Z of Ornamental Plants in Chapter Three for advice about specific plants.*

BEFORE
What the plant may look like before you prune, so that you can compare with the 'after pruning' photograph.

PRUNING
Easy-to-follow instructions.

Technique 1

Pruning
● Clip small-leaved plants such as box with shears (or a hedgetrimmer if the plant is large). For large-leaved plants such as spotted laurel (*Aucuba japonica*), use secateurs as shears can damage leaves which then turn brown and die.

● If trimming in spring only remove growth produced the previous year. Remove the current year's growth if clipping from mid-summer onwards.

● Clip back newest growth without cutting into old wood if possible.

● A trim like this will leave the plant looking tidy for another year. Once you start this kind of shaping it is likely to be required at least annually.

Newest growth
Older growth
Old wood

Newest growth
Older growth
Newest growth
Older growth

After pruning

27

DIAGRAM
An illustration that shows you where to aim for when pruning.

DETAIL
Detailed photograph shows you where to cut.

AFTER
What the plant will look like after pruning, so you know what to expect.

BUXUS

BOX

Box, which is widely used for hedging

A–Z OF ORNAMENTAL PLANTS
(Chapter Three)

COMMON NAMES
Widely used common names are given after the Latin name. If you know only the common name, look the plant up in the index to find the Latin equivalent.

(see Chapter Five, page 184) and topiary, is very amenable to pruning: just clip it to shape with shears (Technique 1). As a border shrub,

CROSS–REFERENCES
Cross-references to other chapters, such as Maintaining Hedges, or to general advice for the plant, or to the appropriate pruning method in the Basic Techniques chapter.

BUPLEURUM

Bupleurum fruticosum is the only species hardy enough to grow permanently outside in Britain.

It flourishes in mild seaside areas and also does well on chalk. No routine pruning is required, but you can clip the bush to shape (Technique 1) if it begins to grow too large. To encourage new growth when it begins to look neglected, cut out one stem in three (Technique 5).

Because the plant is not dependably hardy in cold areas it is sometimes grown as a wall shrub. In time it will become a tangle of twiggy wood if left unpruned, and the branches may eventually trail on the ground. To regenerate an old bush like this, cut it down to within 5–10cm (2–4in) of the ground in mid- or late spring. It should make plenty of new growth by the autumn, but you will lose the flowers for a season.

BUXUS

BOX

Box, which is widely used for hedging (see Chapter Five, page 184) and topiary, is very amenable to pruning: just clip it to shape with shears (Technique 1). As a border shrub, however, it should not require annual pruning. If a neglected old specimen has to be cut back hard it should regrow well if this is done in mid- or late spring. It is possible to reduce the height and spread of an old specimen quite drastically, but this is best done in stages over two or three years. This more severe pruning must be done with secateurs, loppers or a saw.

After planting To improve the shape of a new plant, shorten all the shoots by a third between early and late spring. If planting at any other time of the year, do this pruning the following spring.

Buxus sempervirens

56

C

CALLICARPA
BEAUTY BERRY

The hardy species commonly have a twiggy, upright shape young, and freely produce sh the base. With age the branch become more horizontal, and badly placed branch that is sp shape can be removed. Othe pruning is not usually necess do prune, do it in spring and retain as much of the young w possible.

Callicarpa bodinieri

CALLISTEMON
BOTTLE BRUSH

Callistemons can only be gro outside in the most favourable where they do best in the pro a sunny wall.

AFTER PLANTING
The general pruning advice applies to well-established plants. 'After planting' tells you how to improve those shrubs that benefit from early pruning soon after planting.

After planting To improve the shape of a new plant, shorten all the shoots by a third between early and late spring. If planting at any other time of the year, do this pruning the following spring.

PHOTOGRAPHS
Most of the entries are illustrated with representative species to help you identify the plant you're looking for.

SPECIFIC ADVICE
How to deal with shrubs that need pruning by a method not described in the Basic Techniques chapter. Also possible problems to look out for and what to do about them.

No routine pruning is required, but if the shrub becomes particularly congested cut out a few of the oldest branches in spring or late summer. These will be replaced quickly by new shoots (though these may take several years to flower).

A – Z of Ornamental Plants

...outine pruning is necessary. ...inctive bottle-brush flowers ...ed at the ends of the strongest ...so pruning is likely to be ...ntal to flowering. If the plant is ...becoming congested, however, ...one or two of the oldest shoots ...erate the shrub from the base.

...on citrinus 'Splendens'

CALLUNA
HEATHER, LING

...pruned, heathers become ...r and untidy with age, but it is a ...nd easy task to clip over them ...ears annually in early spring ...ique 3). If you have a large ...bed, an electric hedgetrimmer ...more convenient, but use it ...re.

...sing will encourage new growth ...re flowers, but be careful not to ...k into old wood, especially ...sing an electric hedgetrimmer. ...young growth will hide the ...stems that build up over the ...out eventually bare patches will ...It is when this begins to ...that the plants should ...aced.

Calluna vulgaris 'Elsie Purnell'

CALYCANTHUS
ALLSPICE

Several forms of allspice, C. floridus, are grown. All create spreading shrubs which shoot from the ground, but C. floridus 'Fertilis' has a particularly neat shape. C. occidentalis is more spreading and open, with horizontal branches.

Special cases If you have very dwarf varieties, such as C. vulgaris 'Foxii Nana' and 'Mullion', leave these unpruned (though you can deadhead them carefully if you want to improve their appearance).

A few varieties have very tall, upright growth with long flowering shoots, and you must be careful not to cut these too far back into old wood: make sure you leave some of the previous year's growth below the pruning point.

Sometimes varieties with coloured foliage, such as the very attractive, yellow 'Ruth Sparkes', may occasionally produce all-green shoots. Remove these shoots promptly, cutting back to the point of origin.

Calycanthus floridus

No routine pruning is required, but if the shrub becomes particularly congested cut out a few of the oldest branches in spring or late summer. These will be replaced quickly by new shoots (though these may take several years to flower).

CAMELLIA

These glossy-leaved evergreen shrubs are best grown in dappled shade or a sheltered position to protect them from wind and the blossoms from spring frost. If flowers are damaged by frost, this will not harm the shrub. Sometimes, however, the young spring growth itself is damaged. Leave such shoots until you can see where new growth is going to occur, then cut out the damaged section.

No routine pruning is required but shorten straggly shoots in mid-spring, after flowering.

Deadheading will improve the appearance of the plant, and is particularly worthwhile on varieties that produce masses of bloom. This is because the energy they would otherwise spend producing seeds will

57

PRUNING TIMES
You should not try to prune by specific dates, but according to the progress of the seasons and their effect on plant growth in a particular year in your particular garden. For example, if our advice is to prune forsythia in *late spring*, after flowering, in most places in a normal year this would be in May. However in very mild areas flowering may start in March. Conversely, if spring is very late one year, you may have to delay pruning until June.

If you are in doubt about when a season begins use the following list as a guide, but always be prepared to make adjustments to suit local conditions.

Early spring	March
Mid-spring	April
Late spring	May
Early summer	June
Mid summer	July
Late-summer	August
Early autumn	September
Mid-autumn	October
Late autumn	November
Early winter	December
Mid-winter	January
Late winter	February

CHAPTER ONE

PRUNING ESSENTIALS

PRUNING AND training are very practical elements of gardening, and a knowledge of plant growth helps you to understand why pruning works and allows you to tailor general instructions to meet your specific needs. Pruning is not only about removing unwanted shoots but also about stimulating the growth of other Its effect on the level of growth hormone in the shoots and dormant

buds helps shape the plant, while the removal of a bud can affect the growth and development of other shoots.

On some shrubs, apical buds are very dominant and there are few side branches. Others have slow-growing apical buds with a less dominant chemical control over the buds behind, making the plant much bushier and more 'twiggy'.

Buds may lie dormant, embedded in the bark until something triggers them into growth, such as the removal of a dominant bud by pruning. Shoot buds provide the future framework of a plant, and they can be thought of as compact undeveloped branches

waiting to be stimulated into growth. It is worth studying buds as you prune, and learning to 'read' them with the growth habit of the plant.

Pruning does not necessarily reduce the height of a plant unless repeated regularly, because previously dormant buds will simply replace the removed shoots and continue upward growth. It will, however, produce a bushier tree or shrub, which is why removing the main growing tip is often important in formative pruning for young trees.

The time of year that you prune can also have an effect on subsequent growth so follow the timing recommendations as closely as possible.

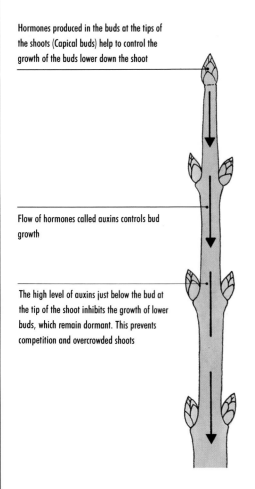

Hormones produced in the buds at the tips of the shoots (Capical buds) help to control the growth of the buds lower down the shoot

Flow of hormones called auxins controls bud growth

The high level of auxins just below the bud at the tip of the shoot inhibits the growth of lower buds, which remain dormant. This prevents competition and overcrowded shoots

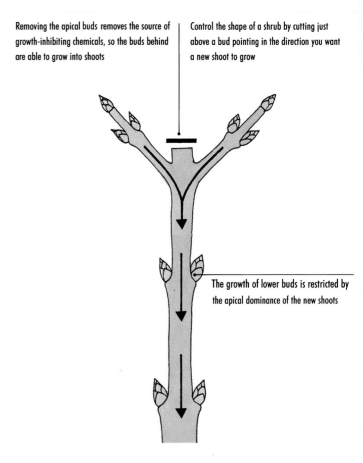

Removing the apical buds removes the source of growth-inhibiting chemicals, so the buds behind are able to grow into shoots

Control the shape of a shrub by cutting just above a bud pointing in the direction you want a new shoot to grow

The growth of lower buds is restricted by the apical dominance of the new shoots

The effect of the constant removal of the apical buds can be seen clearly in this hedge. Allowed to grow with the apical buds intact, the hedge becomes a tall tree, but if the apical buds are constantly removed through clipping or pruning, the tree fails to form a trunk and instead becomes a compact mass of small branches.

When to prune

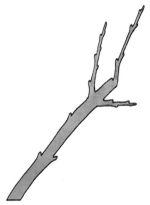

If you prune in winter when the plant is dormant, little internal activity will be taking place, but regrowth will be extensive when the plant does start to grow again.

Pruning in spring and early summer often produces thin growth with narrow angles between old and new shoots.

Pruning in mid- or late summer has the least effect on new growth. There is a risk that shoots produced late will be less able to resist cold damage, so it is generally best avoided for plants of borderline hardiness.

How Pruning Works

PRUNING HELPS to shape a plant not only by the immediate effect of removing a branch or shoot, but also by causing new shoots to grow from dormant buds. This knowledge can be put to practical use when you wish to improve or change the shape of a tree or plant.

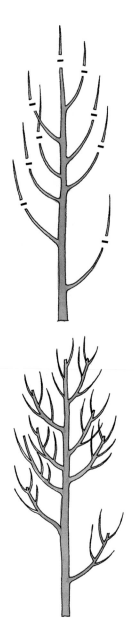

Inhibiting the growth of the apical bud is likely to increase the chances of dormant buds further back starting to grow. Forcing the stem into a horizontal or downward position is one way to do this, and tying the shoots down is a technique used in some forms of training (see festoon plums, page 212).

To thin out a shoot or branch to shape a tree or shrub, or to let in more light (important for fruit crops), prune back to its point of origin. As no dormant buds remain, normally new shoots will not grow to replace it.

For a new shoot to grow to replace the old one, do not cut back to its point of origin, but to a bud that will be stimulated into growth. Some dormant buds may be difficult to detect, but usually they are clearly visible.

MAKING THE RIGHT CUT

To reduce the risk of infection from fungi and bacteria, make a sloping cut in the same direction as the new bud. Avoid cutting so close to the bud that you risk damaging it, but do not leave a long stump as this is more liable to become infected.

 Make a clean, sloping cut, running away from the bud.

 Any stump or snag above the bud will be starved of sap and die. Infection could then spread into the healthy shoot. Cut near to a bud.

Do not make a sloping cut towards the bud. This leaves a snag and allows rainwater to accumulate round the bud and may cause it to rot.

Nicking and notching

These two words are used by some gardeners interchangeably; others use nicking to imply a cut below the bud and notching for a cut above the bud.

Nicking a small crescent or triangle of bark below a dormant bud will inhibit growth. These methods are mostly used for fruit trees, to promote or inhibit the development of specific buds. May is an appropriate time for this kind of growth control.

Notching a small crescent or triangle of bark above a dormant bud tends to stimulate it into growth.

SECATEURS

A GOOD PAIR of secateurs is essential. There are two main types of cutting action: bypass or curved secateurs produce a very clean cut, but only if the blade is sharp. Anvil secateurs have an action that resembles a pruning knife (see page 18). They cut with less effort but are more likely to leave a ragged result.

Comfort is, of course, very important, and is something you can only judge by comparing a few pairs; be sure to open them and make a cutting action. A large, strong hand may find a pair that opens wide and has a strong spring no problem to use, but someone with a smaller hand might find the same pair awkward. The comfort of the size and shape of the handle also depends very much on personal preference.

Weight and balance should also be taken into account when testing the secateurs for comfort, especially if you anticipate using them for a long period.

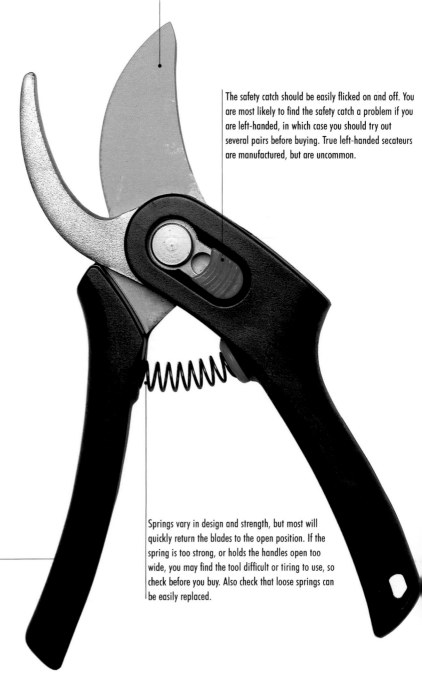

Blades need to be sharp. It is worth checking that they are easy to sharpen. If you are buying an expensive pair, make sure replacement blades and other parts are available.

The safety catch should be easily flicked on and off. You are most likely to find the safety catch a problem if you are left-handed, in which case you should try out several pairs before buying. True left-handed secateurs are manufactured, but are uncommon.

Springs vary in design and strength, but most will quickly return the blades to the open position. If the spring is too strong, or holds the handles open too wide, you may find the tool difficult or tiring to use, so check before you buy. Also check that loose springs can be easily replaced.

Handles are nearly all plastic or plastic-coated nowadays. Bare metal is cold and uncomfortable to hold in the winter. A bright colour, such as orange, is practical: it makes the secateurs easier to spot if you lay them down while working.

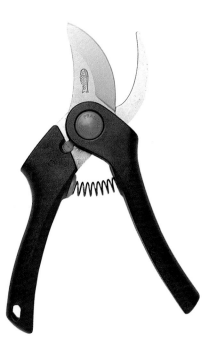

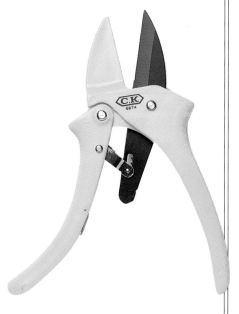

Bypass secateurs have a sharpened convex blade that cuts against a broad concave or square blade. Provided you keep the blades sharp, this type will make clean cuts and is easy to use. Some people prefer these because the tip of the blade is generally narrower and easier to push into a tight area, and the curved 'hook' of the top blade helps to hold the shoot during the cut, although the pivot must be kept tight.

Anvil secateurs have a single sharp cutting blade that slices through the shoot held against a flat anvil (some anvils have a groove to allow sap to run off easily). The anvil is made of a soft metal such as brass or an alloy, or even plastic, so that the cutting blade is not blunted too rapidly. If you find that the stems tend to slip out between the blades, choose one with a swing anvil which has a leverage system that enables the blade to make a parallel approach to the anvil.

Ratchet secateurs are useful if you have a weak grip as they complete a cut in several small movements. They should make pruning easier for you if you find conventional secateurs hard work.

SECATEUR CARE

● Sharpen the blade as soon as it shows signs of becoming blunt.
● Do not try to cut branches thicker than the secateurs are designed for. Most secateurs are suitable for pruning shoots up to about 12mm (½in) thick. For thicker woody stems and branches use long-handled pruners. Above 2.5cm (1in) use a saw.

● Dead wood is harder than living wood – avoid cutting dead branches thicker than 6mm (¼in). For thicker branches use a pruning saw.
● Avoid forcing secateurs to cut through shoots that are too thick by using a twisting movement: it will damage them.

● If you find it difficult to cut through a branch, try cutting at a slight angle rather than square.
● If using bypass secateurs, ensure that the cutting blade is on the plant side of the cut, so that any bruised tissue is on the side to be discarded.

OTHER TOOLS

MOST PRUNING can be done with secateurs, but if you have old shrubs with thick stems, or prickly or thorny shrubs, long-handled pruners or loppers are advisable – not only for comfort and ease of use but also because they make a cleaner cut without risk of straining the tool. For coping with trees or very old shrubs with very thick stems, a pruning saw is a worthwhile investment. If you have major branches to be removed from a tree that demands a chainsaw, it is advisable to employ a professional tree surgeon who will have special equipment and the proper training for the job.

Long-handled pruners (also called loppers or branch cutters; both anvil and bypass types available).

● The long handles make it easy to reach into a prickly shrub, or to cut into the base of any shrubs without having to bend down.

● The long handles make light work of cutting thick shoots in comparison with secateurs. Bypass types may be slightly easier to manoeuvre into a confined space.

● The longer the handle, the more leverage you will have and the less effort will be required to cut through the branch, but the handles also add weight and can make the tool more cumbersome to use.

● More complex types are available for cutting larger limbs; but are only useful if doing a lot of pruning.

Tree pruners (also called tree loppers)

● Useful for removing modest-sized branches from an established tree instead of using a ladder.

● A wide variety of designs is available and some have saw and fruit-gathering attachments.

● A hooked end is placed over the branch to be cut, and a cord or rod mechanism operates the cutter.

● Consider the maximum reach you are likely to need: 2.4m (8ft) is typical, but some are over 3m (10ft) long, others as short as 1.8m (6ft). Some tree pruners have telescopic handles.

● A saw attachment is useful because it enables you to tackle thicker branches – but bear in mind that sawing above your head can be tiring.

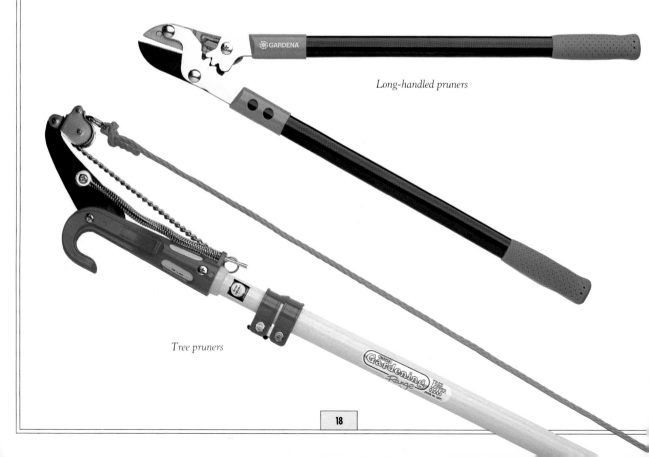

Long-handled pruners

Tree pruners

HARD TEETH

Some saws have specially heat-treated teeth that makes them harder than normal. These should stay sharper for longer, but you cannot sharpen them yourself, and the cost of having new teeth reground on this kind of saw may go a long way towards the cost of a new saw.

Grecian saw.

Straight saw

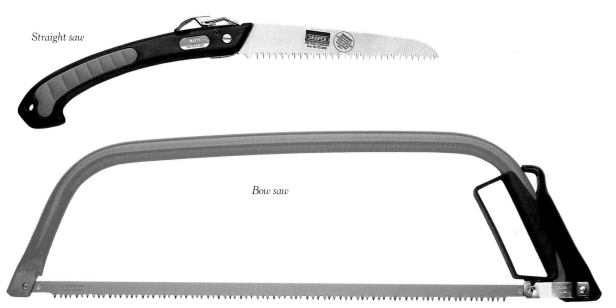

Bow saw

Bow saws
- Fast-cutting.
- Useful for sawing logs and really thick branches (over 12.5cm (5in)).
- Cut on the push and the pull stroke.
- Have a replaceable blade: a 53–60cm (21–24in) blade is suitable for most jobs.
- 'Triangular' bow saws have one end that is narrower than the other, which is useful for getting into awkward places between branches.

Straight pruning saws
- These are the most useful all-round saws for pruning.
- They have widely angled teeth that cut only on one stroke but that help prevent sticking in sappy wood.
- The narrow, tapered end makes them easier to get between branches.
- Their fairly fine teeth can make sawing hard work.
- Some have teeth on both sides, fine on one, coarse on the other. In a confined area you could damage other branches while you saw.
- Available in folding form which makes them safer to carry around.

Grecian (curved) saws
- Very useful for intricate jobs.
- The blade is narrow and curved, ideal for getting into tight places among the branches.
- Convenient for above head-height sawing as the teeth, which are on one side only, point backwards, so cut on the pull stroke.
- Available in folding form which makes them safer to carry around.

Pruning knives

- Less convenient to use than secateurs.
- There is a knack to using one successfully. A proper pruning knife has a curved blade that makes it easier to bite into the shoot as you cut towards yourself.
- Useful for smoothing the edges of large saw cuts (a wood rasp will do for large branches).
- May be useful to buy a general-purpose garden knife that is useful for cutting string, harvesting vegetables, and other jobs.

Hand shears
(also called hedge shears)

- Useful for shaping a new hedge, for clipping topiary, and for clipping back formally shaped shrubs and conifers in the border. Small-leaved shrubs overhanging a path can often be dealt with quickly and effectively with shears.
- Convenient for pruning heathers after flowering.
- Can be tiring to use, but keeping the blades sharp and not too tightly adjusted will help.
- If blades are too slack, they will not cut efficiently.
- Most have straight or slightly curved blades. Those with wavy or serrated edges tend to cut through mature wood more easily but can be more difficult to resharpen.
- A notch in one or both blades, usually close to the handle, is used to hold and cut thick twigs.
- Handles vary in shape and materials, but they make little difference in use.

TOOL CARE

- Wipe tools clean with a cloth; a dish-washing brush and hot water will remove sap accumulation. Then, to prevent rust, coat the blades thinly with oil before putting away your tools. Using a paintbrush is a good way to oil a saw.
- If your saw does not have a protective cover for the blade, make one from thick card and slip the blade into this for carrying or storing.
- Keep secateurs, shears and knife blades sharp. You can usually do this yourself with a sharpening stone, and there are devices available to help you sharpen secateurs and shears. If in doubt, take them to a professional sharpener once a year.
- Bow saws have replaceable blades, so sharpening is unnecessary. Saw teeth can sometimes be sharpened at home, but not hardened teeth. Unless you are sure of what you are doing, have saws sharpened professionally.

Pruning knives

Hand shears

Electric hedgetrimmer

Powered hedgetrimmers
- Invaluable for taking the labour out of hedgetrimming, and saving time.
- For a large garden petrol trimmers are useful where the hedges are far from a power supply, but they are heavy and noisy.
- For a small garden, mains electric trimmers are more satisfactory.
- Electric trimmers are lighter to use, less noisy, and generally cheaper.
- Powered hedgetrimmers are potentially hazardous tools. Risk of accident can be reduced by choosing a tool with good safety features .
- Reciprocating blades means both blades move, rather than one cutting against a stationary blade. These generally cause less vibration and should be less tiring to use.
- There is no ideal number of teeth, but the more per given length, the smoother the finish is likely to be. For thicker shoots it is better to have more widely spaced teeth.
- Rechargeable trimmers are suitable for small hedges or for parts of a large garden where a convenient mains supply is not available.

- Rechargeable trimmers are lightweight and give greater safety in the garden as they have no trailing mains cables.
- The longer the blade, the quicker you will be able to cut your hedge, though power source also affects cutting time (you will probably cut more hedge for a given blade length with a more powerful petrol hedge-trimmer than with an electric one).

Safety features
- Look out for two-handed switches, which mean you must have both hands on the trimmer to operate it.
- Blade brakes should stop the moving blades in less than half a second.
- A lock-off switch requires two separate actions to turn the machine on, reducing the risk of accidental starting.
- A deadman's handle cuts off the power as soon as pressure is released.
- Blade extensions are metal bars that extend beyond the cutting blades, to reduce the risk of contacting moving blades.

Using a hedgetrimmer safely
Powered hedgetrimmers are potentially dangerous, but following these simple rules will minimize the risk from these useful tools:
- Always protect the circuit with a residual current device (RCD).
- Never use during or just after rain.
- Take the lead from the hedgetrimmer over your shoulder and secure it at the back in a belt to avoid a trailing cable that could be cut by the blades.
- Start at one end with the cable behind you, and gradually work away from it so that any trailing cable is always behind you.
- Use the trimmer with smooth upward or horizontal strokes to reduce the chances of cutting the cable.
- Always disconnect the power supply before cleaning the tool or making any adjustments.

BASIC TECHNIQUES

Mastering the nine methods illustrated in this chapter, some of which are as simple as clipping a hedge with shears, will enable you to tackle with confidence almost any routine pruning task.

These basic techniques are suitable for established shrubs. Young or newly planted trees and shrubs may require special treatment as indicated in the A–Z section.

This chapter also tells you how to deal with common problems such as cutting out diseased, damaged and dead wood and how to control unwanted growth.

PRUNING OUT PROBLEMS

FEW SHRUBS and fewer trees require routine pruning, but once a year it is worth checking them to identify and deal with any developing problems. The pictures show how.

Cut out diseased wood
Cut out areas of wood that have started to die back as a result of frost damage, previous pruning wounds, or just disease infection. This ensures that dead wood does not harbour disease spores and stops infection spreading.

Cut back to sound, healthy wood, just above a bud.

Die-back on a cluster-flowered rose

Wood infected by diseases like coral spot (*Nectria cinnabarina*) should be cut out as soon as the problem is noticed. This disease often lives on dead branches, but can become parasitic on live tissue, causing die-back.

Burn the prunings or put them with the refuse for disposal, but do not compost them as this could spread the disease.

Coral spot on a large-flowered rose

Cut out dead or damaged shoots
Remove any damaged areas, cutting back to firm, undamaged wood. Even if the plant is not diseased now, injuries like this are an invitation to infection that may then spread to healthy parts of the shoot.

Pruning out damaged shoots on a broom (Genista)

Eliminate badly crossing branches
Cut out crossing branches that rub against each other or cause congested growth. This will improve the appearance of the plant and reduce the risk of infections entering through wounds caused by friction damage.

Removing a badly crossing branch on a lilac

Prune out all-green shoots on variegated plants
Many variegated shrubs and trees tend to revert by producing all-green leaves. Cut out affected shoots as soon as these are noticed, as the green shoots will be more vigorous and, in time, may dominate the plant.

Euonymus japonicus 'Aureopictus', which reverts to green very easily if pruning is neglected

Eliminate multiple shoots growing from a wounded area

When a branch is removed from a tree, a number of shoots sometimes develop around the cut area. These should be removed, as they are usually ill-placed and will cause overcrowding if allowed to remain. Cut them off at the base, flush with the branch or trunk.

Unwanted shoots being removed from a Prunus serrula

Remove basal shoots

These shoots, also known as suckers, are a problem on grafted plants such as lilac (*Syringa vulgaris* varieties) and roses. Some trees grown on their own roots, such as *Rhus typhina*, may also produce unwanted shoots from the roots. Remove them from the base of the tree to maintain a clear, uncluttered trunk, and from grafted or budded shrubs to prevent the rootstock gradually dominating the plant.

Cut off basal shoots below the ground if possible. On a grafted plant it is important to trace the shoot down to its point of origin, then pull or cut it off close to the main stem. Wipe the stem clean before using secateurs, so that the blades are not damaged by grit.

These basal shoots are being removed from a lilac

Cut out winter damage

Shrubs, especially evergreens that are not totally hardy, may be damaged by a very severe winter. It is not always frost that causes the damage; often cold winds are the culprit.

The youngest leaves at the tips of the shoots are the most likely to suffer winter damage, but provided the rest of the plant is alive and undamaged new growth should soon replace them. To reduce the risk of diseases becoming established in the damaged tissue, and to improve the appearance of the bush, cut back affected shoots to healthy wood.

This Choisya ternata *has been damaged by cold winds and severe frost*

1

CLIPPING TO SHAPE

IF YOU WANT to grow shrubs such as box (*Buxus sempervirens*) and *Berberis darwinii* perhaps in a lawn or container, they will look better if regularly clipped.

Plants listed on page 186 as suitable for formal hedges generally respond well to this kind of shaping.

Before pruning
Many evergreens can be
clipped to a formal shape.

Buxus sempervirens 'Elegantissima'

Pruning

● Clip small-leaved plants such as box with shears (or a hedgetrimmer if the plant is large). For large-leaved plants such as spotted laurel (*Aucuba japonica*), use secateurs as shears can damage leaves which then turn brown and die.

● If trimming in spring only remove growth produced the previous year. Remove the current year's growth if clipping from mid-summer onwards.

● Clip back newest growth without cutting into old wood if possible.

● A trim like this will leave the plant looking tidy for another year. Once you start this kind of shaping it is likely to be required at least annually.

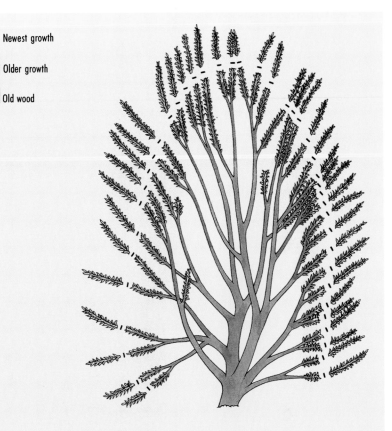

Newest growth
Older growth
Old wood

After pruning

Newest growth

Older growth

Newest growth

Older growth

2

REDUCING NEW GROWTH BY HALF

Do NOT LET brooms (*Cytisus*), and shrubs such as genistas, become straggly and bare at the base. Shorten the new growth annually, and start while they are still young, as they do not produce new shoots from old, dark wood.

Cytisus × praecox 'Allgold'

Before pruning
Prune plants such as these once the flowers have faded and before the seedpods mature.

Pruning

● Cut back all the new green shoots to encourage fresh branching and bushy growth.

● Cut each shoot back by about half way along the new green growth. Do not cut into old dark wood but remove any dead shoots.

● After pruning the shrub will look neater and more compact. Do not expect new shoots to grow low down from the old, dark wood.

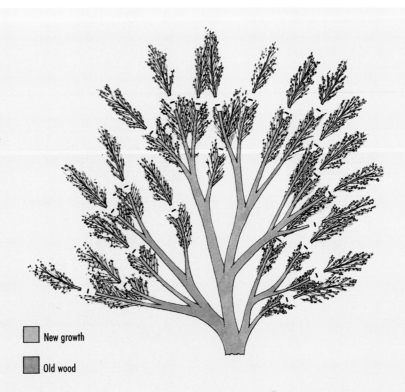

☐ New growth

☐ Old wood

New growth

Old wood

New growth

After pruning

PRUNING BY DEADHEADING

PRUNE HEATHERS and certain other plants by clipping them over with shears to deadhead them. This will make the plants look tidier, keep them low and compact, and improve flowering.

Before pruning
Heathers require regular pruning if they are to remain compact.

Winter-flowering heather.

Pruning

● Once the flowers start to die trim them back with shears. With winter-flowering varieties wait until spring.

● Trim the shoots back close to the base of the current year's growth (or that of the previous summer if pruning winter-flowering heathers in spring). Do not cut into old, dark wood.

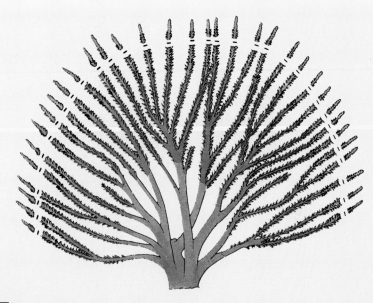

☐ Old flower

☐ Current year's growth

☐ Last year's growth

☐ Old wood

Old flower   Current year's growth

After pruning

4

SHORTENING SIDESHOOTS

THE CALICO BUSH (*Kalmia latifolia*), *Convolvulus cneorum*, and sun roses (*Cistus*) flower on sideshoots produced the previous year. These, and similar slow-growing summer-flowering shrubs, will remain shapely without pruning, but you can stimulate more sideshoots and therefore more flowers by reducing new shoots by two-thirds after flowering.

Before pruning
You can increase the number of flowers the bush is likely to carry next year if you prune after flowering.

Cistus × purpureus

Pruning

● Select those shoots that have flowered. This new growth is softer and paler.

● Cut just above a bud about two-thirds down from the tip of each sideshoot that has flowered.

● If you want to improve the shape of an old bush do not prune back too far. Only cut into the previous season's growth and then only to a point where there is a young shoot.

● After pruning, the plant will retain its attractive shape and may not look very different from a distance, but this technique will help to keep the plants compact and encourage prolific flowering the following year.

Flowered shoot

Previous season's growth

Old wood

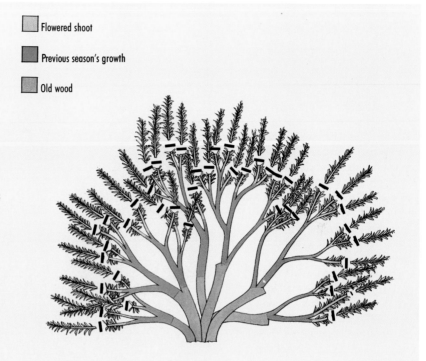

Flowered shoot

After pruning

5

CUTTING OUT ONE STEM IN THREE

MANY SHRUBS can be kept compact and vigorous with plenty of new growth if you cut out one stem in three each year. This very useful technique prevents shrubs becoming too woody and tangled with age, and will help those plants grown for their flowers to bloom well on vigorous wood as the oldest shoots are replaced.

The technique is useful for three groups of shrubs: those that flower early on shoots that grew the previous year, such as forsythias and flowering currants (*Ribes sanguineum*), those that flower prolifically for most of the summer (such as shrubby potentillas), and some plants grown for their foliage, such as variegated dogwoods (like *Cornus alba* 'Elegantissima').

Start this type of pruning when the shrub has been established for about three years. Then if you prune annually you will always be removing a third of the oldest wood each year to keep the plant looking compact and vigorous.

Forsythia 'Beatrix Farrand'

Before pruning
Prune spring-flowering shrubs such as this forsythia soon after flowering. Check the A-Z entry for the best timing.

Pruning

● Remove one stem in three, cutting them back to the base, just above ground level. Choose the oldest or weakest branches to cut out first.

● After the old and weak shoots have been removed, continue with those that will open up the centre of the bush or improve the shape. You may not be able to see a bud to cut to, in which case leave a short stump. This can be removed when the new growth starts.

● After pruning the bush may look a little sparse, but new shoots will soon grow to fill the space.

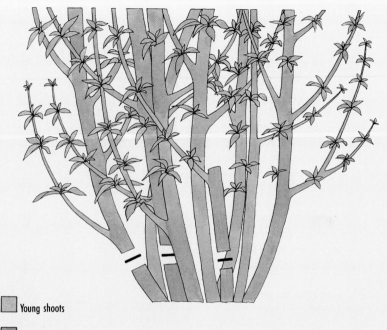

☐ Young shoots

☐ Oldest shoots

After pruning

Oldest shoot

Young shoot

6

CUTTING BACK TO THE GROUND

USE THIS TECHNIQUE to improve the appearance of plants that throw up canes from a spreading clump, or to clear the old growth to make way for new shoots.

Some shrubs, such as the white-stemmed *Rubus cockburnianus* and *R. biflorus*, produce new canes each year. The old canes are best cut to ground level or just above in early or mid-spring.

Others, notably ceratostigmas and hardy fuchsias, form a woody framework of live wood in mild areas, but where the winters are severe all the top growth may be killed even though the roots and crown will probably survive. Where the top growth has been killed, the plant should be cut back to the ground or just above, to allow replacement shoots to grow.

Rubus cockburnianus

Before pruning
The white bloom on the stems of *Rubus cockburnianus* is most pronounced on young shoots, and by cutting out the old ones plenty of attractive young canes will be produced without the growth becoming too congested. Other shrubs may require cutting back close to the ground because the top growth has been killed (this often happens with fuchsias in cold areas).

Pruning

● Working from one side of the bush, and wearing gloves if pruning *Rubus cockburnianus*, cut all the stems off just above the ground. It is not necessary to worry about cutting back to a bud as new shoots will be produced from ground level.

● After pruning, little will be visible except the short stumps of old shoots, but new ones will begin to appear within weeks, and by the end of the season will be as long as those just removed.

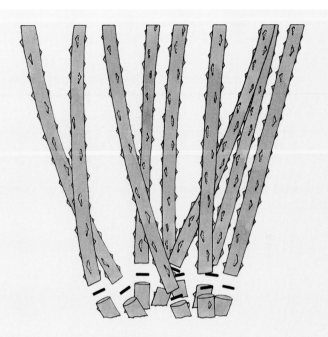

▢ Previous growth

After pruning

7

CUTTING BACK TO A FRAMEWORK (A)

PLANTS GROWN FOR their colourful young stems, such as dogwoods and *Salix alba*, will have the best colour if you regularly prune hard to stimulate new shoots. The same technique can be used to induce larger leaves on compact growth on plants like golden cut-leaf elder *Sambucus racemosa* 'Plumosa Aurea', and to produce the more attractive juvenile foliage on eucalyptus.

Allow the plants to become established for a season after planting, then prune them to within 5cm (2in). of the ground in early spring. This will encourage plenty of low growth that will form the framework in future years.

Annual pruning will produce compact, low growth, but the plant may become weakened and produce mainly thin stems unless you also mulch and feed generously after pruning. Pruning every second year produces plenty of tall, thick shoots which do not have to be fed.

Once this pruning system has become established and a basal framework of shoots has formed, prune as shown.

Salix alba 'Chermesina' (syn. 'Britzensis')

Before pruning
Prune in early spring, before the new leaves appear, annually or every second year.

Pruning

● Cut back each stem to an outward-facing bud about 5cm (2in) from the stump of hard wood.

● Within weeks of pruning, strong new shoots will grow.

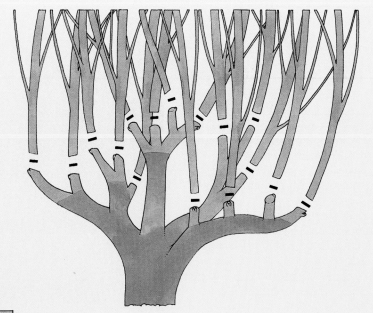

☐ Previous year's growth

☐ Old wood

Outward-facing buds

Previous year's growth

Old wood

After pruning

8

CUTTING BACK TO A FRAMEWORK (B)

ALTHOUGH THIS technique is similar to that used to stimulate shrubs grown for coloured stems or large leaves (Technique 7), pruning should start the first spring after planting and be an annual task.

Buddleia davidii and other shrubs that flower on shoots produced during the current season, such as *Hydrangea paniculata*, will produce larger flowers on more compact plants if you prune hard to a framework of shoots every spring as this stimulates vigorous growth from the base. If not pruned these shrubs tend to produce smaller flowers on leggy plants.

Buddleia davidii

Before pruning
Prune in early spring, when growth is no more advanced than on the plant shown.

Pruning

● Cut back all the previous season's growth to within about two buds of the stump of old wood. This usually means leaving about 5cm (2in) of last year's stem.

● If the bush has become very large and congested, cut one or two old stems down to ground level so that more of the plant's energy goes into producing better flowers on fewer but better-placed shoots. You will probably have to use long-handled pruners for this.

● After pruning, only stumps will remain, but vigorous new shoots will soon grow and many shrubs will produce 1.8m (6ft) stems within a season.

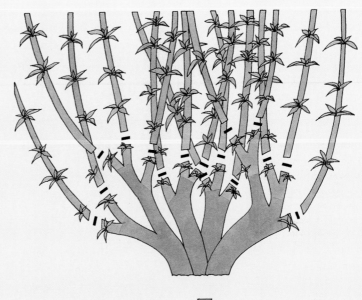

Previous season's growth

Old wood

Previous season's growth

Old wood | New shoot

After pruning

9

CUTTING BACK
GREY-LEAVED
PLANTS

REGULAR PRUNING will prevent grey-leaved plants grown for foliage effect, such as the curry plant *(Helichrysum angustifolium)* and cotton lavender *(Santolina chamaecyparissus)*, becoming straggly and losing their neat, compact form. Start when they are young, as cutting back hard into old wood may spoil or kill the plant. Prune regularly each spring.

Before pruning
Plants like this cotton lavender are compact and attractive when young, but soon become leggy with sparse growth if not pruned.

Santolina chamaecyparissus

Pruning

• If new growth is present at the base, cut the stems back to within 5–10cm (2–4in) of the ground.

• On an established or neglected plant with a woody framework and no new shoots growing from the ground, be careful not to cut into old, dark wood. Confine the pruning to shoots produced the previous year that are still soft, cutting them back to within 5–10cm (2–4in) of the old dark wood.

• After pruning, the plant will look sparse but new shoots will soon grow, producing a much more attractive plant.

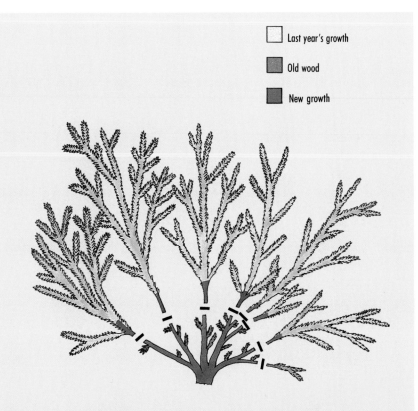

☐ Last year's growth

▨ Old wood

▨ New growth

After pruning

Last year's growth

New growth

Old wood

A–Z OF ORNAMENTAL PLANTS

This directory of trees, shrubs and climbers will tell you whether a particular plant benefits from pruning and, if so, how and when to do it. In many cases regular pruning is unnecessary, but when it is beneficial the most appropriate technique has been selected.

Entries are listed under the names by which the plants are likely to be sold in nurseries and garden centres. If plants have been renamed, but the new names are not yet in popular use, they will be found in the index with a cross-reference to the appropriate entry.

A

ABELIA

Abelias flower mainly on shoots produced the previous year, but may also flower on shoots formed early in the current year, which is why some species have a very long flowering season. All abelias produce new shoots each year, so remove some of the old wood annually (Technique 5) to encourage plenty of young, vigorous growth and improve flowering.

Abelias are fairly hardy, but except in mild areas some winter damage is possible. Evergreen species are likely to lose most of their leaves in cold areas. Wait until early spring when there are signs of new growth so that you can see which shoots are damaged and need removing.

Semi-evergreen species such as *A.* × *grandiflora* are sometimes grown as wall shrubs in cold areas, with growth tied to supporting wires. Tie in the main shoots regularly and leave the fast-growing sideshoots unpruned as these will produce the following year's flowers. If you do not tie in the main shoots as they grow, many of these flowering sideshoots will face the wall and be spoilt.

Young plants require no pruning for the first three or four years other than the removal of winter-damaged shoots.

ABELIOPHYLLUM

WHITE FORSYTHIA

There is only one species, *A. distichum*, which flowers in early spring on growth made during the previous year.

No regular pruning is required. If the bush is neglected or very tangled and flowering is poor, prune by Technique 5 in mid- or late spring, after flowering. Remove the oldest and poorest-flowering shoots first. However, this should not be an annual task.

ABIES

FIR

Make sure young trees develop only one strong leading shoot. No regular pruning is necessary and firs seldom produce new shoots from old wood.

For solutions to conifer problems see Conifers, page 176.

Abies nordmanniana 'Golden Spreader'

ABUTILON

The hardiest species is *A. vitifolium*, which requires the protection of a warm wall or a mild climate to do well. The other species likely to be grown outdoors permanently is *A. megapotamicum*.

Both these species are likely to suffer damage due to very cold weather during winter, and can be short-lived. Therefore prune in mid-spring once new growth can be seen and winter damage assessed.

First remove frost-damaged and dead shoots. Then, if the plant is outgrowing its space, clip it back to size using Technique 1. Clip soft growth on *A. megapotamicum* with shears, but use secateurs for *A. vitifolium*.

In favourable areas *A. vitifolium* will make a large, free-standing shrub. In this case just remove dead or damaged wood in mid-spring then cut off two-thirds of each new shoot in early summer (Technique 4).

Abelia × *grandiflora*

ACACIA

MIMOSA, WATTLE

Acacias are best grown in a conservatory although a few species can be grown outdoors against a sunny wall in very mild areas.

No regular pruning is required other than to remove dead or damaged wood after a hard winter. Where climate and conditions suit, some acacias may grow large and tree-like. If it is necessary to restrict size, cut the plant back by up to two-thirds of its height after flowering.

Acacia dealbata

ACER

MAPLE

Most maples grow into large trees, but many of the Japanese maples, *A. japonicum* and *A. palmatum* varieties, take the form of large bushes or small trees. The majority require no routine pruning, but box elder is a special case (see below).

The Japanese maples are susceptible to spring frosts and cold spring winds, which may cause the opening leaves to shrivel and drop, and in severe cases may kill the tips of the shoots. Leave the plant to see if it recovers: new

leaves may grow and the plant recover fully, but if the tips start to die back, prune back to living wood. Young plants are particularly vulnerable, and the best solution is to plant in a sheltered position where cold spring winds and late frost are less likely to be a problem.

Sycamore, *A. pseudoplatanus*, and *A. platanoides* need no routine pruning. If they grow too large or overhang a boundary, it is best not to tackle the job yourself but to consult a professional tree surgeon.

Problems Most maples bleed badly if pruned in spring, so leave non-essential pruning until the tree is dormant. Coral spot fungus is sometimes a problem on damaged or pruned shoots, so apply a wound paint to the cut surface after pruning.

Acer negundo, which has several common names, including box elder, box maple and ash-leaved maple, can be grown as a multi-stemmed bush-like tree or as a standard with a single clear trunk. It is grown mainly for its foliage and 'Elegans', with yellow-edged foliage, is one of the most popular varieties. 'Flamingo' has pink variegation early in the year, changing to white with age.

If grown purely for foliage, you can pollard box elder each spring if you start with a young plant (see page 171). This will restrain the height and produce larger leaves. 'Flamingo' responds well to this treatment.

If grown as a tree, however, variegated box elder should be pruned as little as possible. Pruning may stimulate unsightly clusters of sideshoots to develop on branches and often the vigorous shoots that grow from a pruned area have all-green leaves.

Any variegated box elder may produce shoots with all-green leaves

Acer negundo

from time to time. Prune these back to their point of origin as soon as you notice them.

Young grafted plants sometimes produce shoots from the rootstock. Remove these at their point of origin. **Maples with beautiful bark** Maples with very attractive bark are best grown with a clear trunk unmarred by low branches. If necessary, remove lower limbs while they are still small, to produce a clear unblemished trunk.

Acer griseum

Species to treat this way include the paperbark maple, *A. griseum*, and the snakebark maples, *A. capillipes*, *A. davidii*, *A. pensylvanicum* and *A. hersii* (syn. *A. grosseri* var. *hersii*).

Multi-stemmed trees Most maples are grown as standard trees with a clear trunk, but some look good as multi-stemmed trees, which gives them a more shrub-like appearance. If not already trained this way, you will need to start with a young plant (see multi-stemmed birch, page 169).

Species suitable for growing as multi-stemmed trees include *A. circinatum*, *A. ginnala* and *A. negundo*. The Japanese maples, *A. japonicum* and *A. palmatum*, may naturally form small multi-stemmed shrub-like trees.

After planting For a clear stem, see page 167.

Acer japonicum 'Aureum'

ACTINIDIA

The two species most commonly grown are the Chinese gooseberry or kiwi, *A. chinensis*, and the kolomikta vine, *A. kolomikta*, with its pink, white and green leaves. Both are vigorous climbers that require regular pruning to keep them under control.

It is important to provide a suitable support, otherwise the shoots twine around each other and become a tangled thicket that makes pruning difficult. The kolomikta vine is usually trained against a wall, tied in to horizontal wires. The shoots can be spaced out as they grow, for neatness and good cover.

Do not prune until the vine has filled its allotted space, then prune in stages to keep it contained. Once shoots have outgrown their bounds by about 60cm (24in), cut them back to within about 15cm (6in) of their point of origin. This is a summer job, best done as you tie in the new growth, and it may be necessary to do this several times.

Shorten these summer-pruned shoots again during the winter. Cut back to one or two buds from their point of origin.

If the plant is mature and becoming overcrowded, cut out a few of the oldest shoots each year and tie in young replacement shoots growing from close to the base.

If the plant is growing up a large pole or tripod, allow the shoots to cascade down when they reach the top. However, during the summer cut back any shoots that grow too long. During winter cut out some of the oldest shoots close to the base but only as long as there are young ones to replace them. This will help to prevent the plant becoming tangled and untidy.

Actinidia kolomikta

AESCULUS

HORSE CHESTNUT

The common horse chestnut, *A. hippocastanum*, makes a very large tree in time. It can be pollarded if the branches start to cause an obstruction (see page 171), but this is a job for a professional tree surgeon and the tree will look misshapen for a couple of years. Crown thinning can be a more attractive option, but still requires the services of a professional.

The red horse chestnut, *A.* × *carnea*, often forms large burrs (swellings with masses of shoots) on the trunk and main branches. These corky eruptions look unsightly but are unlikely to harm the tree. Do not attempt to remove this mass of corky tissue as it often penetrates deep into the trunk or branch, so healing may be difficult.

In general no routine pruning is required, but remove lower branches of large trees in winter if they are becoming an obstruction or casting too much shade. The smaller, more shrubby species, such as *A. parviflora*, are unlikely to need pruning.

After planting Horse chestnuts are often sold with side branches. For a clear stem, see page 167.

AILANTHUS
TREE OF HEAVEN

Only one species is widely grown, *A. altissima*. It is fast-growing and young plants tend to be spindly, but this soon improves as the tree gets bigger. Although it is usually grown on a single trunk, you can grow it as a multi-stemmed tree (see page 169).

Remove any shoots produced by the roots away from the main trunk.

You can also grow the tree of heaven as a coppiced shrub for its large, decorative foliage. The plant will produce shoots of about 1.2–1.8m (4–6ft) annually if you cut it back close to the ground each winter (see Technique 7). If you prune this hard, feed annually and keep the plant watered.

After planting For a clear stem, see page 167; for a multi-stemmed tree, see page 169; for a shrubby plant cut down to just above ground level in late spring.

Ailanthus altissima

AKEBIA

Akebias are climbers with slender twining stems which are usually tied in to horizontal wires against a wall. The plant's main attraction is its fragrant chocolate-purple flowers, but these can become lost among a lot of leafy growth if the plant grows vigorously.

No routine pruning is required, but remove any dead wood in winter or early spring. If akebia outgrows its allotted space, just cut out enough shoots to contain the plant, removing some of the oldest first.

If training the plant against a wall or fence, remove the tips of the developing shoots in spring in order to encourage branching. Then direct the new growth to fill the space. Tie in the new shoots to supporting wires, or they will tend to slump to the ground and become a tangled mass.

If the plant is scrambling freely into a tree or over an old tree stump, you only need to remove dead or damaged wood in late winter.

Akebia quinata

ALBIZIA
PINK MIMOSA, SILK TREE

Albizia julibrissin is an attractive and fast-growing tree, but suitable only for the mildest areas. It is best given wall protection even in favourable regions

as it is easily damaged or killed by a sudden frost.

No routine pruning is necessary, but the tree is fast-growing where conditions suit. If necessary, cut the previous year's growth back to five or six buds in spring to restrict its size.

Albizia julibrissin

ALNUS
ALDER

These deciduous trees and shrubs grow well in moist places, particularly by water. Although they require no routine pruning, you can develop an attractive tree with a clear trunk if you gradually remove branches up to 1.8m (6ft). If you prefer a pyramidal shape, however, leave the lower branches, as they will probably sweep down to the ground in time. Thin out side branches if overcrowded.

Some alders, particularly the grey alder, *A. incana*, tend to form several leading shoots and can become shrub-like. If you want a tall tree cut out competing stems to leave just one, which will eventually become the main trunk when the tree has developed.

A few alders, such as the green alder, *A. viridis*, naturally form shrubs. These need no routine pruning.

After planting Alders are usually sold with side branches. Decide whether you want your tree to have a clear trunk, or branches low down, and ..prune accordingly. For a clear trunk, see page 167.

ALOYSIA

LEMON VERBENA

The species usually grown *Aloysia triphylla*, previously known as *Lippia triphylla*, is also often sold as *L. citriodora*. This deliciously fragrant-leaved shrub is not very hardy and is liable to be damaged in a severe winter, so prune just as the new growth is beginning in spring, when it is easier to assess winter damage.

Prune dead or damaged shoots back to live wood as the buds break (this may mean cutting back into old wood). If an unattractively shaped plant results, prune all the main shoots to about 30cm (12in) above the ground, to stimulate new, even growth. During the growing season, shape the bush by pinching out the tips of shoots.

If you live in an area where your plant comes through the winter relatively unscathed and builds up a permanent framework of branches, prune by Technique 5.

AMELANCHIER

JUNE BERRY, SERVICEBERRY, SHADBUSH, SNOWY MESPILUS

Amelanchier canadensis, *A. lamarckii* and *A. laevis* are very similar. They are sometimes confused when offered for sale, but cultivation and pruning techniques are the same. All have masses of white flowers in spring and brilliant autumn colour.

Most amelanchiers are grown as

Amelanchier canadensis (spring)

shrubs or multi-stemmed trees but, by ensuring all side branches are removed in stages during the formative years, a small tree can be produced. Such formative training is usually done at the nursery.

If you have a plant like this, be prepared to remove any shoots that form on the trunk, as amelanchiers have a tendency to develop strong side-shoots. Otherwise, no routine pruning is required. It may be necessary to remove any weak or crowded shoots every few years to contain the plant and achieve an open, balanced appearance. Do this in late spring once the flowers are over. The plants can be cut back hard if desired.

There are a few species, such as *A. humilis* and *A. stolonifera*, which form a thicket of stems. These need no routine pruning.

After planting For a clear stem, see page 167.

Amelanchier canadensis (autumn)

AMPELOPSIS

Ampelopsis brevipedunculata (syn. *A. glandulosa* 'Brevipedunculata') is a strong-growing climber suitable for growing through trees or along sheds and walls. Training and pruning are neither practical nor necessary in this situation. Simply clip it back when it outgrows its space; you can do this with shears if the growth is still soft.

If it is trained up a pole or similar support, prune it back annually in winter, while dormant, to two or three permanent branches and tie them to the support. These will form the framework. Cut back each sideshoot growing from the framework to the lowest bud. The plant will shoot freely from the spurs (or stumps) formed by this hard pruning, and the development of a tangled mass of foliage will be avoided.

Less vigorous ampelopsis species, such as *A. brevipedunculata* 'Elegans' and *A. megalophylla*, are best trained as a series of main stems, or rods, like a grape vine (see page 229). Each winter, prune the previous summer's growth back to the permanently trained main stem, cutting back to one bud. This will keep the plants tidy and relatively untangled while still providing good summer cover.

ANDROMEDA

BOG ROSEMARY

This low-growing evergreen needs no routine pruning. However, you can clip the shrubs over after flowering (Technique 3) to deadhead the plants and make them look tidier.

ARALIA
ANGELICA TREE

Aralias make large shrubs or small trees, but size depends as much on conditions as pruning. No routine pruning of the branches is required, but remove any diseased or damaged stems in spring. Do not prune hard unless absolutely necessary as this may stimulate unwanted shoots round the base of the plant.

These shoots can be a problem and spoil the plant's dramatic shape. It is especially important to remove any that develop around the base of variegated forms of *A. elata*. Variegated aralias are grafted on to a rootstock of the green-leaved species. Shoots from the rootstock will be all-green and much more vigorous than those of the variegated variety and may quickly dominate the plant.

ARAUCARIA
MONKEY PUZZLE TREE, CHILE PINE

The monkey puzzle tree, *A. araucana*, is the only species likely to be grown outdoors. It is important to allow plenty of space for the symmetrical branches to grow without restriction as a good shape is very important for this tree to look its best.

If the leading shoot is killed or damaged, a number of buds will form near the original growing point. Let these grow a little, then select the strongest to form the new leading shoot and remove the others. If the tree is still young, tie the new main stem to a temporary stake.

No routine pruning is required.

ARBUTUS

The strawberry tree, *A. unedo*, is one of the most popular species. Like the rest of the genus it is evergreen. It can be trained with a single trunk, as a multi-stemmed tree, or left unpruned to form a dense bush.

Those species with especially attractive bark, such as the Grecian strawberry tree, *A. andrachne*, and the Killarney strawberry tree, *A. × andrachnoides*, should be grown with a tall, clear trunk. An established specimen of *A. menziesii* may need to have the lower branches removed to expose more of the trunk.

Arbutus will usually regenerate readily from old wood. If the tree has been damaged in a storm, or young branches appear to have been injured or killed during a very severe winter, wait to see whether new growth appears. If it does, be prepared to cut back the old growth hard. The shape may be spoilt in the short term but the tree will often outgrow the damage.

Arbutus × andrachnoides

ARCTOSTAPHYLOS
BEARBERRY, MANZANITA

The species usually grown are woody, ground-cover plants although the genus does include some small trees.

No routine pruning is needed, but the ground-hugging *A. uva-ursi* may need cutting back once it fills its allotted space. Trim the shoots with secateurs whenever necessary as shears leave a hard, formal edge, which is inappropriate for this plant.

Arctostaphylos uva-ursi 'Point Reeves'

ARISTOLOCHIA
DUTCHMAN'S PIPE

The hardy woody species usually grown is the climbing Dutchman's pipe, *A. durior*.

No routine pruning is required as long as the plant has space to grow unrestrained.

It is difficult to keep the plant tidy even when it is trained to wires against a wall, or up a pergola or pole. Remove surplus shoots in late winter, and at the same time cut back long shoots by a third.

ARTEMISIA

There are both herbaceous and shrubby artemisias. The latter include lad's love or southernwood, *A. abrotanum*, and common wormwood, *A. absinthium*.

Prune these two species by Technique 9 in mid-spring, to prevent the plant becoming leggy and the growth sparse. Other shrubby species only need leggy or frost-damaged growth removed in spring when this becomes necessary.

After planting To stimulate fresh young growth, cut back the existing stems to within 2.5–5cm (1–2in) of the ground if planting in spring. If planting at any other time, leave stems unpruned until the following spring, then prune by Technique 9.

Artemisia 'Powis Castle

ARUNDINARIA

BAMBOO

Old canes offer some support and protection for new ones, routine pruning is not required. Thin out the old canes by cutting them back to ground level if the clump becomes too congested, and chop off underground stems to contain the plant's spread.

Arundinaria viridistriata

ATRIPLEX

The salt bush or tree purslane, *A. halimus*, grows wild on cliffs and can be used as a coastal hedge. Clipping in spring will keep plants compact.

If it is grown as a shrub, no routine pruning is necessary, but if the plant begins to open out and look thin in the centre clip it with shears (Technique 1) – or shorten the ends of the shoots with secateurs if you want a less formal outline – to encourage denser growth and a better shape.

Atriplex halimus

AUCUBA

The spotted laurel, *Aucuba japonica*, is the species most widely grown.

Despite its name the species itself has plain foliage; only its varieties have spotted or variegated leaves.

No routine pruning is required, but if the shrub begins to outgrow its space trim it back in mid-spring (Technique 1). If grown as a hedge, trim in mid- or late summer. Use secateurs not shears, otherwise the cut leaves will turn brown and look unsightly.

After planting To help create a good shape, shorten all the previous year's growth by about one-third, between early and late spring. If planting at any other time, wait until the following spring before pruning.

Aucuba japonica 'Variegata'

AZARA

Several species can be grown in sheltered areas with mild winters. The easiest and most successful way to grow them is as free-standing bushes planted in front of a wall. However, you can select about eight shoots branching from close to the base and tie these fan-like to horizontal wires fixed to the wall. Sideshoots will grow from this framework of shoots to cover the wall eventually. If the plant becomes congested, prune back some of the sideshoots to the fan-like framework in late spring.

Azaras grown as bushes or small trees require no routine pruning.

Azara serrata

BAMBUSA

BAMBOO

The more vigorous bamboos spread quickly by underground stems. The best way to restrict the spread is with a solid barrier buried about 45cm (18in) deep. Old paving stones or slabs would do the job. If the clump becomes congested, remove some of the old canes by cutting them back to ground level – best to wear gloves for this task. Otherwise routine pruning is unnecessary.

BERBERIDOPSIS

CORAL BERRY

After many years the branches of this evergreen climber may become a little crowded, in which case thin them by cutting out a few of the oldest thick shoots and weakest thin ones. Otherwise no routine pruning is necessary.

BERBERIS

BARBERRY

Most berberis require little in the way of regular pruning, except the occasional removal of old shoots to encourage new growth and create an attractive shape. Left unpruned, some species become large, with dense growth, and may outgrow their space.

Deciduous species, such as *B. thunbergii* and *B.* × *wilsoniae*, are traditionally pruned in late winter, but you may prefer to wait until early or mid-spring, by which time you can see if any shoots have died by the absence of new growth. Prune evergreen species after flowering (usually this means late spring).

To improve the shape of mature deciduous or evergreen berberis that are becoming untidy or have outgrown their space, cut back one-third of the stems to just above ground level (Technique 5), or to healthy young shoots close to the base. This will reduce the number of flowers produced the following spring but improve the appearance. Young plants only require long, straggly shoots trimming back for a good shape.

Remove any crossing, badly placed or diseased shoots in early spring.

Berberis dictyophylla

The white-stemmed berberis, *B. dictyophylla*, is grown mainly for its stems, which are attractive in autumn and winter when the white 'bloom' is prominent. Encourage the production of strong young shoots by cutting out a third of the oldest stems each year (Technique 5), even if the plant is young and still compact.

Dwarf berberis *B. thunbergii* 'Atropurpurea Nana', *B. buxifolia* 'Nana' and other dwarf berberis do not require regular pruning when grown in a border, but some can be shaped as formal hedges or individual specimens.

Formal clipping Berberis that are suitable for hedging (such as *B. darwinii*), can also be clipped into a formal shape with shears immediately after flowering is over.

Grafted plants Most berberis are raised from cuttings or seed, but a few (such as *B. linearifolia* and *B. × lologensis*) are sometimes grafted on to another species, such as *B. thunbergii*. Grafted plants may occasionally produce some weak shoots from the rootstock. If this happens, cut them back to the main stem.

Berberis × lologensis

BETULA
BIRCH

Most birches form large trees, and no routine pruning is required once they are mature. They have attractive bark and are most frequently grown as single-stemmed trees, with a clear trunk to about 1–2m (4–7ft).

To create this clear trunk, remove the lower branches in late summer over a period of two or three years after planting. Do not prune between early winter and late spring as wounds tend to bleed badly.

Dwarf species, such as *B. nana*, should not be pruned except to remove any dead or diseased shoots.

Betula papyrifera

Multi-stemmed trees The common silver birch, *Betula pendula*, is sometimes grown as a multi-stemmed tree to appear like a small clump of separate trees. To create this effect, cut the tree back to near ground level after planting. Do not do this with varieties such as *B. pendula* 'Dalecarlica' and *B. pendula* 'Youngii', as these will have been grafted and you will simply

encourage the rootstock to grow.

The same technique can be used with other species. *B. nigra* can easily be induced to divide at ground level to form a large bush with a rounded head. It will often divide naturally low down to produce two or three main stems. If you want a single-stemmed tree prune out any competing shoots.

After planting For a small weeping tree, allow the head of *B. pendula* 'Youngii' to develop naturally at the graft height. For a taller specimen that will make more of a focal point, train the leading shoot to about 3m (10ft) to a stake until the wood has hardened enough to remain rigid.

Bark peeling Many species, such as *B. nigra* and *B. utilis*, have bark that flakes and peels. This can be part of their attraction, but for a cheery winter effect you may want to expose the bright new bark beneath by gently peeling off the flakes in late autumn.

BUDDLEIA

BUTTERFLY BUSH, ORANGE BALL TREE

Some of the most popular buddleias should be pruned hard each spring to keep them compact and encourage large flowers. Others are best pruned moderately, in summer. The most widely grown buddleia is the common butterfly bush, *B. davidii*. It is typical of those that flower at the ends of shoots produced in the current year. Prune it annually otherwise it will become leggy with flowers at the ends of tall stems. In a small garden buddleias are best cut back close to the ground each spring using Technique 8. Start when the plants are young so that they never become too woody and neglected. If there is more room, say at the back of a large border, cut back to a framework (Technique 8).

In an exposed position, cut about a third off each stem in late autumn to reduce wind damage in winter. Finish pruning in mid-spring.

Other species that you should treat in this way are *B. crispa*, *B. fallowiana* (hard pruning improves the silvery foliage as well as the flowers), *B. forrestii*, and *B. nivea*.

Buddleia 'Lochinch' is a hybrid between *B. davidii* and *B. fallowiana*. Prune using Technique 8, or leave it unpruned to make an attractive, very large shrub. If it gets out of hand, cut it back hard: it should regenerate.

Buddleia × *weyeriana* is a hybrid between *B. davidii* and *B. globosa*. Normally it does not require pruning, but if it becomes too large or if flowering begins to deteriorate, cut back the previous year's shoots during the spring to about 10cm (4in) from their point of origin.

Buddleia alternifolia (the fountain buddleia), *B. globosa* and *B. colvilei* all flower on wood produced during the *previous* year, so spring pruning is

Buddleia alternifolia

inappropriate. Cut out a third of the old stems as soon as the flowers drop (early- to mid-summer), using Technique 5. If you fail to prune the plant periodically, the lower branches will begin to die as new ones produced above them shut out light, and the whole plant becomes congested and unattractive. If you have a neglected bush that has become very large and overgrown, try cutting the whole bush back hard: it should regenerate and, after two or three years, make an attractive shrub again.

Standard trained *Buddleia alternifolia* can be trained into a standard. Start with a young plant. Select a strong shoot and tie it to a supporting stake to form the main stem. Remove any other shoots growing from the base of the plant. Remove sideshoots from the bottom two-thirds of the main stem until it has reached 0.9–1.2m (3–4ft). The plant can then be allowed to grow normally, and the top pruned using Technique 5, leaving the main stem untouched.

Wall-trained Most buddleias are grown as free-standing shrubs, but some of the less dependably hardy species and hybrids, such as *B. fallowiana*, *B.* 'Lochinch' and *B.* × *weyeriana*, can be successfully fan-trained against a wall.

To form a fan, select about five strong shoots to tie in to the support wires after planting, then prune out all others. If there is space, allow a few more shoots to grow from the base the following year, and tie these in too. Prune back to the framework and not to the ground. Periodically cut out some of the old framework branches if there are suitable young replacement shoots growing from the base of the plant. (Otherwise cut out surplus new basal shoots to avoid overcrowding.)

After planting In spring prune back *B. davidii* and *B. globosa* to within 5cm (2in) of the old wood. If planting at other times, wait until the following spring before pruning.

Buddleia davidii

BUPLEURUM

Bupleurum fruticosum is the only species hardy enough to grow permanently outside in Britain.

It flourishes in mild seaside areas and also does well on chalk. No routine pruning is required, but you can clip the bush to shape (Technique 1) if it begins to grow too large. To encourage new growth when it begins to look neglected, cut out one stem in three (Technique 5).

Because the plant is not dependably hardy in cold areas it is sometimes grown as a wall shrub. In time it will become a tangle of twiggy wood if left unpruned, and the branches may eventually trail on the ground. To regenerate an old bush like this, cut it down to within 5–10cm (2–4in) of the ground in mid- or late spring. It should make plenty of new growth by the autumn, but you will lose the flowers for a season.

Buxus sempervirens

BUXUS
BOX

Box, which is widely used for hedging (see Chapter Five, page 184) and topiary, is very amenable to pruning: just clip it to shape with shears (Technique 1). As a border shrub, however, it should not require annual pruning. If a neglected old specimen has to be cut back hard it should regrow well if this is done in mid- or late spring. It is possible to reduce the height and spread of an old specimen quite drastically, but this is best done in stages over two or three years. This more severe pruning must be done with secateurs, loppers or a saw.

After planting To improve the shape of a new plant, shorten all the shoots by a third between early and late spring. If planting at any other time of the year, do this pruning the following spring.

CALLICARPA
BEAUTY BERRY

The hardy species commonly grown have a twiggy, upright shape when young, and freely produce shoots from the base. With age the branches become more horizontal, and any badly placed branch that is spoiling the shape can be removed. Otherwise pruning is not usually necessary. If you do prune, do it in spring and always retain as much of the young wood as possible.

Callicarpa bodinieri

CALLISTEMON
BOTTLE BRUSH

Callistemons can only be grown outside in the most favourable areas, where they do best in the protection of a sunny wall.

No routine pruning is necessary. The distinctive bottle-brush flowers are formed at the ends of the strongest shoots, so pruning is likely to be detrimental to flowering. If the plant is old and becoming congested, however, remove one or two of the oldest shoots to regenerate the shrub from the base.

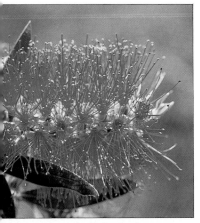

Callistemon citrinus 'Splendens'

CALLUNA

HEATHER, LING

Left unpruned, heathers become straggly and untidy with age, but it is a quick and easy task to clip over them with shears annually in early spring (Technique 3). If you have a large heather bed, an electric hedgetrimmer may be more convenient, but use it with care.

Pruning will encourage new growth and more flowers, but be careful not to cut back into old wood, especially when using an electric hedgetrimmer. Dense young growth will hide the woody stems that build up over the years, but eventually bare patches will appear. It is when this begins to happen that the plants should be replaced.

Special cases If you have very dwarf varieties, such as *C. vulgaris* 'Foxii Nana' and 'Mullion', leave these unpruned (though you can deadhead them carefully if you want to improve their appearance).

A few varieties have very tall, upright growth with long flowering shoots, and you must be careful not to cut these too far back into old wood: make sure you leave some of the previous year's growth below the pruning point.

Sometimes varieties with coloured foliage, such as the very attractive, yellow 'Ruth Sparkes', may occasionally produce all-green shoots. Remove these shoots promptly, cutting back to the point of origin.

Calluna vulgaris 'Elsie Purnell'

CALYCANTHUS

ALLSPICE

Several forms of allspice, *C. floridus*, are grown. All create spreading shrubs which shoot from the ground, but *C. floridus* 'Fertilis' has a particularly neat shape. *C. occidentalis* is more spreading and open, with horizontal branches.

No routine pruning is required, but if the shrub becomes particularly congested cut out a few of the oldest branches in spring or late summer. These will be replaced quickly by new shoots (though these may take several years to flower).

Calycanthus floridus

CAMELLIA

These glossy-leaved evergreen shrubs are best grown in dappled shade or a sheltered position to protect them from wind and the blossoms from spring frost. If flowers are damaged by frost, this will not harm the shrub. Sometimes, however, the young spring growth itself is damaged. Leave such shoots until you can see where new growth is going to occur, then cut out the damaged section.

No routine pruning is required but shorten straggly shoots in mid-spring, after flowering.

Deadheading will improve the appearance of the plant, and is particularly worthwhile on varieties that produce masses of bloom. This is because the energy they would otherwise spend producing seeds will instead create more growth for the following year's display.

Rejuvenating an old camellia You ·can rejuvenate an old, overgrown camellia with weak, scraggy growth by cutting back into old wood. It is best to do this over a couple of years. In the first season cut back all the lower branches to the main stem in spring, but retain a cluster of shoots at the top of the central stem to manufacture food. By the following spring, buds on the old wood should have started to grow, at which point the top can safely be cut off to leave a compact plant with vigorous new shoots growing from the base.

After planting Young plants can be improved by shortening the pale young growth. If you do this for the first two or three years you will. encourage thick, bushy growth to the base of the plant.

Camellia 'Anticipation'

CAMPSIS

TRUMPET CREEPER, TRUMPET VINE

The trumpet vine flowers on growth produced during the current year, so you can cut it back hard if you need to control its spread.

Prune the previous year's growth to two or three buds in winter or early spring. If new growth is required to fill a gap, reduce the length of these replacement shoots by about a third to encourage firmer stems.

The trumpet vine has aerial roots that help it to cling to a support, but if it is wall-trained for protection, tie new growth to horizontal support wires.

After planting To encourage basal growth that will make a better-looking plant, cut back shoots to within 15cm (6in) of the ground in winter.

Campsis radicans

CARAGANA

PEA TREE

These unusual small trees, such as *C. arborescens* and its varieties, and shrubby species such as *C. pygmaea*, should not be pruned when mature. *Caragana arborescens* 'Pendula' is grafted on to the top of a straight stem to form a small weeping tree.

After planting For a clear stem, see page 167. *C. arborescens* 'Lorbergii' is often grown for its foliage rather than its flowers, in which case prune back all the shoots by at least two-thirds, between late winter and mid-spring.

Caragana arborescens 'Pendula'

CARPENTERIA

C. californica, the only species, requires no regular pruning until the shrub becomes too large or badly shaped. Then you should cut out one stem in three (Technique 5) in late summer to maintain a supply of healthy young growth. If neglected, the older shoots eventually become thin at the top and bear fewer flowers.

The shrub does best in mild areas, and may be damaged where winters are very cold. In the latter case it may be necessary to cut back to healthy, undamaged wood. The plant will regenerate, even if you have to cut back hard, though it may take a couple of seasons to recover.

Carpenteria californica

CARPINUS

HORNBEAM

Hornbeam is sometimes used as a hedging plant (see Chapter Five, page 164) and will tolerate clipping, when it resembles a beech and holds on to its dead leaves in winter. When grown as a tree, on the other hand, it requires no routine pruning.

After planting For a clear stem, see page 167.

Carpinus betulus

CARYOPTERIS

BLUEBEARD, BLUE SPIRAEA

The plant usually grown in gardens for its lovely blue flowers is *C. × clandonensis*. This should be treated almost like a herbaceous plant with the stems cut back annually to 2.5–5cm (1–2in) above ground level in mid- to late spring (Technique 7) to reduce the amount of dead wood and encourage more flowers.

Caryopteris incana does not need cutting back so hard. Just remove the dead tips of the shoots as the buds break in spring.

After planting If planting in spring, cut back all growth to within 2.5–5cm (1–2in) of the ground when new shoots emerge from near the base. If planting at any other time of the year, wait until the following spring before cutting back.

Caryopteris × clandonensis

CASSIA

Yellow-flowered *Cassia corymbosa* is best grown against a sunny wall in mild areas. Train a framework of branches to a support of trellis or horizontal wires. Prune back the previous year's shoots to within one or two buds of the framework branches as soon as the buds begin to break in the spring.

Cassia corymbosa

CASSINIA

GOLDEN HEATHER

Cassinia fulvida alone is likely to be hardy enough to grow in the open, and then only in mild areas. Its branches are sticky when it is young and in summer the shrub bears many small white flowers.

Cut out one stem in three (Technique 5) each year in late summer to improve the shape and to stimulate healthy young growth. Cut any straggly branches back to their point of origin for a tidy appearance.

CASTANEA

SWEET CHESTNUT, SPANISH CHESTNUT

Sweet chestnuts make large trees and need plenty of space. Attempts to restrain their size by pruning will spoil the natural shape. However, established trees sometimes produce shoots from the base or the trunk and these should be removed promptly.

Varieties with variegated leaves tend to revert easily to green. Cut out any green shoots to their point of origin.

Castanea sativa

CATALPA

INDIAN BEAN TREE

Catalpa bignonioides is usually grown as a tree with a clear trunk. The white, somewhat frilly flowers of summer are followed by long beans which persist after the leaves have fallen.

No routine pruning is required, but it will tolerate cutting back to modify the shape if necessary as even old branches produce new shoots readily. You can remove any low branches that make mowing difficult but the removal of large branches is a job for a professional tree surgeon.

C. bignonioides 'Aurea' looks attractive as a multi-stemmed tree or large shrub.

After planting If you want a tree with a clear trunk and the early training has not already been done, let two or three shoots grow from the base, then select the strongest to form the main stem. Prune out the weaker shoots, and tie the main stem to a 2.4m (8ft) stake.

Between late summer and early spring, remove side growths on the main stem for about two-thirds of its length, until the required height for the canopy is reached. Leave on any leaf rosettes that are not producing any new shoots.

For a multi-stemmed catalpa tree, see page 169.

CEANOTHUS

CALIFORNIAN LILAC

Both deciduous and evergreen species and hybrids are grown for their haze of blue flowers, but the method of pruning differs.

Deciduous ceanothus Cut back all the branches in spring as the leaves begin to appear to about 7.5–10cm (3–4in) from the point of origin of the previous year's growth (Technique 8). Without regular pruning the shoots become weak and flowering performance poor.

Evergreen ceanothus Routine pruning is not essential for evergreen species but to encourage new growth it is worth cutting two-thirds off each new shoot after flowering (Technique 4). Evergreen ceanothus are often grown against a wall for protection. Secure the branches to a strong trellis or training wires, and tie in new shoots in early summer and again in early autumn. If they become bare at the base, try planting another shrub in front to disguise the unattractive part.

Evergreen ceanothus are sometimes damaged in a cold winter and in unfavourable areas they may even be killed. If severely damaged, cut back to healthy living wood to stimulate new growth from the base.

After planting If planting a *deciduous* ceanothus in early or mid-spring, cut the shoots back to within 5cm (2in) of the old wood to encourage good branching from the base. If planting at any other time, wait until the following spring before pruning.

Evergreen species should not be pruned after planting.

Ceanothus × veitchianus

CEDRUS

CEDAR

Most cedars grow into large trees, spreading with age, and require no regular pruning. It is important to allow plenty of space and good light all round the tree. If it is cramped by other trees or shrubs, or if planted too near a building, growth often becomes unbalanced and the appearance of the tree is spoilt. During the early years, train a single leading shoot until the required height is reached. The leading shoot on a young deodar, *Cedrus deodara*, often arches over or droops. There is no need to tie this to a supporting stake.

As the cedar grows, remove any dead wood from underneath or at the ends of branches, but bear in mind that cedars do not shoot readily from old wood.

For general advice on pruning conifers, see page 176–7.

Cedrus deodara

CELASTRUS

CLIMBING BITTERSWEET

If this brightly fruiting climber is growing into a tree or over a dead stump, no routine pruning is necessary. If it is growing against a wall or up a pergola, annual pruning *is* required. In late winter remove overcrowded branches and cut back the main shoots by half.

Celastrus orbiculatus

CERATOSTIGMA

HARDY PLUMBAGO, SHRUBBY PLUMBAGO

Pruning the low-growing *C. plumbaginoides* is very simple: just cut back the previous year's growth to the ground (Technique 6) in early or mid-spring. In cold areas this growth will probably be killed during the severe winter weather anyway.

With taller species, such as *C. willmottianum*, cut back to living wood old shoots that have flowered as the buds begin to break in spring. This may mean cutting them back close to ground level.

After planting Cut back the previous year's growth to within 5cm (2in) of the old wood if planting in early or mid-spring. If planting at any other time wait until the following spring before pruning.

Ceratostigma plumbaginoides

CERCIDIPHYLLUM

Cercidiphyllum japonicum, the one usually grown, tends to develop multiple stems and these can be allowed to grow naturally to form a large, multi-stemmed shrub or tree. If you would prefer a tree with a single clear trunk, select the strongest stem and train it upright. Then remove any other competing stems as early as possible.

CERCIS

The Judas tree (*C. siliquastrum*) naturally makes a large rounded shrub with multiple trunks. When well-established it is normal for it to produce flowers directly from the trunk or main branches. No routine pruning is required, but if you want a tree with a clear trunk some branches may have to be removed once the plant is five or more years old. *C. canadensis* and *C. racemosa* are more likely to form small trees and are easier to train with a single trunk than *C. siliquastrum*.

After planting For a clear stem, see page 167.

Cercis siliquastrum

CHAENOMELES

FLOWERING QUINCE, JAPONICA

Chaenomeles look best grown against a wall or fence and will benefit greatly from regular pruning. If grown as a bush, no routine pruning is required, but it is worth thinning out overcrowded branches after flowering.

Wall training If it is grown against a wall or fence, train a framework of shoots to horizontal wires, like a fan. During the first few years of training (during which time the plant will not flower well), cut back to five leaves all shoots growing away from the wall unless you need them to tie into a gap. Cut back to two leaves any further sideshoots that are produced from these shortened shoots. This treatment will help to build up clusters of buds to ensure that plenty of flowers are produced.

Once the plant is flowering well, prune in spring after flowering, cutting back the previous year's growth to two or three buds.

If the plant becomes very congested, remove some of the shoots after the leaves have fallen.

CHAMAECYPARIS

CYPRESS

This large group of conifers includes some that are suitable for intensive clipping as a hedge (see page 181). Cypresses, including the many dwarf varieties, do not normally require any pruning. If a developing tree forms two leading shoots, prune one out (see Conifers, page 176–7).

The size and growth rate of some cypresses are often underestimated. For control of vigorous species, see page 177.

Chamaecyparis lawsoniana 'Winston Churchill'

CHIMONANTHUS

WINTER SWEET

The one usually grown is *C. praecox* (syn. *C. fragrans*). Its scented flowers in winter are produced on wood formed during summer.

Pruning a young shrub is likely to delay flowering. With an established plant, cut out one stem in three (Technique 5) in early spring to encourage new growth. New shoots will then be produced freely from the shrub's base.

Wall specimens Winter sweet can be trained against a wall. Prune all shoots growing away from the wall and those that have flowered to within 5–10cm (2–4in) of the base in late winter or early spring.

If growth becomes congested, cut out a few of the old branches completely, then tie in a number of young replacement shoots drawn from the base of the plant.

Cutting back sideshoots to two leaves on a Chaenomeles

Chimonanthus praecox

CHOISYA

MEXICAN ORANGE BLOSSOM

Choisyas require no regular pruning, but it may be necessary to remove winter damage. Although hardy in most areas, in a position exposed to severe wind chill, the glossy evergreen foliage may suffer. Remove entirely any badly frost-damaged shoots in early spring to encourage new growth from the base. If it is only the leaves at the end of the shoots that are affected, cut back to healthy foliage.

Although not essential, you can keep the foliage looking young and fresh on a mature shrub by cutting back one-third of the oldest branches close to the ground after flowering (Technique 5). This will encourage new shoots from the base.

Choisya ternata

Choisya ternata 'Sundance'

Autumn flowers *Choisya ternata* bears fragrant white flowers in spring, but it will often continue to bloom intermittently through the summer until the autumn. You can encourage autumn flowers by cutting back shoots that have flowered by about 25–30cm (10–12in) as soon as the first spring flowering is over.

CISTUS

SUN ROSE

Always prune with caution, as cistus seldom shoot again from old wood (with the exception of a few species, such as *C. monspeliensis* and *C. parviflorus*). To increase flowering reduce the length of each shoot by two-thirds (Technique 4) in late summer. Cut out dead or damaged shoots in spring, but if all the young growth has been killed by severe weather the plant is unlikely to survive.

After planting Encourage compact and bushy plants by pinching out the growing tips of shoots several times during their first and second years of growth. Be careful not to pinch off all the young growth.

Cutting out an old damaged shoot on a Cistus

CLADRASTIS

These trees, which bear wisteria-like flowers in summer, require no routine pruning. However, if you have to remove a branch, do so in late summer as the wood tends to bleed heavily at other times.

The wood of the yellow wood tree, *C. lutea*, is brittle. Old trees that have branched low may require bracing or supporting in some way in order to reduce the risk of damage in high gales. The other alternative is to cut them back.

CLEMATIS

Clematis are relatively simple to prune once you have discovered which group they belong to.

If you know the name of the species or variety, look it up in the table opposite. If you don't, follow the guidelines below to determine the correct pruning group. It is crucial to get the right group – if you prune at the wrong time you could cut off all the flowering shoots. If you don't prune at all you may end up with tall bare stems and all the flowers out of sight at the top.

If you grow several different kinds of clematis it would be a good idea to write brief instructions on the back of each label.

WHICH GROUP?

Decide which of the three groups below most closely describes your plant, then prune accordingly. If:

● It has relatively small flowers and blooms in spring or early summer, prune as **Group 1**.

● It has large flowers and blooms in early or mid-summer, and possibly some further flowers in autumn, prune as **Group 2**.

● It flowers later, from mid- or late-summer onwards into the autumn, prune as **Group 3**.

GROUP 1 CLEMATIS

These flower in spring and early summer on shoots produced the previous year, and generally have large numbers of relatively small flowers. *C. macropetala* and *C. montana* are well-known examples.

When to prune Prune after flowering, but only if necessary. Do not prune in the winter, otherwise you will cut off the shoots and lose the new season's flowers.

Clematis montana 'Tetrarose'

How to prune Regular pruning is usually unnecessary, especially if the plant is growing into a tree or over some other natural support. A plant growing along a fence or one that has become too large for its support should have dead wood and surplus growth removed after flowering to keep the plant within its allotted space. Do not worry about cutting back to a particular point; just remove enough growth to confine the plant.

GROUP 2 CLEMATIS

These flower in early to mid-summer, and sometimes again in autumn, on shoots produced the previous summer. Many of the large-flowered hybrids fall into this group.

When to prune Prune immediately after flowering, but only if the plant needs restricting. An old, dense plant that has become overgrown and neglected can be pruned hard in late winter: the following summer's flowers will be sacrificed, but the plant will look better in future years.

How to prune Minimal pruning is required unless the plant has become completely overgrown. If the shoots are very tangled, take them from their

Clematis 'Mrs Cholmondeley'

supports, space them out and retie them, cutting out any that are surplus. Cut back those that have to be removed to the lowest pair of buds, close to ground level.

Encouraging a second flowering

Group 2 clematis sometimes produce a second crop of flowers in the autumn. You can encourage an extended flowering period by cutting back half of the stems in late winter or early spring. The plant will produce an early batch of large flowers on the old stems from the previous year, and the new shoots that grow from the pruned stems will produce a display of smaller flowers in the autumn.

GROUP 3 CLEMATIS

These flower in late summer and autumn, on shoots produced in the

Clematis 'Niobe'

current year. They tend to become bare at the base if not pruned regularly.

When to prune Prune in late winter or early spring.

Clematis 'Ville de Lyon'

How to prune Cut the plant back to the lowest pair of plump, healthy-looking buds you can find. These will be about 30–90cm (12–36in) above the ground. This may mean cutting off green, healthy shoots, but the plant will reshoot from the base and be better for it.

DOUBLE TROUBLE

Do not prune varieties with double flowers unless absolutely necessary as they produce double flowers only on old wood. Flowers that are produced later in the season on new wood are usually single.

Because double varieties need to develop old wood before double flowers appear, do not be disappointed if the flowers are single the first time they flower after planting.

WHICH CLEMATIS TO PRUNE WHEN

Species/variety	Group 1	Group 2	Group 3
'Abundance'			○
alpina	○		
armandii	○		
'Barbara Dibley'		○	
'Barbara Jackman'		○	
'Beauty of Worcester'		○	
'Bees' Jubilee'		○	
'Belle Nantaise'		○	
'Belle of Woking'		○	
calycina	○		
chrysocoma	○		
'Comtesse de Bouchaud'			○
'Daniel Deronda'		○	
'Duchess of Albany'			○
'Duchess of Edinburgh'		○	
× durandii			○
'Elsa Späth' (syn. 'Xerxes')		○	
'Ernest Markham'			○
'Etoile Violette'			○
flammula	○		
florida		○	
'Gipsy Queen'			○
'Hagley Hybrid'			○
'Jackmanii'			○
'Jackmanii Superba'			○
'Lady Betty Balfour'			○
'Lady Northcliffe'		○	
'Lasurstern'		○	
'Lincoln Star'		○	
'Lord Nevill'		○	
macropetala	○		
'Madame Edouard André'			○
'Marie Boisselot'		○	
'Miss Bateman'		○	
montana	○		
'Mrs Cholmondeley'		○	
'Nelly Moser'		○	
'Niobe'			○
orientalis			○
'Perle d'Azure'			○
'Rouge Cardinal'			○
tangutica			○
texensis			○
'The President'		○	
'Ville de Lyon'			○
viticella			○

CLERODENDRUM

Only two species can be grown outdoors in a temperate climate, and they require different treatment. *Clerodendrum bungei* is tender and likely to be cut down by frost in most places. However, in mild areas if it is planted in a protected position an established plant will usually produce new shoots in spring. Cut the shoots to ground level in spring (Technique 6), as this will increase the size of both flowers and foliage.

Clerodendrum trichotomum is slightly hardier. It is a large, slow-growing shrub with a bushy habit and requires no routine pruning.

CLETHRA

The most commonly grown is *Clethra alnifolia*, the white alder or sweet pepper bush. *C. tomentosa* is similar in its downy shoots and white bell-like flowers. No routine pruning is required for either, but the clump will become a thicket in time as shoots develop from soil level. Remove at ground level some of the oldest shoots and any very thin ones every two or three years in winter. If the thicket has spread too far and become very dense, with weeds that are difficult to remove growing within the base, dig up the plant and replant selected pieces with plenty of vigorous new shoots and

roots. Take the opportunity to add some garden compost and nutrients to the soil.

Species that form large shrubs or even small trees, such as *C. acuminata*, *C. barbinervis*, and *C. monostachya*, require no routine pruning. However, they sometimes produce new shoots from low down, and these can replace any very old or weak branches that should be pruned out.

The lily-of-the-valley tree, *Clethra arborea*, requires winter protection except in the very mildest areas. If part of the tree is killed during a cold winter, it may be possible to select a healthy shoot arising from the base to train as a replacement.

Clerodendrum trichotomum 'Fargesii'

Clethra alnifolia

CLIANTHUS

PARROT'S BILL, LOBSTER CLAWS

The parrot's bill, *C. puniceus*, is a climber which must be grown against a sunny wall for protection, even in the most favourable areas.

To encourage bushy growth pinch out the growing tips of young plants several times. Tie in any long shoots to fill vacant space. Once established, prune annually in spring, when you can see which stems are dead by the lack of new growth. Also remove some of the oldest shoots to make room for those just starting to grow.

COLLETIA

ANCHOR PLANT

These curious, spiny shrubs rarely have leaves but produce fragrant flowers in autumn. No routine pruning is required, but shorten any heavy old branches that have become bent with age. If new shoots arise from old wood at the base of the plant, retain these to replace old branches, which can then be cut out.

After planting If the plant is a poor shape, or too spindly, prune the previous season's growth to within 5cm (2in) of the old wood in spring.

COLUTEA

BLADDER SENNA

Colutea arborescens is a bushy shrub with a long flowering season. The yellow pea-like flowers are followed by bladder-like seed pods.

Prune out one stem in three (Technique 5) in late spring, to help keep the shrub compact and neat. As flowers are borne on the current

season's wood, this method of pruning ensures constant replacement of the oldest wood.

CONVOLVULUS

The convolvulus most likely to be grown in a shrub border is *C. cneorum*. Cut two-thirds off each new shoot in late summer (Technique 4), to encourage a supply of new silvery leaves and whitish flowers for the following year. This technique also prevents old shoots becoming long and woody, and subsequently untidy.

Convolvulus cneorum

CORDYLINE

CABBAGE PALM

The species hardy enough to grow outdoors in mild areas is *C. australis*, sometimes called the Torbay palm. *C. indivisa* can also be grown outdoors in very mild areas.

No routine pruning is required, but the lower leaves that die as the plant develops a tree-like stature can be removed in late spring to improve the overall appearance.

Cordyline australis

CORNUS

DOGWOOD

This large group of plants includes shrubs and trees that require very different pruning techniques. Tree species and some shrubby dogwoods need no routine pruning, but those grown for their coloured stems should be pruned regularly.

For coloured winter stems *Cornus alba* and *C. stolonifera* varieties, grown for their red winter stems, and the yellow-barked dogwood, *C. stolonifera* 'Flaviramea', should be pruned by cutting back hard to a stubby framework of stems in spring using Technique 7.

After planting Cut back *C. alba* varieties, whether grown for foliage or

Cornus 'Norman Hadden'

stems, and *C. stolonifera* to within 5cm (2in) of old wood in spring. If planting at any other time of year, it is best to wait until the following spring before cutting back.

For ornamental foliage Some shrubby dogwoods have attractively variegated foliage. These are best pruned to encourage large leaves even if they also have coloured stems. With shrubs such as *C. alba* 'Elegantissima' and *C. alba* 'Spaethii', cut out one stem in three (Technique 5). The best time to do this is in mid-spring.

The varieties of *C. florida* with variegated foliage do not require regular pruning.

Some dogwoods grown for their attractive foliage become tree-like in time. The pagoda tree, *C. alternifolia* 'Argentea', and the wedding-cake tree, *C. controversa* 'Variegata', develop attractive tiered branches and do not require any routine pruning. However, on particularly old trees it may be necessary to remove twiggy growth or shoots that are spoiling the tiered appearance.

The variegated cornelian cherry, *C. mas* 'Variegata' needs no pruning but can be cut back regularly to within two buds of the old wood after flowering to keep it small, compact and shrubby.

Flowering dogwoods *Cornus florida* is a shrubby species grown primarily for its very attractive and showy white bracts (petal-like leaves). It requires no routine pruning.

Chinese or Japanese dogwood, *Cornus kousa* and Pacific dogwood, *C. nuttallii*, are also trees that have attractive bracts. They require no routine pruning.

After planting Some dogwoods will form a large shrub or a small tree, and this depends on their early pruning and training.

Cornus mas, *C. alternifolia* and *C. controversa* all branch naturally near the base to form multiple stems unless you specifically select and train a clear stem (see page 167). Frequent pruning from an early stage will keep it shrubby.

Cornus alba 'Sibirica'

COROKIA

The wire-netting bush, *C. cotoneaster*, and *C.* × *virgata*, both need a sheltered position or mild climate as they are not fully hardy. Fortunately they produce new shoots freely from old wood if damaged by frost. Cut out any dead or damaged stems in early spring. Normally, however, no routine pruning is required.

CORONILLA

Grown for their attractive foliage and yellow pea-like flowers, these sun-loving shrubs benefit from the protection of a wall in cold areas. To encourage a supply of new shoots, and to prevent the plant becoming too woody, remove one shoot in three in mid-spring (Technique 5).

Coronilla valentina

CORYLOPSIS

COWSLIP BUSH

These shrubs have leaves resembling those of hazel. They need no routine pruning. However, if the plant becomes large and congested, remove a few of the oldest and thickest shoots at ground level after the fragrant flowers are over.

Corylopsis willmottiae

CORYLUS

HAZELS, FILBERTS

The hazel often grown in gardens is the variety *Corylus avellana* 'Contorta' with corkscrew-like branches. Once it has reached a reasonable size (when it is about five years old), cut out one stem in three (Technique 5) in mid-spring. Repeat this every second or third year, but not annually.

Those grown for their coloured foliage, such as golden *C. avellana* 'Aurea' and the purple filbert, *C. maxima* 'Purpurea', benefit from annual pruning. Cut out one stem in three (Technique 5) for a supply of strong new shoots with brightly coloured foliage.

The Turkish hazel, *Corylus colurna*, grows into a tree and needs no routine pruning. Remove any shoots that appear at ground level.

Corylus colurna

COTINUS

SMOKE BUSH

The smoke bush, *Cotinus coggygria*, is naturally bushy with rounded leaves and a haze of fine flowerheads in summer. To prune for flowers *and* foliage, cut out one stem in three (Technique 5) in mid-spring.

If you prefer a large shrub with masses of flowers, leave the bush unpruned, except to remove any dead or diseased wood in spring.

For a compact foliage plant, cut down the stems to a framework of stubs close to ground level (Technique 7). You will sacrifice flowers, but this technique improves the appearance of purple-leaved varieties.

Cotinus obovatus, on the other hand, needs no routine pruning.

After planting To encourage a bush of good shape, shorten all the previous year's growth by about one-third in spring. If planting at any other time, however, wait until the following spring before pruning.

Cotinus coggygria 'Foliis Purpureis'

COTONEASTER

This large group of plants includes both evergreen and deciduous species that range from ground-huggers to large shrubs of almost tree-like proportions. Few need routine pruning, and this is to limit size.

Species that may need constraining include large shrubs such as *C. simonsii* and *C. wardii*, and low spreaders like the fishbone cotoneaster, *C. horizontalis*, and the prostrate *C. × suecicus* 'Skogholm'. Cut out one stem in three each year (Technique 5) once they have filled their allotted space.

Prune deciduous species in late winter or spring before the leaves open, evergreens in mid-spring. Most cotoneasters reshoot even if cut back hard into old wood, though this is not normally necessary. Take care not to spoil the natural shape of the plant by heavy pruning.

'Tree' cotoneasters A number of cotoneasters, including prostrate ground-huggers, are sometimes grafted on to a stem of an upright species such as *C. bullatus* to produce a very small tree. One such is the so-called weeping cotoneaster, *C.* 'Hybridus Pendulus'. However, it may also be grown on its own roots with the stem trained against a stake.

Standard and half-standard cotoneasters require no routine pruning, but remove any shoots that appear on the main stem as soon as you notice them.

Cotoneaster horizontalis in autumn colour

CRATAEGUS

THORN, HAWTHORN, QUICKTHORN, MAY

Hawthorns, *Crataegus monogyna* and *C. oxyacantha* (syn. *C. laevigata*), tolerate close clipping and make good wildlife hedges. When they are grown as trees, however, they require no routine pruning.

After planting Hawthorns make attractive small trees with a round head of branches on a clear stem. Remove any sideshoots that appear on the stem below the required level of branching. Do this in stages, gradually raising the height of the branches above the ground, if the tree is young.

Crataegus oxyacantha 'Rosea Flore Pleno'

Late winter or mid-spring are the best times to do this.

If the tree already has a clear stem of the required height, prune back all the previous year's shoots by about two-thirds between late winter and mid-spring, to encourage a densely branched tree to form.

CRINODENDRON

LANTERN TREE

Crinodendron hookerianum is the only species hardy enough to be grown outdoors, and even then it requires a mild area. It needs shade, otherwise the foliage can be scorched by the sun.

No routine pruning is required, but if the shrub becomes too large, cut out one stem in three (Technique 5) in mid-summer.

CRYPTOMERIA

JAPANESE CEDAR

Crypotomeria japonica is the only species but it has many varieties with foliage differing in form and colour. None requires routine pruning.

Prune only for problems (see Conifers, pages 176–7).

X CUPRESSOCYPARIS

LEYLAND CYPRESS

The Leyland cypress (× *C. leylandii*) is widely used for tall hedges and screens (see page 186). Given adequate space it makes a noble tree which requires no routine pruning.

The Leyland cypress is a fast-growing tree that sometimes becomes larger than planned. Cutting out the top will check the growth and is unlikely to kill the tree, but some dieback may occur from the cuts. New branches should continue the upward growth, though the tops will probably be wider than before. The process will have to be repeated every few years to control their growth. High summer is a good time to do this kind of 'topping'.

An alternative solution is to cut the tree down close to the base, but leaving a sideshoot with a growing tip. Tie this to a cane to make it grow upright. The process can be repeated once the new growth becomes too large, but it is most likely to succeed with reasonably young trees that still have sideshoots close to the base.

Prune only for problems (see Conifers, page 176–7).

CUPRESSUS

CYPRESS

Cypress species grow into large trees, but there are also dwarf varieties and varieties with coloured foliage. None of these requires routine pruning.

Prune only for problems (see Conifers, page 176).

CYTISUS

BROOM

The appearance of most brooms can be improved from an early age by regular pruning which prevents these short-lived plants becoming leggy and bare at the base. Cut back growth made within the last year by half (Technique 2), as soon as flowering is over. Don't cut into bare wood as this will kill the plant. New shoots seldom grow from old wood.

The pineapple broom, *C. battandieri*, may grow into a small tree in mild areas, but usually it stays shrubby.

If *C. battandieri* is trained against a wall, prune in mid-summer by cutting off surplus branches that cannot be trained into a space, or that are growing away from the wall. Tie in new branches to fill spaces or extend the cover.

Cytisus battandieri

D

DABOECIA

St Dabeoc's heath or Irish heather, *D. cantabrica*, is widely grown in its many varieties. To keep the plants compact and well covered with foliage, lightly trim with shears (Technique 3) early on in the spring.

Danae racemosa

Routine pruning is not essential, but for plenty of young and attractive shoots cut out one stem in three (Technique 5) in spring each year. Do this annually so that all of the oldest shoots will be removed before they become unsightly.

Daboecia cantabrica

DANAE

ALEXANDRIAN LAUREL

The only species, *D. racemosa*, is a low-growing shrub that produces shoots from a spreading root system. Cut out dead or dying shoots at ground level in spring, just as new growth is commencing.

DAPHNE

Of the many species grown variously for their sweet-smelling flowers, foliage or colourful fruits (beware, these are poisonous), none requires routine pruning. However, it is worth cutting out straggly shoots in early spring to keep the plants tidy. If you prune severely, flowering will suffer for a year.

Some dwarf and spreading species, such as *D. blagayana* and *D. cneorum*, develop long trailing branches after a few years which sometimes become bare. Instead of pruning them out, try pegging these branches down in the soil and cover over with gritty compost so that they root to form new plants.

Daphne cneorum

DAVIDIA

DOVE TREE,
POCKET-HANDKERCHIEF TREE

This lovely tree looks best growing alone in a lawn but it may be ten years before the large white petal-like bracts appear. Once established no routine pruning is required.

After planting The dove tree tends to develop a bushy habit if not trained with a clear trunk. For a clear stem, see page 167.

Davidia involucrata

DESFONTAINIA

The only species, *D. spinosa*, is a compact slow-growing shrub which requires no routine pruning. If you have to prune for problems such as dead or diseased wood, early spring is the time to cut back to healthy wood.

Desfontainia spinosa

DEUTZIA

Deutzias branch freely from the ground, and flower mostly on short lateral shoots from the previous year's growth. To encourage flowering, cut out one stem in three (Technique 5) in mid-summer, immediately after the flowers have fallen.

Some species, such as *D. gracilis*, are slightly tender and the flower buds and young shoots may be killed by a severe late spring frost. If this happens, cut back dead stems to strong living wood in early summer.

Deutzia × rosea

DIERVILLA

BUSH HONEYSUCKLE

These deciduous shrubs are similar to weigelas and are pruned in the same way. Cut out a third of the shoots in mid-summer after flowering, removing the oldest shoots first (Technique 5). This will stimulate bushy growth. As diervillas flower on the current season's growth, cutting back hard will not affect flowering and for this reason you can also prune in the spring.

Diervillas form spreading clumps which in time may become too large and congested. If this happens, dig up the plant and replant a young, vigorous portion of the parent.

DIPELTA

These shrubs produce stems with attractive peeling bark and showy blossom. They shoot freely from the base and old wood tends to become congested, so it is a good idea to prune out one stem in three (Technique 5) in early or mid-summer.

DISANTHUS

There is just one species, *D. cercidifolius*, which naturally forms a rounded bush. No routine pruning is required. Prune for problems in spring as the leaves open.

DORYCNIUM

These low-growing shrubs, now sometimes listed as *Lotus* species, produce shoots that usually die back to a woody rootstock each winter. Leave the dead shoots on as protection over winter and prune them back to the young basal shoots in the spring (Technique 6).

After planting If planting in spring, cut back all the shoots to within 2.5–5cm (1–2in) of the ground provided you can see new shoots emerging from near the base. If planting at any other time, wait until the next spring before cutting back.

DRIMYS

Winter's bark, *D. winteri*, is the species most usually grown. It develops into a conical-shaped tree or a large shrub. No routine pruning is required, but any spreading branches can be removed to confine the plant if it outgrows its allotted space. Cold winds in winter can damage the evergreen foliage and may also kill shoots. In spring cut back any damaged branches to new growth. In cold areas the likelihood of such damage will be reduced if the plant is grown in the shelter of a wall.

Disanthus cercidifolius (autumn)

Dorycnium hirsutum

E

ELAEAGNUS

These hardy shrubs and trees require no regular pruning, but they tolerate cutting back to shape if necessary, and some, particularly *E. × ebbingei*, are used for hedging (see page 186–7). Shorten any straggly shoots in mid- or late spring.

Elaeagnus usually grows freely from old wood. To encourage new growth on an old plant, or to restrict size, cut out one stem in three in mid-spring (Technique 5). This is unlikely to be necessary until the plants have become well established for some years and most plants can be kept within bounds by cutting them back with secateurs.

Oleaster, *Elaeagnus angustifolia*, can be trained into a spreading tree by removing the lower shoots from the central leading stem. In time the branches tend to grow long and heavy and are prone to storm damage. Therefore, it is wise to prune back the tips of the branches every few years.

After planting To form a shapely plant, shorten all the previous year's growth by one-third if planting in spring. If planting at any other time, wait until the following spring before doing this.

Retaining variegation Variegated varieties of *E. pungens* sometimes produce all-green shoots, and these should be removed to prevent the bush becoming dominated by the more vigorous green branches. Branches with green leaves also spoil the appearance of the shrub.

Elaeagnus pungens 'Maculata'

Pruning out shoots with all-green leaves can be done at any time of year except the early summer. New leaves at this time are often slow to develop new variegation, so be patient, otherwise you may spoil the shape of your plant by over-zealous pruning.

EMBOTHRIUM

CHILEAN FIRE BUSH

Embothrium coccineum can be grown outdoors in mild areas where it makes a large shrub or small tree. Its position in the garden and the climate will dictate size and shape so let the plant grow freely; it will often develop branches from the base.

No routine pruning is required, but shorten straggly growths after flowering is over. Pruning out problems, such as dead or damaged stems, should be done in early spring.

Embothrium coccineum

ENKIANTHUS

These spring-flowering shrubs colour well in autumn. They need no routine pruning, but early spring is the time to prune out any frost-damaged shoots or deal with an overgrown specimen. If the plant has to be cut back quite severely, it will usually produce plenty of new growth.

Enkianthus campanulatus

ERICA

HEATH, HEATHER

Most heaths and heathers are easy to prune. Just clip off dead flowerheads to improve the appearance and encourage new foliage and more flowers (Technique 3). The best time to do this depends on the species: prune Dorset heath, *E. ciliaris*, bell heather, *E. cinerea*, and Corsican heath, *E. terminalis*, in late summer; *E. carnea* (syn. *E. herbacea*), *E. × darleyensis*, and *E. erigena* (syn. *E. mediterranea*) in late spring; cross-leaved heath, *E. tetralix*, and Cornish heath, *E. vagans*, in mid-spring. Do not prune late autumn and winter-flowering species during winter, but wait until spring when new growth is about to start.

Tree heaths, such as *E. arborea*, need different treatment to improve their appearance and flowering. Cut two-thirds off each new shoot (Technique 4) in early summer. The more tender taller heaths, such as *E. lusitanica*, should be left unpruned unless there is a specific problem that needs to be solved, such as frost damage. This species often recovers well after the dead and damaged shoots have been removed in spring.

When pruning any heather it is important not to cut back into old wood as instead of new growth you will be left with unsightly bare patches.

Trimming tips If you have a large bed of closely planted heathers, an electric hedgetrimmer will save time, but there is a risk of cutting into old wood. Garden shears are easier to control, but can be tiring to use. You might find shearing easier if you cut at a time when the shoots are damp. *However, do not use an electric hedgetrimmer in damp conditions.*

Collect up the dead heads and clippings and put them straight on to a sheet of canvas or polythene as you work for easy clearing up.

In a bed where heathers are densely planted, trim the plants round the edge first, then do the central area by placing your feet carefully between the plants and moving as little as possible. Trampling on heathers can spoil their effect as a ground-covering carpet.

Erica × darleyensis

ESCALLONIA

Shrubby escallonias have neat glossy foliage studded with many flowers in summer. Most respond well to pruning and *E. macrantha* is often cultivated as a clipped hedge (see page 186–7).

To encourage new growth on a well-established shrub, cut out one stem in three (Technique 5) in mid-summer after flowering. This may not be necessary every year, however, and if the plant is growing well and looks good and healthy, the best course of action is to leave it alone.

Some species are not particularly hardy, but they grow readily from old wood. Even if most of the plant has been killed during an exceptionally severe winter, it may re-grow from undamaged shoots. Therefore, wait until late spring or early summer before pruning to see whether any new shoots are produced.

Escallonia 'Edinensis'

EUCALYPTUS

GUM TREE

Gum trees rapidly grow tall, but they can be cut down to the ground to produce shoots from the base and thus form shrubby plants.

The leaves of eucalyptus change shape as the tree becomes older. On a young plant the leaves are usually rounded, but on a mature shoot they are generally elongated or sickle-shaped. The foliage on a young tree is much more attractive, and useful in flower arrangements. The best way to ensure a eucalyptus keeps producing this attractive foliage is to prune it almost to the ground each year or every second year, so that the shoots are always young.

To prune a shrubby plant, cut it down to just above ground level (Technique 7) in late spring each year or every second year if you want taller shoots. Cutting back regularly produces bushy growth with much larger leaves.

Most species have very attractive bark, and where there is space for a tall tree, a specimen with a single trunk makes a striking feature.

Trees require no routine pruning once established. Exceptionally severe winters may kill parts of even the hardiest species, but a tree is rarely killed completely and new growth is often generated from the remaining branches, even directly from the trunk. Cutting out the dead wood is a job for a tree surgeon as the branches are likely to be large and some distance above the ground. The tree can usually be saved, even if its outline is spoilt. However, it is only worth trying to salvage a particularly fine specimen.

After planting It is essential to decide at an early stage whether you want your eucalyptus to be a short, sturdy

Eucalyptus gunnii

shrub or a tall single-trunked or multi-stemmed tree. For a tree with a clear trunk see page 167.

If the plant seems very weak, cut back the main stem to about 45cm (18in) from the ground and new shoots will be produced from the stump. Select the strongest of these shoots when it is 30–60cm (12–24in) long to train as the main stem, then cut out all the others flush with the stump.

If the tree already has a strong single stem with branches at the appropriate height, prune the previous year's growth back by about two-thirds in spring. This will encourage the formation of dense foliage with bigger leaves (at least while the tree is young).

For a multi-stemmed tree with several trunks Cut the young tree back to about 45cm (18in) above the ground, and select the required number of shoots, which will soon grow from the stump. Remove any surplus shoots. Once the shoots are about 1.8m (6ft) high begin to remove sideshoots to produce clear stems below the foliage.

For shrubby growth Cut the plant back to about 30cm (12in) above the ground in the spring. If planting at any other time, wait until the following spring before cutting back. New shoots will soon be produced, and you should prune these to within a couple of inches of the old stump each year.

Eucalyptus pauciflora

EUCRYPHIA

Eucryphias prefer to grow in light shade or in a clearing among trees, and competition from other plants largely determines whether they make a dense shrub or a small tree. They do not respond well to pruning. Therefore only prune for problems. Any damaged branches should be removed in early spring.

Euonymus fortunei 'Silver Queen (*adult form*)

Eucryphia × *intermedia* 'Rostrevor'

EUONYMUS

Euonymus vary from ground-hugging evergreens to small deciduous trees or large shrubs, but none of them requires routine pruning.

The deciduous species usually grown are winged euonymus, *E. alatus*, and spindle, *E. europaeus*, which has poisonous fruits. The spindle can safely be pruned back to reduce the height and spread if it becomes too large.

The evergreen Japanese euonymus, *E. japonicus*, tends to form a dense shrub, though it can grow into a small tree and is often used for hedging (see page 186). The variegated varieties are more attractive for a shrub border. Some of these are likely to produce all-green shoots, and unless these are cut right back to their point of origin the plant may quickly be dominated by the more vigorous green growth.

Variegated varieties of the evergreen *E. fortunei*, such as 'Emerald Gaiety' and 'Emerald 'n' Gold', are widely planted as ground cover. They also look good as individual shrubs at the front of a border, and if planted at the base of a wall the shoots will grow upwards, instead of horizontally along the ground.

No routine pruning is required for *E. fortunei* varieties, but if you want to encourage denser ground cover cut back the previous year's growth in early spring. However, this should only be done once or twice, and is not an annual job once the plants are well established. If old plants begin to look neglected, cut out one stem in three (Technique 5) in early spring. If the plant is trained against a wall, simply prune back any shoots that are straying from their allotted space in spring.

After planting Evergreen euonymus need all the previous year's growth shortened by about one-third after planting in spring. This will encourage bushiness. If planting at any other time, wait until the following spring before pruning.

Juvenile or adult? *Euonymus fortunei* varieties are usually seen as low-growing or climbing plants, which are usually juvenile forms. Adult forms have a different habit of growth: instead of the shoots being slender and trailing, they become erect and bushy, with larger leaves. 'Carrierei' and 'Silver Queen' are shrubby.

EXOCHORDA

To keep these shrubs flowering well cut one stem in three (Technique 5) in early summer, after flowering. The plant freely produces shoots from ground level, and it is sometimes necessary to remove some of these while they are still young to avoid the possibility of overcrowded growth on a mature specimen.

F

FABIANA

Fabiana imbricata is an uncommon, slightly tender shrub, normally grown at the foot of a south-facing wall. It needs no routine pruning but shorten long shoots after flowering to improve the shape if necessary.

If a branch is damaged or broken by a high wind, cut it back and new shoots will grow.

FAGUS

BEECH

The common beech, *F. sylvatica*, makes a very large tree, best seen as an isolated specimen in a garden where it has plenty of space to grow

Fagus sylvatica 'Tortuosa'

unhindered. Big, old specimens tend to shed branches unexpectedly. If this happens seek advice from a professional tree surgeon.

No routine pruning is required when beech is grown as a tree, but it will tolerate regular clipping when grown as a hedge (see page 181).

Other varieties are more suited to a small garden. The weeping purple beech, *F. sylvatica* 'Purpurea Pendula', which is slow-growing with branches often cascading down to the ground, needs no routine pruning.

The contorted beech, *F. sylvatica* 'Tortuosa', forms a network of congested branches. Do not thin these out (other than to remove dead wood) as this dense growth is a characteristic of the tree.

The Dawyck beech, *F. sylvatica*, 'Fastigiata', is narrow and upright with naturally twisted side branches. Do not attempt to remove these to form a clear trunk: it should have a narrow outline, with branches to the base.

X FATSHEDERA

This is a hybrid of a variety of *Fatsia japonica* and an ivy, *Hedera helix* 'Hibernica'. The plant has a sprawling habit with shoots that tend to grow erect and then flop. It can be left unpruned to form a bushy, spreading shrub with time, but if you cut out one stem in three (Technique 5) in mid-spring each year it will stimulate more young shoots and produce a tidier, more shapely plant.

× *Fatshedera lizei*

FATSIA

FALSE CASTOR OIL PLANT

Fatsia japonica requires little pruning, but if it grows too large for its allotted space remove the oldest stems at ground level in spring. You can keep the shrub compact and ensure that it produces plenty of attractive young leaves by cutting out one stem in three in mid-spring each year (Technique 5); generally it shoots readily from old wood. A balanced shape is important, to the appearance of *F. japonica*, so cut back any shoots that seem to be spoiling the outline in mid-spring.

Fatsia japonica

FEIJOA

GUAVA, PINEAPPLE GUAVA

Although this will make a large free-standing shrub in mild areas, it is usually grown with the protection of a wall. It should be planted a little distance, about 18in (45cm), in front of a wall so that it can grow naturally.

No routine pruning is required, but it may be necessary to restrict the spread. Do this by gradually pruning back into the main framework of the plant annually, in mid-summer after it has flowered.

FICUS

FIG

When the fig, *F. carica*, is grown for its fruit, special pruning methods apply (see page 230), but you can grow it in mild areas as a very decorative shrub with large, attractive leaves.

If given space the plant will make a spreading shrub, but you can restrict its size if you need to by pruning back all of the over-large shoots. Take them far enough back to hide the cut end from view.

If the plant becomes really overgrown and untidy, try cutting it back hard to just above ground level in spring. You may find that nature does this job for you, killing the top growth during the winter.

Fortunately the fig has great powers of rejuvenation and new growth normally easily regrows even after such drastic treatment.

Vigour can also be restricted by planting where the roots can be confined (in an area of paving, for example – insert slabs or some other kind of barrier vertically into the soil to limit the horizontal spread of the roots), or by root pruning (see page 173) where this is practical.

FORSYTHIA

GOLDEN BELL BUSH

Forsythias flower on shoots produced in the previous year, so pruning should always be done soon after flowering to give new shoots time to mature.

To improve the overall shape and encourage flowering (very old branches do not flower so well), cut out one stem in three (Technique 5) annually, in mid-spring.

Forsythia suspensa usually needs to be trained against a wall for support. The sideshoots that have flowered should be cut back hard in mid-spring to within one or two buds of the old wood. This will keep growth compact and close to the wall, though new shoots will arch away from the wall.

Forsythia hedge

Forsythia suspensa

Clipping a hedge Forsythias, particularly *F. intermedia* 'Spectabilis', can be planted and trained as a hedge. The plants should be clipped with shears in mid-spring after flowering. Remove about 15cm (6in) from each shoot unless you need to restrict spread. If the hedge is not too long a better result will be achieved using secateurs.

The same technique can be used to create any geometric outline, though the shaping will take several years.

Usually growth is so vigorous that another clipping will be necessary later in the summer, even though you risk clipping off some of the following year's flowering shoots.

FOTHERGILLA

Fothergillas, which are grown mainly for their colourful autumn foliage, send up woody, twiggy stems from the ground. They require no routine pruning. Do not cut off the low shoots as these help to keep the plant covered with foliage close to the ground.

FRAXINUS

ASH

These hardy trees are easy to grow, provided that the soil is not too dry. They do not require any routine pruning at all.

Be careful not to damage the leading shoot in the early years, otherwise the shape of the tree will be spoilt as competing main shoots produce a narrow V-shape.

FREMONTODENDRON

Fremontodendron californicum is the species normally grown. It is not hardy enough to be grown as a free-standing shrub except in the mildest areas, and is usually trained against a wall.

To increase flowering and control the size once the plant is well established, cut two-thirds off each new shoot (Technique 4) in early spring. Tie in new shoots to fill any gaps. This is also the time to remove any winter-damaged shoots.

Health warning The dusty down from the stems can be irritating to the skin and eyes.

Fothergilla major

Fremontodendron californicum 'Pacific Sunset'

FUCHSIA

Some fuchsias, such as *F. magellanica*, are hardy enough to be left outdoors without winter protection. In all but the mildest climates the top growth will be killed in the winter, and pruning consists of cutting back the old or dead stems to ground level (Technique 6) in mid- or late spring. Despite this apparently drastic pruning new shoots will appear in profusion.

In particularly mild areas, the top growth may survive the winter and the woody branches can be left unpruned to form an attractive, tall, spreading shrub. To keep a flowering hedge in good shape, prune back the sideshoots in the spring, as the new buds break.

Very old bushes that have retained woody shoots from year to year can be cut back hard to encourage new growth from the base. Fuchsias shoot freely from old wood, and flower on shoots produced in the current year, so they are very tolerant of hard pruning if necessary.

Standard fuchsias must be overwintered in a greenhouse or conservatory as the main stem is vulnerable to frost damage. Prune the head in spring once new growth is evident. Shorten the previous year's shoots to within a couple of buds of the main stem, and cut out completely any very weak shoots. Pinch out the growing tips from the new shoots several times as they grow, to produce a bushy, rounded head.

Fuchsia 'Tom Thumb'

G

GARRYA

SILK TASSEL BUSH

Garrya elliptica is the species usually grown. It can be treated as a free-standing bush in mild areas; elsewhere it is best grown against a wall for protection. It responds well to pruning, and sideshoots can be cut back hard to a framework of main branches against a wall.

Generally, however, the best way to prune a garrya, whether free-standing or planted close to a wall, is to cut out one stem in three (Technique 5) in mid-spring each year. This will keep the shrub within bounds.

GAULTHERIA

Gaultherias can be grown without pruning, especially the creeping partridge-berry or winter-green, *G. procumbens*. However, to encourage new growth and maintain the plant's vigour, cut out one stem in three (Technique 5) in mid-summer.

Gaultheria shallon forms spreading thickets of upright shoots. If necessary, chop off pieces from around the edge of the plant with a spade in mid- or late spring to restrict its spread. If the plant becomes overgrown and invasive, cut all growth to the ground in early spring. It will soon reshoot.

GENISTA

BROOM

Most genistas thrive without any routine pruning, but it can be helpful to thin out crowded shoots on an old plant after flowering to help keep the bush open. Also, occasional pruning can help prevent the plant from becoming leggy.

Some species respond to more specific treatment. *G. lydia* and the Mount Etna broom, *G. aetnensis*, can have their new shoots cut back by half (Technique 2) in late summer, but avoid cutting back into old wood. If the plant looks attractive then it is better to leave it alone.

Spanish gorse, *G. hispanica*, forms a low, compact hummock. Clip over with shears immediately after flowering to deadhead it; removing a couple of inches (about 5cm) of the stems will help to keep it compact.

Garrya elliptica

Gaultheria procumbens

Genista hispanica

GINKGO

MAIDENHAIR TREE

The maidenhair tree resents pruning, and shortened shoots may die back further. If the main stem forks, however, cut out the weaker branch as soon as possible, so that the tree grows with one strong leading shoot.

Ginkgo biloba 'Pendula'

GLEDITSIA

Honey locust, *Gleditsia triacanthos*, and its popular golden variety 'Sunburst', require no routine pruning once they reach tree size. However, they benefit from early pruning, and this encourages dense branching.

After planting see page 167. To encourage dense branching prune the previous year's growth back by two-thirds between late winter and mid-spring. Restricting the size will also stimulate the formation of large leaves. If planting in summer or autumn, it is best to wait until the following winter before pruning.

Gleditsia triacanthos 'Sunburst'

Gleditsia triacanthos

GREVILLEA

A few species are suitable for growing outdoors but these succeed only in mild sheltered areas. They are best planted close to a wall for protection, although they cannot be trained effectively against a wall.

Prune in spring when winter damage can be assessed. Cut back any dead or damaged shoots to a point where new growth can be seen. Prune back any long, straggly shoots which are spoiling the shape of the plant.

Grevillea rosmarinifolia

GRISELINIA

Griselinia littoralis is the only species hardy enough to survive outdoors during mild winters. No routine pruning is required, but the shrub can be clipped (Technique 1), preferably with secateurs to avoid damaging the large leaves. The shrub can be cut back hard if it is necessary to do so, and it will reshoot from old wood.

Shorten any straggly growths in mid-spring or late summer to improve the shape.

Griselinia littoralis is sometimes used for hedges in seaside areas, where it tolerates wind and salt spray well (see page 186).

After planting Shorten the previous year's growth by one-third in spring to ensure the shrub develops a good, bushy shape. If planting at any other time, wait until the following spring before pruning.

Griselinia littoralis 'Variegata'

H

HALESIA

MOUNTAIN SILVERBELL,
SNOWDROP TREE

Although halesias will make small trees, they have spreading, low branches that provide good cover close to the ground. These low branches should be left unpruned.

The species usually grown, *H. carolina* and *H. monticola*, are also sometimes sold with a short single trunk. Any branches that have to be removed because they are in the way or have been damaged should be dealt with in autumn. Routine pruning is unnecessary.

Halesia monticola vestita

X HALIMIOCISTUS

To encourage new flowering shoots on these evergreen shrubs, cut two-thirds off each shoot (Technique 4) in late summer. Be careful not to cut back into old wood as such severe pruning can kill these plants. Once they begin to deteriorate it is best to propagate replacement plants from cuttings taken in summer.

× *Halimiocistus wintonensis*

HALIMIUM

These evergreen flowering shrubs do well by the seaside. To encourage new flowering shoots cut two-thirds off each new shoot (Technique 4) in late summer. Take care not to cut into old wood because you could kill the plant as a result.

Halimium umbellatum

HAMAMELIS

WITCH HAZEL

Witch hazels have a rather spreading shape and the branches often grow horizontally close to the ground. No routine pruning is required and it is better not to remove any branches unless really necessary. Better to achieve a balanced shape by growing the plant in good light and with plenty

of space than to attempt to create a symmetrical bush by pruning.

If necessary, to improve the overall shape or restrict the spread of the tree remove individual branches in early spring.

Hamamelis mollis

Hebe × franciscana 'Variegata'

HEBE

SHRUBBY VERONICA

Most hebes have very compact mound-forming or carpeting growth and for these routine pruning is unnecessary.

Many hebes are of borderline hardiness and may be damaged during a severe winter: the leaves will become brown and the stems bare. Do not be tempted to prune these damaged shoots until spring, for they may afford the plant a little extra protection. Wait until the new growth appears, then it will be clear how much of the dead or damaged shoots will have to be cut off. Start by pruning back to the first strong new bud developing on each shoot, but be prepared to cut back further about a month later to produce a better-shaped bush.

If the shrubs become leggy, prune back hard in mid-spring. Fortunately hebes will usually shoot from old wood, whether hard pruned or cut down by frost, and sometimes they grow new leaves along bare stems. The appearance of hebes will be improved if you pick off the dead flowers or developing fruits.

Special cases Some hebes do benefit from regular pruning. Large-leaved varieties with bold flowers, such as *H.* 'Great Orme' and *H.* 'Midsummer Beauty', can be cut back to the ground (Technique 8) in mid-spring to encourage vigorous new foliage and plenty of flowers. Some gardeners do this annually, but you may prefer to do it only every third or fourth year to rejuvenate the shrub.

Small-leaved, low-growing varieties such as *H. pinguifolia* will respond with vigorous new growth if you prune out one stem in three (Technique 5) in late summer. Without this kind of pruning to maintain a supply of young shoots, very old plants can become straggly and bare in places.

Variegated hebes, such as *H. andersonii* 'Variegata' or *H.* × *franciscana* 'Variegata', sometimes produce shoots with all-green leaves. Cut these out at their point of origin as soon as you notice them. A few hebes, such as *H. hulkeana*, produce many large seed capsules which should be removed.

After planting If planting large-leaved hebes (as opposed to those with scale-like leaves) cut back all the previous season's shoots to within 5cm (2in) of old wood in early or mid-spring. If planting at any other time, wait until the following spring before cutting back. Do not prune those with scale-like leaves.

HEDERA

IVY

Ivies can be grown for years without any pruning. However, those grown up a wall or fence look neater after being clipped with shears in late spring or early summer if they are within reach. Do not be afraid to clip close with shears if the ivy is well-established. It will look bare for a few weeks but new leaves will soon grow. Always make the effort to trim ivy from around windows and gutters using secateurs, cutting back far enough to allow for a season's growth – usually 30–61cm (1–2ft).

The large-leaved ivies such as the Persian ivy, *H. colchica*, and Canary Island ivy, *H. canariensis*, are sometimes grown over pergolas or arches. These need no routine pruning, but once they become large it may be necessary to cut out one stem in three to reduce the amount and

weight of foliage. Cut them close to the ground, then wait a week or two for the foliage to wilt so that you can easily identify the stem you have cut, and remove it. This may need to be done every year if space is restricted.

Ivies grown as ground cover need no routine pruning, but you may wish to cut them back to prevent them growing up the trunks of trees or overtaking other shrubs. If you do this each spring, it should be easy to pull up the creeping shoots. Cut them back to leave a clear area of about 30cm (12in) around shrubs.

'Tree Ivies' When some ivies reach a certain height (which varies with the plant) and maturity, the leaves become more oval in shape and the plant then produces non-clinging, bushy flowering shoots.

If cuttings are taken from this adult growth, the young plants will retain the adult characteristics and are known

Hedera colchica 'Dentata Variegata'

Hedera canariensis 'Variegata'

as 'tree ivies'. These will grow into round, self-supporting bushes up to 1.8m (6ft) tall that flower and fruit freely. Tree ivies need no routine pruning, but you can cut them back to size or clip them into shapes.

Limiting damage Ivies will not damage sound brickwork. But if it needs pointing the weaknesses may be made worse by the self-clinging ivy roots. Be especially careful not to let the shoots grow under wall tiles as the thickening branches will loosen them in time. They may then be lifted and broken by a gale if not by the thick shoots themselves. In the same way shoots can damage interwoven fences as they creep between the wooden strips and prise them apart.

Do not let ivy scramble into gutters, which will soon become blocked.

Ivies are not parasites. As they use trees only for support, they are unlikely to harm an old and well-established tree. The roots will, however, compete for water and nutrients, so do not let ivies grow up young trees. Ivies may also smother trees and hedges, especially formal ones, though they provide useful cover in a wildlife hedge.

Hedera colchica 'Dentata Variegata'

HELIANTHEMUM

ROCK ROSE, SUN ROSE

An annual trim will keep these plants compact and encourage more flowers the following year, with the possibility of a second, smaller, show of flowers in the autumn.

Cut two-thirds off each new shoot in early or mid-summer (Technique 4) after flowering. Use shears to make the job easier.

Helianthemums nummularium

HELICHRYSUM

The shrubby helichrysums, such as the curry plant, *H. angustifolium*, benefit from routine pruning to improve their overall appearance. Cut back the previous year's growth to within 5–10cm (2–4in) of the ground in mid-spring (Technique 9).

If you want a larger plant, cut to within 5–10cm (2–4in) of a framework of old wood.

Species such as *H. splendidum*, that are not dependably hardy and only suitable for mild areas and protected places, are best grown in a sheltered position and cut back to a small framework of short shoots in the same way as a buddleia (Technique 8), in mid-spring.

After planting Prune *H. angustifolium* hard after planting in spring. When new shoots can be seen emerging from near the base, cut back all the previous year's growth to within 5cm (2in) of the ground. If planting at any other time, wait until the following spring before doing this.

Helichrysum angustifolium

HIBISCUS

TREE HOLLYHOCK, TREE MALLOW

The hardy species popular as a late summer- and autumn-flowering shrub is *H. syriacus*. No routine pruning is necessary, but you can cut out individual branches to control the size of an old specimen if necessary. Early spring is the time to deal with winter-damaged shoots or other problems.

Hibiscus syriacus 'Blue Bird'

HIPPOPHAË

Sea buckthorn, *Hippophaë rhamnoides*, is the species commonly grown and does not need routine pruning. However, if the plant becomes too large, or you want to encourage new shoots, cut out one stem in three annually (Technique 5) in mid-spring. Wear gloves and eye protection as these plants have vicious thorns.

Hippophaë rhamnoides

An overgrown and neglected old plant can be cut back to 5–10cm (2–4in) above ground level in early spring with a good chance of regeneration, but you will sacrifice berries on female plants for a couple of years.

Hippophaë salicifolia is less common and will form a small tree with a 1.2–1.8m (4–6ft) trunk. Keep the trunk clear of sideshoots.

Male and female Orange berries are a feature of the sea buckthorn, but if your plant is not fruiting, pruning is unlikely to help. The male and female flowers are carried on separate plants, so you need plants of each sex for berries otherwise the female flowers will not be pollinated.

HOHERIA

Hoherias are not dependably hardy and some require a mild climate to do well. If they are damaged or even killed back to the ground during a severe winter, give them time to show signs of life. They will often shoot from the base and regenerate well.

No routine pruning is required, but if the shrub grows too large cut out individual oversized branches as necessary in mid-spring.

Hoheria lyallii

HOLODISCUS

OCEAN SPRAY

Holodiscus discolor flowers on leafy arching shoots that are produced on the previous year's growth. Routine pruning is not essential, but on overgrown plants it is worth cutting out one stem in three (Technique 5) annually in early spring to encourage new growth. Young shoots are produced from the base to replace the older ones.

HYDRANGEA

Varieties of the popular *H. macrophylla*–mopheads and lacecaps–benefit from the old brown flower heads being left on during the winter as this helps to protect the flower buds from frost damage. Remove the flower heads in spring when the leaves show green. At the same time remove any

Hydrangea macrophylla

very thin or very old shoots close to ground level, to open up the shrub and improve its shape.

Hydrangea arborescens benefits from the same treatment as *H. macrophylla*.

Hydrangea paniculata will have larger flowers on stronger stems if you prune the main branches to within two buds of their bases (Technique 8) in mid-spring.

To maintain the flower and foliage size of *H. villosa*, cut out one stem in three (Technique 5) in mid-spring.

Hydrangea petiolaris, the climbing hydrangea, needs no routine pruning if growing against a large tree for support, but when trained against a wall it will be necessary to restrict growth once the allotted space has been filled. Cut back shoots that have outgrown their space during the summer, taking them back to their point of origin. Cut back any shoots that grow outwards from the wall in spring. Remove up to a third of the shoots each spring, and spread the job over three or four years, so that flowering is not affected.

Other hydrangeas do not need routine pruning. Any problem such as damaged growth or the need to restrain excessive growth can be dealt with in mid-spring.

After planting *Hydrangea arborescens* and *H. paniculata* will grow bushier if you cut back all the shoots to about 5cm (2in) of old wood if planting in early or mid-spring. If planting at any other time, wait until the following spring. Other species do not require this treatment.

Oversized shrubs If you have an oversized mophead or lacecap hydrangea and do not mind sacrificing the flowers for two or three years, try cutting it down to 5–10cm (2–4in) above ground level. It will reshoot from the base.

HYPERICUM

ST JOHN'S WORT

Most hypericums benefit from having one stem in three removed in early spring (Technique 5). This will prevent the plants becoming old and

Hypericum calycinum

woody, and the new shoots produced in the spring and summer are encouraged to give some late flowers.

Cut the rose of Sharon, *H. calycinum* down to ground level annually in early spring to get rid of the old foliage and stimulate plenty of large flowers. This is a tough plant, so do not be afraid to prune it drastically.

Varieties grown mainly for foliage effect, such as *H. × moserianum* 'Tricolor' and *H.* 'Summergold' are best pruned close to the ground (Technique 8) each spring then fed and mulched. If you are not able to do this, only prune every second spring.

After planting Most hypericums, and particularly *H. calycinum*, *H.* 'Elstead', *H.* 'Hidcote' and *H. × moserianum*, are best cut back hard after planting in spring. Prune all the previous season's growth back to within 5cm (2in) of the old wood, cutting just above a bud. If planting at any other time, wait until the following spring before pruning.

HYSSOPUS
HYSSOP

Hyssopus officinalis is an attractive aromatic shrub that is often grown in the herb garden, sometimes as a dwarf hedge, or it can be grown at the front of a shrub or mixed border. Cut it back to within about 7.5cm (3in) of the ground (Technique 9) during early spring.

If growing hyssop as a low, informal hedge, clip lightly with shears in early or mid-spring, just enough to shape the plants and trim off any undesirable long shoots.

Hyssopus officinalis

I

IDESIA

The igiri tree, *Idesia polycarpa*, makes a small or medium-sized tree in time, with branches arranged in horizontal tiers. It is slow-growing and needs no routine pruning but any damaged branches can be removed in spring.

ILEX
HOLLY

Hollies are usually grown as shrubs, but they will make small trees in time. They can also be clipped into pyramids and standards with ball-shaped heads. Although no routine pruning is necessary, they will tolerate hard pruning, and they are sometimes used for hedging (see page 186). The best time to prune is in early spring.

Variegated hollies sometimes produce shoots that have all-green leaves. Cut these out at their point of origin as soon as they are noticed.

If shoots are growing from the stem or base of a holly trained with a clear stem, remove these back to their point of origin.

After planting If you want a bushy holly, shorten the previous year's growth by one-third if planting during the spring. If planting at any other time, wait until the following spring before pruning. Although most hollies benefit from this formative pruning, do not prune box-leaved holly, *I. crenata*, or perny holly, *I. pernyi*, at all after planting.

Ilex aquifolium 'Aurea Marginata'

If you want a holly tree, try to buy one with the initial training already done. However, if you want to train it yourself, start with a young specimen. Form the trunk by removing two-thirds of the sideshoots from the main stem, starting from the bottom. Gradually remove more sideshoots over the next couple of years until the trunk has grown to the required length.

Ilex aquifolium 'Golden Queen'

ILLICIUM

The two species most likely to be grown are *I. anisatum*, a slow-growing large shrub or small tree, and *I. floridanum*, a shrub with dense growth. No routine pruning is required for either of these species, although the latter may need wayward branches cutting out in spring. Old branches can be removed at ground level as new shoots of *I. floridanum* are usually freely produced from the base.

INDIGOFERA

INDIGO BUSH

The indigo bush, *I. gerardiana* (now known as *I. heterantha*), is often grown against a wall in cold areas, but in mild districts can be left unpruned to make a large free-standing shrub. To keep a shrub shapely in cold areas by encouraging new growth, cut each new shoot back by two-thirds annually (Technique 4) in late summer. Other shrubby species that are suitable for growing outdoors should be pruned in the same way.

If the indigo bush is badly damaged by a cold winter, try cutting it down to 5–10cm (2–4in) above ground level in mid-spring; it should grow again from the base. Otherwise just shorten frost-damaged shoots to healthy wood.

After planting Prune back the previous year's growth to within 5cm (2in) of old wood before new growth starts in spring. If planting at any other time, wait until the following spring before pruning.

Indigofera gerardiana

ITEA

SWEETSPIRE

The species most widely available is the holly-leaved sweetspire, *I. ilicifolia*. It is grown as a free-standing shrub in mild areas, elsewhere, for protection, it may need to be grown near a wall. Normally it needs no routine attention, but any winter damage can be pruned out in early spring.

Mature plants may become congested, with a reduction in the number of flower tassels. If this happens, cut out a third of the oldest stems each year (Technique 5) in mid-summer to rejuvenate the plant.

Other species, such as the hardier Virginian sweetspire, *I. virginica*, and *I. yunnanensis* can be treated in much the same way.

Itea ilicifolia

J

JASMINUM
JASMINE

Most of the hardy jasmines are climbers, but one of the most popular, the winter jasmine, *J. nudiflorum*, is more of a sprawly shrub with long, flexible stems that benefit from the support of a wall or trellis. To encourage more flowers, cut out one stem in three (Technique 5) in mid-spring as soon as flowering is over.

Jasminum humile and the primrose jasmine, *J. mesnyi* (syn. *J. primulinum*), are not dependably hardy except in the mildest areas, but should be pruned in the same way as winter jasmine. As these species flower at different times, prune *J. mesnyi* in early summer and shrubby *J. humile* in late summer. The plant is usually hardy, but if a severe winter kills the top growth, cut back to

ground level.

True climbing species, such as *J. beesianum*, *J. officinale*, and *J. × stephanense* normally require no routine pruning. However, once a plant becomes too large or overcrowded, thin out the shoots after flowering. Cut them back to their point of origin, but remove only sufficient shoots to contain the plant.

JUGLANS
WALNUT

Walnut trees need plenty of space to develop their spreading branches and will not start to produce nuts until they are about 15 years old. Pruning of any kind should be avoided if possible because the trees bleed profusely when cut. Remove any dead or crossing branches in early summer.

After planting For formative pruning to produce a clear trunk see page 167.

Young trees are damaged by late spring frosts. If the main shoot is killed allow several replacement shoots

to grow for a year, then reduce these to one that is in a good position to become the new main shoot.

JUNIPERUS
JUNIPER

Junipers range from large trees to dwarf, ground-hugging shrubs. They require no routine pruning, but see Conifers (page 176) for advice on how to deal with possible problems.

Juniperus chinensis

Jasminum mesnyi

Juglans regia

KALMIA

Kalmias produce their cup-shaped flowers on two- or three-year-old stems. Therefore it is best not to prune these handsome shrubs unless really necessary. If a shrub becomes too big, cut out one stem in three (Technique 5) annually, in mid-summer, after flowering is over. This is also a good time to prune out any dead or damaged material.

The calico bush or mountain laurel, *K. latifolia*, sometimes looks weak and straggly if conditions do not suit, and severe pruning will not help as regrowth is often slow. Improve the growing conditions (all kalmias like moist lime-free soil).

The sheep laurel, *K. angustifolia*, often becomes woody with age, and if the main stems bend over and become exposed the shrub looks unattractive. You can cut out the worst-affected stems to just above soil level, as the plant will usually produce new growth readily. If an old bush reaches this stage, the best solution is to remove the oldest one-third of the shoots annually (Technique 5).

The bog myrtle, *K. polifolia*, always remains small and compact so normally no pruning is required.

KERRIA

JEW'S MALLOW

There is only one species, *K. japonica*, and it makes a bushy shrub that produces new straight shoots from ground level. It should be pruned regularly to encourage the production of vigorous new shoots. These flower in the second year.

Cut out one stem in three (Technique 5) in early summer, after flowering is over.

The shrub spreads to form a large clump of upright shoots, and it may be necessary to chop off portions round the edge with a spade if the plant outgrows its allotted space.

There is a variegated variety and this sometimes produces all-green shoots. Cut these back to their point of origin as soon as noticed.

After planting Cut back the previous year's growth to within 5cm (2in) of the old wood if planting in early or mid-spring. If planting at any other time, wait until next spring to prune.

Kalmia latifolia 'Clementine Churchill'

Kerria japonica 'Pleniflora'

KOELREUTERIA

The species usually grown is the golden or Chinese rain tree, *K. paniculata*. No routine pruning is required. If the tree fails to flower reliably once it is well established, this is likely to be because of unsuitable conditions (it needs a warm climate and good light), in which case pruning will not help.

After planting If you buy a tree already trained as a standard, prune the previous year's shoots back by about two-thirds, to encourage a denser branch formation.

If the tree is less than 1.5m (5ft) tall, support it with a cane and remove two-thirds of the sideshoots, working up from ground level (leaving any leaf rosettes without shoots). Continue to extend the height of clear stem over the next couple of years until the desired length for the trunk is reached.

KOLKWITZIA

The beauty bush, *K. amabilis*, is the only species. It needs regular pruning to keep the plant vigorous, a good shape and with plenty of flowers. Cut out one stem in three (Technique 5) in mid-summer, after flowering.

Kolkwitzia amabilis

+ LABURNOCYTISUS

PINK LABURNUM

A very unusual tree, + *L. adamii* combines the living tissue of two different plants: *Laburnum anagyroides* and *Cytisus purpureus*. Individual branches bear either yellow laburnum flowers or pink cytisus flowers (sometimes both occur on the same one). This is the character and attraction of the plant, so do not attempt to prune out parts of the tree with one or other of the flowers.

No routine pruning is required, and it may even be resented. Prune only if there is a specific problem such as a damaged branch.

Just occasionally, however, the laburnum will dominate, and there is a risk of the complete tree having laburnum flowers. If this appears to be happening, prune out some of the stronger laburnum shoots to redress the balance.

Koelreuteria paniculata

+ Laburnocytisus adamii

LABURNUM

Laburnums are fast-growing and tend to branch freely, so early training is important. Pruning should be avoided as bleeding may occur and large wounds do not heal easily. If you have to remove a large branch, do so in mid- or late summer as the wound is then less likely to bleed than in spring.

After planting For a clear stem, see page 167. If you would prefer a bushy tree with branches low down, allow a number of the sideshoots to grow so that the tree develops a well-balanced shape.

Laburnum arches Laburnum tunnels are a feature of some large gardens, but you can achieve a more modest version in a small garden by growing laburnums over an arch or a pergola. *L.* × *watereri* 'Vossii' responds well to the pruning required, has long flowers and produces few (poisonous) seeds.

To begin training, tie in young growth to the support, especially where the shoot has to bend, but check the ties annually to make sure they are not too tight. Once the stem has set into a curve tying is unnecessary.

Remove crossing branches and any that are badly placed (those that would grow into the arch, for example) at an early stage. In winter, prune the previous season's shoots back to just one or two buds from the old wood.

LAPAGERIA

CHILEAN BELLFLOWER

Lapageria rosea is only hardy enough to be grown outdoors in the mildest areas, and then it requires a sheltered wall and partial shade. It is usually tied to horizontal wires stretched along the wall.

Cut out the weakest stems in spring before growth starts.

Lapageria rosea

LARIX

LARCH

Larches are unusual among conifers because they shed their needles in winter. They need no routine pruning, but remove shaded lower branches if they start to die. Good light is necessary for a well-shaped tree.

For general advice on pruning for problems, see Conifers on page 176.

Larix decidua

Laburnum × *watereri* 'Vossii'

LAURUS

BAY, BAY LAUREL, SWEET BAY

The species most often grown is bay laurel, *Laurus nobilis*, used as a flavouring in cooking. It can be left unpruned or clipped or cut back hard to shape the bush (Technique 1) in mid-spring. Use secateurs rather than shears as these can slash the leaves causing them to turn brown.

Trim small mop-headed or trained trees twice a year, in mid-spring and again in mid- or late summer, rather than pruning then more severely once a year.

In most areas young bays are particularly susceptible to weather damage. Cold winds will cause the leaves to turn brown at the tips. The plants will usually outgrow this damage as new growth appears, but the scorched leaves are unsightly so try to prune most of them out of a formally clipped specimen in spring.

Occasionally shoots may be killed in a very severe winter, even on a mature plant. If this happens, cut back to live wood once you can see where new shoots are appearing, or cut back the whole bush to about 30cm (12in) above the ground. It will normally re-grow, but the new shoots will take several years to reach a respectable height. This technique should be tried only on a badly damaged or very large old plant that you would otherwise remove altogether.

After planting Bay responds well to training, so it is important to decide at an early stage what type of plant you want. For a bushy plant shorten all the previous year's growth by one-third in spring. If planting at any other time of the year, wait until the following spring before pruning.

Bays can also be trained into small mop-headed trees, pyramids and

Clipped and trained bay

specimens with 'corkscrew' stems. Early formative training is important for these and it is best to buy plants ready-trained.

Trained bays Shaped bays are sometimes grown in pots, but these should be taken into a sheltered position such as a conservatory, porch or greenhouse for the winter, to protect your investment in time or money from the effects of a particularly severe winter.

Ready-trained specimens can be bought from nurseries and garden centres, but tend to be expensive. You can train your own, but you will need a great deal of patience.

Pyramids are the easiest to produce because they are close to the plant's natural shape. Buy a plant with shoots right down to the base and cut the higher side branches back with secateurs, taking the topmost shoots back further if necessary. Hold a straight piece of wood against the plant as a guide to judge how far back you need to cut each shoot to achieve the appropriate taper. Do not prune the topmost shoot.

The initial pruning can be done at any time during the spring or summer, but early spring is best because it allows further shaping to be done in late summer. Do not expect an attractive shape or dense foliage at this stage, but the first year's pruning will stimulate more branching and denser growth to trim to shape later.

In subsequent years go over the plant in spring and mid- or late summer, cutting back each shoot to an appropriate length, using a straight edge as a guide for the taper. Leave the lowest shoots unpruned if you want to increase the width of the base. It will take three or four years before the plant looks really well shaped.

'Lollipop' trees (those with a round head on a clear stem) are very attractive when complete, though they can look unattractive for several years during formative training.

Start with a young plant and remove all sideshoots from the bottom two-thirds of the plant but allow the top to develop. Pinch out the growing tips of the sideshoots at the top of the shrub as soon as they exceed about 30cm (12in) in length.

Continue to remove sideshoots from the bottom two-thirds for the next few years until you have a stem of the required length, then pinch out the tip of the topmost shoot and the growing tips of sideshoots at the top of

the plant. This will produce a denser head of foliage.

In subsequent years continue to pinch out the growing tips each spring, and if necessary prune back the new growth again in mid- or late summer to maintain a good compact head of dense foliage.

LAVANDULA

LAVENDER

Lavenders respond well to routine pruning. To improve their overall appearance, cut back the previous year's growth to new shoots within 5–10cm (2–4in) of the ground in early or mid-spring (Technique 9) just as new growth starts.

If you want a larger plant, cut to within 5–10cm (2–4in) of a framework of old wood. This severe pruning is only suitable for lavenders that have been pruned annually in this way from a young age. On old plants that have not been pruned hard

Bay in tub with brown leaves to be clipped out

Lavandula angustifolia

regularly, just shorten the previous year's growth in spring.

If you have a lot of plants clip them lightly with shears after flowering. This will also remove the dead heads which look unsightly if left on over winter. Prune lavenders used for a low, informal hedge in the same way.

Unfortunately, lavenders have a relatively short useful life, and even with regular pruning may start to sprawl and die back in time. Therefore it is worth taking cuttings in summer to replace plants that cannot be improved by pruning.

After planting When new shoots appear at the base in spring, cut back the previous year's growth to within 2.5–5cm (1–2in) of the ground.

Leptospermum 'Jubilee'

LAVATERA

MALLOW

The tree mallows, *L. arborea* and *L. olbia*, grow tall, so cut a third off the top of each stem in late autumn to reduce the risk of winter wind damage. Finish pruning in mid-spring by cutting back all the previous year's growth to about 15cm (6in) from the ground. Hard pruning encourages flowering and keeps the plant more compact. Do not worry if the new shoots seem slow to appear; there may be little growth until early summer.

After planting Cut back the previous year's shoots to within 5cm (2in) of the old wood, before the new growth emerges. If planting at any other time, wait until the following spring before cutting back.

Lavatera olbia

LEPTOSPERMUM

NEW ZEALAND TEA TREE

If one of these sun-loving evergreens grows too large, cut out one stem in three (Technique 5) in mid-summer. Leptospermums often fail to grow again if you cut back into old wood. So do not prune unless it really is necessary. Remove any straggly branches in mid-spring.

LESPEDEZA

BUSH CLOVER

Lespedeza thunbergii, the species most likely to be grown, benefits from winter protection. The tall stems die in the winter, but are replaced by a mass of new shoots in the spring which will carry the flowers. Cut back the previous year's growth to the ground (Technique 6) in early spring.

After planting Cut the previous year's stems back to the new shoots when these appear at the base of the plant.

Leucothoe axillaris

LEUCOTHOË

Leucothoë fontanesiana is a hardy evergreen with glossy, pointed leaves. Cut out one stem in three (Technique 5) in spring to encourage new foliage to develop.

LEYCESTERIA

The species most commonly grown is the pheasant berry, *L. formosa*, a shrub with green upright stems that are attractive in winter. Remove a third of the oldest shoots annually (Technique 5) to ensure a regular supply of new growth and plenty of flowers.

After planting Cut back the canes to within 5cm (2in) of the ground, in spring before new growth emerges. If planting at any other time, wait until the following spring before cutting back. This might delay the initial flowering but will produce a bushier shrub more quickly.

Leycesteria formosa

LIBOCEDRUS

The incense cedar, *L. decurrens* (now more correctly *Calocedrus decurrens*), requires no routine pruning. For further pruning advice for conifers, see page 176.

LIGUSTRUM

PRIVET

Privet is most familiar as a hedge (see page 186), but it can also be left unpruned to grow as a free-standing shrub in a border, or trained into a geometric shape which is clipped with shears or hedgetrimmer in mid-spring.

Keep an eye open with variegated varieties for all-green shoots and cut these back to their point of origin as soon as noticed.

Privets that have become too large or overgrown can be cut back hard to about 5–10cm (2–4in) above the ground, if necessary, to make a new start with fresh growth.

After planting To develop a well-shaped shrub from an early stage, shorten all the previous year's growth by one-third in spring. If planting at any other time, wait until the following spring before pruning. Do not do this to slow-growing compact varieties like *L. japonicum* 'Rotundifolium'.

The glossy or Chinese privet, *L. lucidum*, will make a small tree, usually on a short stem of about 60–90cm (24–36in). If you want a tree and the plant has not already been trained at the nursery or garden centre, start with a young specimen and remove sideshoots to the height at which you want the foliage to start. Because this can become too heavy for the trunk, a permanent stake is necessary to give the required support.

Ligustrum ovalifolium 'Aureum'

LIQUIDAMBAR

SWEET GUM

Sweet gums naturally grow into large trees with a strong central stem. *L. formosana* is vulnerable to damage by late spring frosts and if this happens the growing tip of the central stem may be killed and competing shoots may develop. Reduce these to one.

Liquidambar styraciflua is the most popular species. The lower branches can be removed to make a longer trunk but, unless you are confident about doing this, consult a tree surgeon. This does not detract from the tree's attractive outline as the branches tend to droop.

After planting For a clear stem, see page 167.

Once you have a tree with a clear stem and branches at the appropriate height, cut all the previous year's growth back by two-thirds between late winter and mid-spring. Cut very thin shoots back even further. This will encourage dense growth that will show off the handsome foliage which turns shades of red, orange and purple in the autumn.

LIRIODENDRON

TULIP TREE

The tulip poplar or tulip tree, *L. tulipifera*, is the best known species. The unusual tulip-shaped flowers do not appear until the tree is about 15 to 20 years old. The elegant spreading shape of the established tree needs no routine pruning, but if two main shoots develop remove one as soon as possible.

After planting If the tree has sideshoots growing from the main stem, remove these up to the height at which you want the branches to develop. With small plants you may

Liquidambar styraciflua

Liriodendron tulipifera 'Aureomarginatum'

have to do this over several years as the plant grows.

If you have a young shrubby plant, remove all but the strongest shoot, then tie this to a 2.4m (8ft) cane to form the trunk. Remove sideshoots from the bottom two-thirds of the stem each year until the required height is reached.

The columnar *L. tulipifera* 'Fastigiatum' should be left unpruned to grow naturally.

LONICERA

HONEYSUCKLE

Honeysuckles are a diverse group of plants. Most are climbers, some are bushy, and one, *L. nitida*, is widely used as a hedging plant (see page 186).

Climbing honeysuckles don't need pruning but can be cut back if they become tangled or too large. They fall into two groups and it is important to determine which group your honeysuckle belongs to.

Those that have their flowers in pairs on the current year's growth, of which the Japanese honeysuckle, *L. japonica*, is the best known, can be pruned drastically if necessary. If they outgrow their allotted space, just clip them to size with shears during the dormant season, mid-winter to early spring, or after flowering.

The climbers that produce blooms at the ends of the shoots in whorls (radiating like the spokes of a wheel), or in clusters, flower on stems that are at least a year old. The majority of climbing honeysuckles, including the popular woodbine, *L. periclymenum*, fall into this group. Prune them as soon as flowering is over by cutting back each flowered shoot to a point where there is a non-flowering young

Lonicera japonica

shoot to replace it. This is often difficult because old and young stems usually twine around each other, and it is usually impractical to cut back all the flowered shoots.

Overgrown climbers Over the years, the stems of climbing honeysuckles become so entwined that pruning is difficult. If the plant simply needs containing, prune all stems back to their support or cut off the highest growth if this has started to cascade down in a curtain of tangled woody shoots. You will sacrifice flowers for a year (unless the species is one that flowers on new shoots, such as *L. japonica*), but this treatment will improve the plant's appearance in the long run.

Lonicera × brownii

Lonicera

If the honeysuckle is climbing over a trellis that needs repair or maintenance and the plant is so well established that it is impractical to untwine the stems, cut the whole plant down in the autumn to about 5–10cm (2–4in) above the ground. If the stems are very tangled, cut them in several places along their lengths and at the base. Leave for a week or two to allow time for the foliage to die and then disentangle the wilted sections.

Vigorous new shoots will grow the following spring and these can be trained in from scratch. You will lose flowers for a year, but the benefits of maintaining the support and making the plant more tidy will make the loss worthwhile.

Shrubby honeysuckles Shrubby honeysuckles, such as winter-flowering *L. fragrantissima*, and *L × purpusii*, and summer-flowering *L. tatarica*, need no regular pruning. However, to keep an old plant within bounds cut out one stem in three (Technique 5) in mid-spring for winter-flowering species,

and after flowering for those that bloom in early and mid-summer.

Lonicera nitida, known by common names that include poor man's box and shrubby honeysuckle, must be clipped hard (Technique 1) in mid-spring if you want a formal outline. To stimulate new growth and control the size of a free-standing plant in a border, prune out one stem in three (Technique 5) annually.

The low spreading privet honeysuckle, *L. pileata*, requires no routine pruning, but if it grows too large, reduce the new shoots by two-thirds (Technique 4) in mid-spring.

After planting Shorten the previous year's growth on *L. nitida* and *L. pileata* by one-third in spring. Allow all other species to grow without pruning until well established.

LUPINUS

LUPIN

The gorgeous yellow-flowered tree lupin, *L. arboreus*, grows fast but tends to be short-lived. Cut out one stem in three (Technique 5) in early spring to keep the plant vigorous. Deadhead after flowering unless you want to leave some pods for seeds. It is a good idea to grow some plants from seed every few years as replacements.

Lupinus arboreus

LYCIUM

The species most likely to be grown is the Duke of Argyll's tea tree, *L. barbarum*. It needs annual pruning to keep it tidy, so cut out one stem in three (Technique 5) in spring or early summer to encourage new shoots.

MAGNOLIA

Although some magnolias are shrubby, others make tall trees. The most popular magnolias for small gardens, such as *M.* × *soulangeana* and its varieties, *M.* × *loebneri* 'Leonard Messel' and the star magnolia, *M. stellata*, are grown as low, branching trees that resemble large shrubs. These require no regular pruning, though it is always worthwhile removing any small crossing branches in the winter if this helps to create a more open and attractive shape.

Most species can be grown as multi-stemmed or single-stemmed trees, but very vigorous species, such as *M. campbellii*, should be grown with a central leading shoot and a clear single trunk. Other magnolias such as *M. kobus* are widely available as single-stemmed or bushy multi-stemmed trees. After formative pruning, trees with a single leading shoot need no routine pruning.

In very mild areas, the evergreen *M. grandiflora* is sometimes grown as a large free-standing tree with a single trunk. Lower branches can be removed to improve the shape. In most places, however, *M. grandiflora* is better grown against a sheltered wall

Magnolia × *loebneri* 'Leonard Messel'

Magnolia grandiflora

for protection. Bear in mind when planting that this tree does grow large and is only suitable for a tall house wall. Remove branches growing away from or towards the wall at an early age, and tie in new shoots in early autumn. New shoots may need to be trimmed annually if the plant grows too large for its allotted space.

Summer-flowering magnolias, such as *M. × highdownensis*, *M. sieboldii* and *M. sinensis*, may with care be reduced in size by removing selected branches if they outgrow their allotted space. Do this in late autumn or early winter.

In general magnolias need little in the way of regular pruning. If shoots or branches suffer damage, these should be removed in mid-summer to reduce the risk of bleeding and to allow time for healing to take place before winter. Magnolias have good powers of recovery and produce new growth from old wood. However, they are prone to infection entering cut surfaces, so if a wound is over 12mm (½in) across, it is worth using a wound paint (see page 173).

After planting For a clear stem, see page 167.

Magnolia × soulangeana 'Lennei'

MAHONIA

The Oregon grape, *M. aquifolium*, is a strong grower that will almost certainly have to be controlled by annual pruning. To help contain the spread and improve the overall appearance, cut out one stem in three (Technique 5) in early summer. Left unpruned, this mahonia will eventually look untidy with fallen leaves and dead twigs. Use a spade or

Mahonia lomariifolia

edging tool to control sideways spread by chopping off underground stems.

Mahonias grown as ground cover benefit from hard pruning to keep them low and compact. Cut them back to about 15cm (6in) above the ground in spring when the old leaves look tatty. This may only be necessary every second year.

Other mahonias, such as *M. japonica*, *M. lomariifolia* and *M. 'Charity'*, have stiff, upright growth that would be spoilt by this form of pruning. To encourage bushy growth in the early years, cut off the flower heads to below the new leaf joints beneath them as soon as flowering is

over. Even if a stem has not flowered, remove the top rosette of leaves to encourage bushy growth. If you want the berries to develop or need a very narrow plant for a confined space, pruning should not become an annual job once initial branching has started.

MALUS

ORNAMENTAL CRAB APPLE

Most ornamental crab apples are grown as small standard trees with clear trunks, but *M. floribunda*, one of the most popular species, is sometimes trained on a short trunk or even as a bush. Unlike apples grown for their fruit (see page 192), ornamental crab apples do not require annual pruning.

Many ornamental crab apples are grafted on a rootstock, so it is important to watch for any shoots that arise from below the point of the graft, which is usually at ground level. Try to remove these at their point of origin as soon as possible.

After planting For a clear stem, see page 167. Some ornamental crab apples are grown on a short trunk only 60–90cm (24–36in) tall, others are given trunks of 1.8m (6ft) or more.

Malus 'John Downie'

MENZIESIA

Menziesias are fairly erect shrubs with branches that originate from below ground level. Annual pruning is unnecessary, but in spring cut out some of the weakest shoots, along with any dead wood, if the branches become congested.

Menziesia ciliicalyx

MESPILUS

MEDLAR

Medlars, *M. germanica*, make attractive, many-branched, spreading trees, though the fruit may not be to everyone's taste.

No routine pruning is required but the central leading shoot is usually cut out when the tree reaches an acceptable height to give a more spreading shape.

Unsightly clusters of shoots resembling a witch's broom are sometimes produced, especially on horizontal branches. If these are not cut back to the branch they will spoil the shape of the tree in time.

After planting Medlars are usually grown as standard trees with a 1.8–2.4m (6–8ft) trunk. Cut the sideshoots back to two or three leaves during the dormant season. Leave on any leaf rosettes that do not form shoots, but remove these once the required length of stem for the trunk has been produced.

Mespilus germanica

Metasequoia glyptostroboides

METASEQUOIA

DAWN REDWOOD

The dawn redwood, *M. glyptostroboides*, the only species, is a large deciduous conifer. It grows tall and straight with a strong main stem. If this stem is damaged, remove all but one of the competing shoots that develop, allowing only the strongest shoot to grow as the replacement.

Do not remove low sideshoots on young trees as the dawn redwood looks particularly attractive with foliage close to the ground.

For further advice on pruning conifers, see page 176.

MORUS

MULBERRY

Mulberry trees make an attractive ornamental feature in a large garden and the delicious fruit is an added bonus on mature trees of the right variety. The two species most likely to be grown are *M. alba* (once cultivated for its leaves, on which silkworms were fed) and *M. nigra*, the species grown for its edible fruit.

Any non-essential pruning should be avoided because the trees are liable to bleed if cut. *M. alba* has a tendency to produce unsightly clusters of thin shoots, sometimes in great quantity, on horizontal branches. Cut these back flush with the branch annually, to prevent them spoiling the tree's shape.

After planting For a clear stem, see page 167.

MYRICA

Myrica gale, the bayberry, and *M. cerifera* tend to be invasive and develop a thicket of shoots. If, in time, these plants become tall and straggly and look untidy, cut them down to ground level in mid-spring. New shoots should soon grow. Apart from this they require no regular pruning.

Myrica californica naturally forms a bush or small tree. It is sometimes killed back to near ground level in a severe winter, but new shoots will grow from any living tissue that survives. Therefore after a very cold winter, wait to see where new shoots appear before pruning out dead wood.

Myrtus communis

MYRTUS

MYRTLE

The common myrtle, *M. communis*, is the species most usually grown. Like other myrtles it needs to be given a sheltered position and is most reliable in mild districts.

If plants are growing well, you can clip or cut them back hard in early summer to create a more formal outline. Any frost-damaged shoots should be removed in early or mid-spring. If the plant is severely damaged, or killed down to ground level by the cold, it may produce new shoots from old wood at the base, so wait to see if this happens before pruning in spring or digging it up.

Morus alba 'Pendula'

N

NANDINA

CHINESE SACRED BAMBOO

Nandina domestica is the only species and is grown mainly for its autumn tints. It also has scarlet or white fruits that ripen in late summer and often persist through the winter. Therefore it is best not to be tempted to remove old flowering spikes as soon as the flowers are over but to concentrate on spring pruning if the plant needs smartening up.

In cold areas nandina often looks ragged and may suffer damage during winter. In a severe winter it may be killed down to ground level. New growth will usually shoot from the roots, however, and the fresh start will often improve the appearance of an old plant. Growth may be slow at first, but the plant should look respectable again by the end of the season.

If an old plant begins to look congested, cut out one stem in three (Technique 5) in mid-spring to induce new growth from the base. If possible, cut the stems right down to soil level to avoid a thicket of dead stumps. This kind of pruning does not need to be carried out every year.

NEILLIA

These plants form a clump of upright shoots from ground level. *N. thibetica* (*N. longiracemosa*) is the species most likely to be grown. To increase the display of pale pink tubular flowers, cut out one stem in three (Technique 5) in late summer.

Shoots are sometimes produced on the spreading roots 30cm (12in) or more away from the main plant. If the plant has to be kept within a certain area, try to remove these at their point of origin by unpacking the soil and following the roots back to the main plant. If this proves difficult they can be chopped off with a spade.

Neillia 'Thibetica'

NERIUM

OLEANDER

The oleander, *N. oleander*, can survive winter outdoors only in the very mildest areas. It is usually grown in a large pot or tub and taken into a conservatory or greenhouse for the duration of the winter.

Cut back the current year's growth by half after flowering (Technique 2). If you need to control the size of a plant, cut back sideshoots to 10cm (4in) from their base.

Danger warning All parts of the oleander are poisonous, so take care when pruning. Wear gloves, and do not let sap get into your mouth.

Nerium oleander

Nandina domestica 'Firepower'

NOTHOFAGUS

SOUTHERN BEECH

These trees need plenty of space to look their best. Some of the deciduous species, such as *N. antarctica*, are dependably hardy. Evergreens, including *N. dombeyi*, can be grown in favourable areas. Although they may lose most of their leaves in a hard winter, new ones should grow readily in spring. *N. dombeyi* usually forms a smaller tree with a spread that can equal its height. The tree becomes very bushy, often with the lower branches horizontal and not far from the ground.

Southern beeches require no routine pruning.

Nyssa sylvatica ,autumn

Nothofagus procera

NYSSA

TUPELO

The species most commonly grown is *N. sylvatica*. If left to its own devices a young plant will tend to make a large shrub that may evolve into a tree. If you want a good-looking tree with a clear trunk, early training is worthwhile. It is also worth removing one or two of the lowest branches of mature trees if this improves the appearance. The remaining branches can be allowed to hang and this displays the autumn colour in an attractive manner. Crooked branches and twiggy growth are natural, so leave them be and do not risk spoiling the shape by over-enthusiastic pruning.

Nyssa sinensis is less common as it is less hardy and more demanding in its soil requirements than *N. sylvatica*, but the same general comments apply.

After planting If you buy a very young tree, less than 1.5m (5ft) tall to train into a tree with a clear, straight trunk, insert a cane after planting. Tie the stem to this before removing sideshoots from the bottom two-thirds of the plant. Leave on any rosettes of leaves without shoots at this stage.

Gradually prune off more sideshoots as the tree grows, to produce a clean stem over the next couple of years, to the height at which you want branching to start.

OLEARIA

DAISY BUSH

These are shrubs for a mild climate where they will provide excellent shelter for smaller plants in seaside areas. In cold districts there may be winter casualties with shoots killed or damaged. Cut out any dead wood in mid-spring. Fortunately daisy bushes grow freely from old wood, so having to cut back a frost-damaged plant causes only a temporary setback.

To encourage a regular supply of new shoots, which will improve the appearance of the bush and keep it flowering well, cut out one stem in three (Technique 5) in mid-summer, after flowering is finished. For hedges, see page 186.

Olearia × scilloniensis

OSMANTHUS

Osmanthus regenerates freely from old wood, so plants can be cut back quite severely if they become overgrown. This ability to shoot freely even when cut back hard makes some species useful hedging plants, and O. × *burkwoodii* (which is also sold as × *Osmarea burkwoodii*) is sometimes used in this way. Other species, such as O. *heterophyllus*, also clip well and can be used for hedging (see page 186).

Although no routine pruning is required, a shrub can be kept within bounds by cutting two-thirds off each new shoot (Technique 4) in early summer. Remove any dead or winter-damaged wood in early spring.

For *Osmanthus decorus*, see entry for *Phillyrea decora*.

After planting To produce a well-shaped bush shorten all the previous year's growth on O. *heterophyllus* by a third after planting in spring. If planting at any other time of year, wait until the following spring before pruning. Variegated varieties of O. *heterophyllus* should not be pruned in this way.

Osmanthus heterophyllus 'Variegatus'

OSMARONIA

Osmaronia cerasiformis will sometimes be found listed under its more recent name, *Oemleria cerasiformis*.

It makes a shrubby thicket several feet across so regular pruning is necessary to restrain it and keep it looking neat. Cut out the oldest third of the stems (Technique 5) in mid- or late spring, after flowering.

Once the shrub fills its allotted space be prepared to chop around the edge of the clump with a spade to remove any unwanted shoots.

Osmaronia cerasiformis

Oxydendrum arboreum

OSTRYA

These medium-sized trees require no routine pruning. The species most often grown is *O. carpinifolia*, the European hop hornbeam, whose lower branches should be allowed to sweep down to eye level so that the fruits and catkins are more easily appreciated.

OXYDENDRUM

SORREL TREE

There is only one species, *O. arboreum*, a large but slow-growing shrub or tree. Try to encourage a strong central shoot by removing any competitors, but do not remove low branches as generally they enhance the appearance of the plant. Otherwise no routine pruning is necessary.

OZOTHAMNUS

These shrubs need a mild climate and a sheltered position. No routine pruning is required, but where conditions suit, they may grow large. If growth becomes congested, prune out one or two old shoots each year close to the base. If the plant is damaged or looks straggly after a severe winter, prune it hard in spring just as the new growth emerges.

Ozothamnus ledifolius

Ostrya carpinifolia

PACHYSANDRA

This ground-carpeting plant should grow for many years without attention, but if old plants seem to need to be rejuvenated, cut back the previous year's growth to about 5cm (2in) above the ground in early spring to stimulate new shoots. This is not an annual job, however.

The only species widely grown is *P. terminalis*, the Japanese, mountain, or wood spurge.

Pachysandra terminalis 'Variegata'

PAEONIA

PEONY

Although the shrubby tree peonies, such as *P. suffruticosa* and *P. delavayi* 'lutea' are hardy, young shoots may be damaged by frost. Prune out dead wood in early or mid-summer when any new growth will be apparent, as it is often difficult to distinguish live from dead wood in winter.

As the fruits ripen, the stem carrying them usually dies back to a bud from which a new shoot will grow. For purely cosmetic reasons, you can cut off these dead pieces of stem once the leaves have fallen.

Paeonia suffruticosa 'Rock's Variety'

PARAHEBE

These low, wiry-stemmed shrubs need a sunny position to grow well. After flowering is over the plants will look better for a trim with shears (Technique 3) to deadhead and improve their shape.

PARROTIA

PERSIAN IRONWOOD

The only species, *P. persica*, has pendulous branches and the lower ones may even grow along the ground. This is part of the plant's beauty, so leave these low branches unpruned unless they create a problem such as making mowing difficult. Branches seldom need thinning, even though they appear crowded.

Although often described as a small tree, without the proper training parrotia usually ends up as a large bush without a trunk. If you want a specimen with a definite trunk up to about 1.8m (6ft), be careful to buy one that has been trained with a clear stem, or start with a small plant and do the formative training yourself.

After planting For a clear stem, see page 167.

Parrotia persica in autumn colour

PARTHENOCISSUS

These self-clinging climbers have tendrils that form discs or pads which cling tightly to a solid surface. The most widely grown include Boston ivy, *P. tricuspidata*, Chinese Virginia creeper, *P. henryana*, and Virginia creeper, *P. quinquefolia*. They grow vigorously and an annual check should be made if planted against a wooden fence or shed, or a building, in case thickening stems are causing problems. Shoots may creep between wooden slats and beneath tiles, and gutters can be blocked with stems and falling leaves in the autumn. The

Parthenocissus henryana

stems should be pruned each autumn to restrict growth near eaves, windows and gutters. Using your own observation from previous years, cut back all shoots to a point where they are unlikely to be a problem next year.

If the plant is trained over a pergola, annual pruning in late autumn or early winter is necessary to control size and keep the plant tidy. Train the main branches up the support, then each year cut the current season's sideshoots back to just above the lowest bud. The new shoots produced each year will hang down to form a curtain.

PASSIFLORA
PASSION FLOWER

The species most likely to be grown outdoors is *P. caerulea*, which in favourable areas will cover a wall or fence to a height of about 2.4–3m (8–10ft) if trained against a trellis or horizontal wires. Establish a framework of branches, spaced about 15–25cm (6–10in) apart, and tie them into position. Once the plant's own tendrils take hold, you can remove the ties. Remove some of the shoots during summer if the plant becomes too tangled and congested for your liking. Each spring prune back the sideshoots that grow from the framework branches to within one or two buds of their point of origin.

Passiflora caerulea

PAULOWNIA
FOXGLOVE TREE

When young, paulownias are fast-growing but vulnerable in cold winters. Young growing tips may be damaged or killed if the wood has not matured. For this reason it is

Paulownia tomentosa grown as a shrub

important to make sure the main stem on a young tree is at least 1.8m (6ft) tall before developing the canopy of branches. If winter damage is a problem, cut back affected shoots on a young tree to a healthy bud.

Paulownias can be pruned severely each spring to induce shrubby growth with exceptionally large foliage. Cut down the stems to 5–10cm (2–4in) from the ground each year before new growth begins (as Technique 7). Feed and water well for the most luxuriant growth and largest leaves.

After planting If you buy a young paulownia to train as a tree with a clear trunk, let it develop strong sideshoots for the first year or two. Remove sideshoots from the bottom two-thirds of this stem between late summer and late spring. Repeat this annually until the paulownia has a clear stem of at least 1.8m (6ft).

PERIPLOCA

This vigorous climber branches freely from the base. If training it up a pergola or similar support it is advisable to trim over with shears in spring to ensure a tidy outline. Cut out some of the weakest shoots at the same time if the plant has become too bushy for its support.

A plant growing through a small tree or along wire supports against a wall will not require routine pruning.

Pernettya mucronata 'Crimsonia'

PERNETTYA

To retain an attractive shape, cut out one stem in three (Technique 5) in mid-spring. The plants can form dense thickets in time. If it becomes necessary to restrict spread, carefully remove shoots and their roots from around the edge of the clump without spoiling the shape of the plant. They can be re-planted elsewhere or given to a friend.

PEROVSKIA

The shoots of Russian sage, *P. atriplicifolia*, are usually killed back to within a few inches of the base in winter weather, but new shoots grow readily in spring.

In mid-spring, just as new growth is beginning, cut back the previous year's shoots to within about two buds of the

base. Usually this will be about 5–10cm (2–4in) above the soil.

Do not remove the old stems before spring, even though the plants would look tidier, as they may provide the plant with a little extra protection during the winter.

Perovskia atriplicifolia

PHILADELPHUS

MOCK ORANGE

Most philadelphus increase in spread quite rapidly which, coupled with the height of some philadelphus, makes regular pruning desirable. Timing is important, however, as they flower on wood produced in the previous year.

Cut out one stem in three (Technique 5) in mid-summer, after flowering. This will encourage a constant supply of new shoots that will flower well on compact plants.

Always bear in mind, however, that the natural height varies widely from one species or variety to another. A variety such as *P.* 'Sybille' is easily kept to about 1.2m (4ft), *P. microphyllus* has a natural height of 60–90cm (24–36in), but varieties such as *P.* 'Virginal' will quickly reach 2.4m (8ft) or more. Regular pruning will improve the overall shape and compactness, but it will not restrict the height of a naturally tall variety.

Philadelphus 'Bouquet Blanc'

A golden problem Most philadelphus are grown for their flowers, but *P. coronarius* 'Aureus' is prized mainly for its foliage as the white flowers do not show up particularly well against yellow leaves.

Like many golden foliage shrubs with soft, thin leaves, if planted in a sunny exposed position, it will often suffer from sun and wind scorch. This results in brown patches on the leaves, which then shrivel and look unsightly. Such damaged foliage makes the plant look very untidy. So after flowering clip off the dead blooms and that part of the stem with damaged leaves to a point where the foliage is unblemished. In addition to this tidying up, cut out one stem in three, as with other philadelphus.

PHILLYREA

Jasmine box, *Phillyrea decora* (now more correctly named *Osmanthus decorus*), can be clipped to shape (Technique 1) in late summer. If you want to restrict the size of the bush without clipping, which will produce a formal outline, prune back long shoots to points well inside the bush in late spring or early summer, after flowering. If the bush is badly overgrown, spread this method of pruning over two or three years, but do not make it an annual job.

Phillyrea angustifolia and *P. latifolia* have dense, twiggy growth and it is more difficult to restrict their size by pruning. If a shrub is damaged, perhaps by heavy snow or high winds breaking stems, try cutting down the plant to 5–10cm (2–4in) above the ground in spring. It should soon shoot freely even if you cut into old wood.

After planting If planting in spring, shorten the previous season's growth by one-third to give the plant a good shape. If planting at any other time of the year, wait until the following spring before pruning.

PHLOMIS

Shrubby phlomis have woody shoots but the tips are soft and prone to winter damage. Fortunately new shoots grow freely from old wood unless the plant is very old.

To encourage plenty of flowers and attractive foliage, cut back the previous year's growth to within 5–10cm

Phlomis fruticosa

(2–4in) of the ground (Technique 9) as soon as new growth appears in spring.

If you want a larger plant, just cut back sideshoots each year to within 5–10cm (2–4in) of a framework of old stems. Plants that have been pruned like this regularly from an early age are more likely to respond well to this treatment than old plants that have not been regularly pruned.

After planting If planting in spring, cut back all the previous year's shoots to within 2.5–5cm (1–2in) of the ground once new shoots emerge from near the base. If planting at any other time, wait until the following spring before doing this.

PHORMIUM

NEW ZEALAND FLAX

Phormiums are grown for their spiky clumps of leaves. Remove any dead or winter-damaged foliage in spring.

PHOTINIA

Although photinias do not need to be pruned annually, they can be cut back in early spring if they become too tall and leggy. Frost-damaged branches of vulnerable species such as deciduous *P. beauverdiana* and evergreen *P. serrulata* can be cut back to living wood.

Strong young shoots are sometimes produced from ground level. These are best removed in spring if they spoil the shape of the plant. However, if the older branches are beginning to lose their vigour and attractiveness, just reduce the number of these basal shoots, allowing some of them to grow to replace the older branches that have become too straggly.

After planting To encourage a good shape, shorten all the previous year's growth by one-third if planting in spring. If planting at any other time of the year, wait until the following spring before pruning.

PHYGELIUS

Phygelius aequalis and *P. capensis*, Cape figwort, are the species commonly grown and these half-hardy evergreen shrubs are usually treated as

Phygelius aequalis

Phormium cookianum (P. colensoi)

Photinia × fraseri 'Red Robin'

herbaceous perennials. If grown in the open border, only advisable in mild areas, prune close to the ground (Technique 6) in spring once there are signs of new growth.

If trained against a wall, a woody framework of main stems tied into supporting wires may survive, and over several years the plant may reach about 1.5–1.8m (5–6ft). Prune by cutting back growth to the main stems in spring.

PHYLLOSTACHYS
BAMBOO

Do not be tempted to remove the old, dead canes annually as they will act as a support and offer some protection to the more supple young canes that can be damaged by heavy rain or snow. However, if the clump becomes too congested, it is advisable to cut out some of the old canes periodically in mid- or late spring.

Phyllostachys viridiglaucescens

PHYSOCARPUS
NINEBARK

The species usually grown is *P. opulifolius*, and this shrub produces young shoots from ground level among the older stems which have peeling bark. Regular pruning will encourage plenty of attractive mahogany-brown new shoots for winter interest. Cut out one stem in three (Technique 5) in mid-spring.

Physocarpus capitatus is less often grown, but is more vigorous and spreading than *P. opulifolius*. It produces many new shoots from the base. It may be necessary to reduce the number of shoots within the clump and remove those growing from around the edge, to restrict its size, unless the shrub is growing in a wild part of the garden where it has enough room to spread.

PICEA
SPRUCE

The genus includes large trees such as the popular Christmas tree or Norway spruce, *P. abies*, and dwarf varieties suitable for a rock garden. Routine

Picea pungens 'Glauca Pendula'

pruning is not required and lower branches should not be removed as the trees look more attractive covered with foliage as close to the ground as possible. Good light from all sides will ensure a symmetrical shape, but for general advice on pruning conifers, see page 176.

Shapely Christmas trees Most people prefer a dense, symmetrically shaped, conical Christmas tree for the home. This can be achieved by regular clipping in spring. Clip a couple of inches from the sides to form a pyramid, starting the third year after planting a small tree, and repeat annually until it is ready for lifting. Be careful not to remove or damage the central shoot. This method is not necessary or practical for trees growing permanently in the garden.

Picea glauca 'Albertiana Conica'

PIERIS

LILY-OF-THE-VALLEY SHRUB

Pieris have the double attraction of white flowers that resemble lily-of-the-valley and bright red leaves in spring. Prune out any dead or damaged branches in early summer. Pieris will usually shoot readily from old wood so do not be afraid to cut them back hard if necessary.

Pieris formosa

PINUS

PINE

These trees, some very large, others small and slow-growing, do not require any regular pruning. However, if the leading shoot has been damaged a whorl of shoots, arranged like the spokes of a wheel, will form at its base. Remove all these except for one, the straightest and strongest, which will form the new leading shoot. For general advice on how to prune conifers, see page 176.

Pinus contorta 'Frisian Gold'

PIPTANTHUS

EVERGREEN LABURNUM

Piptanthus laburnifolius (syn. *P. nepalensis*) is not dependably hardy when grown in the open border, but against a wall it is hardy in most years except in very cold areas. In spite of its common name, it will lose its leaves in a severe winter.

The plant is often short-lived, so to keep it healthy, and vigorous, remove one stem in three (Technique 5) in early summer.

Piptanthus laburnifolius

PITTOSPORUM

Pittosporums are naturally neat in appearance. They are usually reliably hardy in mild areas, but may be damaged or killed in a very severe winter. In cold areas provide winter protection or else be prepared for winter damage and probable losses.

If most or all of the shoots are killed, do not dig the plant up until you have given it a chance to show signs of growth. Cut the plant back close to the ground and it will often produce new shoots. Within a year or two it may be as attractive as before. Fortunately the popular *P. tenuifolium* and its varieties will usually grow readily from old wood and damaged shoots can be cut out with confidence.

Pittosporums need no other regular pruning, but if you want a neatly shaped shrub clip with shears (Technique 1) in late spring. If untrimmed plants become straggly in time, shorten long shoots in mid- or late spring to improve the shape.

After planting To achieve a shapely plant, shorten all the previous year's shoots by one-third if planting in spring. If planting at any other time of the year, wait until the following spring before pruning.

PLATANUS

PLANE

These strong-growing trees respond to early training and once established require no routine pruning.

The London plane, *P.* × *hispanica* (which will also be found under the names *P.* × *acerifolia* and *P.* × *hybrida*), usually has a clear trunk of about 1.8–2.4m (6–8ft) when young. Over the years this can be extended to 4.5–6m (15–20ft), to make the most of the attractive flaking bark. On mature trees the lower branches often hang down heavily: a problem for street trees, but attractive in the garden where there is more space.

Other species are treated in a similar way, but they tend to have a more rounded head and shorter trunk.

Planes regenerate freely from the wood surrounding a cut surface. Street trees sometimes have their main branches cut back, or pollarded, regularly to form a dense crown of young shoots and contain their spread (see page 171). Although they tolerate this treatment, in a garden it is better to let them retain their natural shape.

The best time to pollard trees, or to do any severe pruning, is from late autumn to late winter. However removing branches from large plane trees is a job best done by a professional tree surgeon.

After planting For a clear stem, see page 167.

Pittosporum tenuifolium 'Silver Queen'

Platanus × *hispanica*

Pleioblastus viridistriatus

PLEIOBLASTUS

BAMBOO

Many bamboos have now been renamed, but you may find them listed under the older names by which they are commonly sold. *Pleioblastus viridistriatus*, for example, will still be found under *Arundinaria*.

Bamboos need little pruning. Old canes can be thinned periodically, but this is not an annual job.

POLYGONUM

The rampant Russian vine, *P. baldschuanicum* (now more correctly *Fallopia baldschuanica*), should be given a support, such as an old tree or a shed, large enough to make annual pruning unnecessary.

If the plant has to be contained, just cut it back to within its allotted space during winter or early spring. Bear in mind that it will quickly reach its

previous size, so cutting back will probably become an annual task.

Even plants that do not need to be pruned back will eventually build up a lot of dead wood and this should be removed occasionally.

Polygonum baldschuanicum

PONCIRUS

HARDY ORANGE, JAPANESE BITTER ORANGE

There is only one species, *P. trifoliata*, and it requires no pruning other than to remove any dead or damaged branches in mid-spring. Do not attempt to cut out the crossing branches as this dense growth is characteristic of the plant. Wear gloves to prune this shrub, otherwise the spiny branches will make it a very unpleasant task.

The fruits, which look like small oranges, are only likely to be seen in very mild areas and in other places pruning will do nothing to encourage their production.

POPULUS

POPLAR

These fast-growing deciduous trees should be pruned in early or mid-winter as bleeding can be a problem, especially in spring and summer. Any unsightly clusters of shoots that develop on the trunks of poplars should be removed.

Some species produce new shoots from ground level and eventually form a clump. With most species, such as *P. alba* and *P. canescens*, these are best removed so that the tree retains an attractive shape. Some species can, however, look attractive when grown as a clump in this way. One of these is *P. tremula* (aspen).

Pruning for large leaves Some poplars that have very attractive leaves can be pruned hard regularly (Technique 7) to increase leaf size and the intensity of their colour. You need to start this while the plant is still young, however. Prune *P.* × *candicans* 'Aurora' every year and *P. serotina* 'Aurea' every three to five years.

Populus candicans 'Aurora'

After planting Leave the sideshoots on poplars that look better with a feathered trunk. These include *P. alba* 'Pyramidalis', *P.* × *candicans* 'Aurora', and the Lombardy or Italian poplar, *P. nigra* 'Italica'. However, the sideshoots should be cut back to within 5–10cm (2–4in) of the main stem to encourage denser growth. For a clear stem, see page 167.

POTENTILLA

SHRUBBY POTENTILLA,
SHRUBBY CINQUEFOIL

The many varieties of the shrubby potentilla, *P. fruticosa*, need regular pruning to keep them in good shape and flowering well. Cut out one stem in three (Technique 5) in early spring. This method of pruning will prevent growth becoming congested with old and weak branches that spoil the look of these hardy shrubs.

If you have a very old neglected plant that is flowering poorly and looks untidy, rather than dig it up try cutting it back hard to within 15cm (6in) of

the ground. Remove some of the new shoots to form a bush of neat and manageable proportions. Prune normally (using Technique 5) in all subsequent years.

Potentilla fruticosa 'Daydawn'

PRUNUS

This genus includes many ornamental trees and shrubs, as well as fruits such as cherries and plums (see pages 210–17). Few ornamental prunus require pruning, but the main exceptions are detailed here.

Blackthorn or sloe, *Prunus spinosa*, spreads rapidly and the basal shoots will eventually make a large clump if not restricted. It can be clipped and grown as a hedge (see page 186).

The Chinese bush cherry, *P. glandulosa*, is a compact bush which will flower best if you cut out one stem in three (Technique 5) after flowering.

Laurels, such as the cherry laurel, *P. laurocerasus*, and Portugal laurel, *P. lusitanica*, are tough shrubs that tolerate hard pruning if necessary. No routine pruning is required if the plant is growing in a border, but cut back as hard as necessary, preferably in late winter, if it begins to outgrow its allotted space. Do not be afraid to cut into old wood. An overgrown laurel

Prunus 'Kanzan', *like other Japanese cherries it requires no routine pruning*

Prunus cerasifera 'Pissardii'

will grow new shoots quite easily if you cut it down to about 15–30cm (6–12in) from the ground. Hedges are generally trimmed in late summer (see page 186).

Purple-leaved plums, such as *P. cerasifera* 'Nigra' and *P. cerasifera* 'Pissardii' can be clipped to a formal shape, and even used as a tall hedge (see page 186). Normally, though, they are grown as small trees and require no routine pruning.

The purple-leaf sand cherry, *P. × cistena*, also known as the dwarf crimson cherry, is shrubby. It does not require routine pruning, but can be cut or trimmed fairly hard if necessary in late winter and early spring.

The peeling-bark cherry, *P. serrula*, should be trained with a long, clear trunk so that the shiny red-brown peeling bark can be appreciated, so be prepared to remove some of the lowest branches if necessary. This may stimulate unsightly clusters of shoots to grow from the wounded trunk and these must be removed before they spoil the appearance of the tree. It may take five to ten years from planting for the bark to display its full beauty.

Prunus serrula

Prunus tenella 'Fire Hill'. *This shrubby flowering prunus requires no routine pruning*

The Russian almond, *Prunus triloba*, will flower more reliably if pruned annually. Cut out one stem in three (Technique 5) in early summer. This plant is sometimes grown against a wall, in which case train the branches as a fan (see page 100) then cut the shoots that grow away from the wall back to one or two buds from their point of origin, immediately after flowering is over.

Silver leaf disease Silver leaf disease, *Chondrostereum purpureum*, is a particular problem for *Prunus*. It enters through wounds, generally between early autumn and late spring, so avoid pruning during this period. Whatever the time of year, it is worth using a wound paint on large wounds.

If pruning branches that are already affected by the disease, cut back beyond the limit of the tell-tale brown stain that is visible in the wood.

After planting To train as a tree, see page 188. To avoid the risk of silver leaf disease associated with winter pruning (see above), training should be undertaken between late spring and mid-summer.

Prune *P. glandulosa* and *P. triloba* back to within 5cm (2in) of the old wood in spring. If there are flowers, wait until these are over. If planting at any other time, wait until the following spring before pruning.

If planting the laurels *P. laurocerasus* and *P. lusitanica* in spring, shorten the previous year's growth by one-third to encourage a bushy shape. If planting at any other time, wait until the following spring before pruning.

PSEUDOLARIX

GOLDEN LARCH

Pseudolarix amabilis is best grown with a central stem where there is space for the horizontal branches to spread unrestricted. The lower branches may sweep down almost to ground level, but these are part of the tree's character and should be left alone.

No regular pruning is necessary but for general advice on pruning conifers, see page 176.

PSEUDOTSUGA

The Douglas fir, *P. menziesii*, usually needs no routine pruning in either its tall or its dwarf form. However, if two competing main shoots develop, reduce to one as soon as possible.

The tree is naturally irregular in growth and outline, so do not attempt to shape it by cutting out individual branches. For general advice on pruning conifers, see page 176.

PYRACANTHA
FIRETHORN

Pyracanthas grown as free-standing shrubs require little in the way of pruning, but cut them back hard in late winter if it is necessary to improve shape or control size. Try to cut back the shoots to points close to the centre of the plant, so that pruned branches are inconspicuous.

Wall-trained plants must be pruned annually. If you simply want to keep the plant tidy a clip over with shears in late winter is generally sufficient and will produce a flat, hedge-like finish. If thick or particularly long shoots grow out, cut these back with secateurs to a point well within the plant. For a good show of berries on a more formally trained plant, use the technique described below.

For the first two or three years concentrate on training the shoots to the wall. They are largely self-supporting in time, but tie them to horizontal or vertical wires fixed to the wall for early support. You can train

Pyracantha 'Orange Glow'

them as formal fans or espaliers (as described for apples, pages 196 and 193), or adopt a less rigid approach with branches that snake randomly up the wall.

Once the framework branches have been established, shorten all new sideshoots in mid-summer so that only two or three leaves remain. This will expose the berries to view and encourage more flower buds to develop the following year.

PYRUS
ORNAMENTAL PEAR

The pear most often grown ornamentally is the weeping willow-leaved pear, *P. salicifolia* 'Pendula', but some upright pears such as *P. calleryana* 'Chanticleer' are also decorative. None of these require routine pruning.

For pear trees grown for fruit, see page 206–9.

After planting To encourage a dense canopy, prune back the previous year's growth by two-thirds (weak shoots can be pruned harder) between late winter and mid-spring. If planting at any other time, wait until the following late winter to mid-spring before pruning.

Pyrus salicifolia 'Pendula'

bushy plants, so leave on all the sideshoots and, to encourage a bushier shape, prune the previous year's growth by one-third in spring. If planting at any other time, wait until the following spring before pruning.

QUERCUS

OAK

Many oaks grow into large trees and need plenty of space in which to spread their branches without restraint. There are some varieties with upright growth which form columnar trees, along with a few shrubby species, such as the evergreen Kermes oak, *Q. coccifera*. Oaks do not need routine pruning.

Mature specimens may require surgery for problems such as shoots dying back in the canopy of an English or common oak, *Q. robur*, or to remove a low-spreading branch from a holm oak, *Q. ilex*. The professional help of a tree surgeon should always be sought for this kind of pruning.

Quercus robur 'Fastigiata'

RHAMNUS

BUCKTHORN

Most buckthorns make large shrubs or small trees, although there are a few low-growing species suitable for a rock garden. Evergreen species can be clipped into a formally shaped bush (Technique 1) in mid-summer. Deciduous species are best left unpruned.

After planting The larger species, such as *R. frangula*, are sometimes grown on a clear stem, see page 167.

Evergreen species, such as *R. alaternus*, are more attractive grown as

Rhamnus alpinus

RHODODENDRON

Rhododendrons, including evergreen and deciduous azaleas, will benefit from pruning once they are fully grown (usually after 10 to 15 years), although this is not essential. If at that stage you cut out one stem in three annually (Technique 5) in mid-summer, a regular supply of new growth and more flowers will be encouraged. This should not be necessary for dwarf rhododendrons and azaleas.

Deadheading is beneficial, especially on young plants as it prevents the plant putting energy into seed

Rhododendrons

production. Snap off the dead flowers by hand each year, but be careful not to damage the developing bud behind.

Many attractive rhododendron varieties are grafted on to a rootstock of the ordinary 'wild' rhododendron. If this produces shoots with different flowers these must be removed as they will grow rapidly and overtake the variety you want. These shoots will produce inferior flowers.

Rhododendron ponticum, the 'wild' rhododendron, is sometimes used as a large hedge or informal screen (see page 186). Prune annually after flowering by cutting back shoots to a point within the bush where the cut ends are not noticeable. If this is done annually, after flowering is over, a screen of this type will not become overgrown and unsightly.

Rejuvenating an old bush An old or very large bush may need more drastic treatment if it has outgrown its allotted

space, is flowering poorly or has become mis-shapen and unattractive. Cut the whole shrub back to about 30cm (12in) above the ground in early spring. It may be several months before the stubs produce new shoots. These will not grow much in the first year and you will lose at least one season's flowers, but the following year the shoots usually grow vigorously. You will then have a compact plant that will be easier to control by routine pruning (Technique 5).

Rhododendron 'Amoenum'

RHUS

SUMACH

Some species form trees, others make large shrubs. The most common is stag's horn sumach, *R. typhina* (now more correctly *R. hirta*), which should be grown with a short, clear stem if you want a tree with spreading branches. No routine pruning is required unless there are any weak or crossing branches which should be cut out in spring.

Rhus typhina, especially the variety 'Laciniata', and *R. glabra* 'Laciniata', have magnificent foliage, especially in their autumn colour. To encourage the formation of even larger leaves on a compact shrub, cut the stems back to a short framework of stubs (Technique 7) in mid-spring. Gradually a woody framework will be built up at the base. Cut back shoots to within about 10cm (4in) of this old wood each year in spring.

On a well-established plant too many vigorous shoots may be produced, in which case remove some of them so that the foliage (which is often more than twice the size of that on unpruned plants) can be appreciated. If you prune hard like this, try to compensate by mulching and feeding the plant.

Shoots can arise from the roots often some distance from the plant, especially if it has been injured or pruned hard. Remove these as soon as possible and try to take them back to their point of origin.

After planting To grow *R. typhina* as a tree with a clear stem, see page 167. Alternatively, if you want to grow this or *R. glabra* as a compact shrub with large leaves, prune back the previous year's growth to within 5cm (2in) of the old wood before the new growth emerges in spring. If planting at any other time of the year, wait until the following spring before pruning.

Health warning *Rhus toxicodendron*, the poison ivy or poison vine, should be pruned with care as the sap causes dermatitis. Individual sensitivity varies, but as a precaution always wear heavy duty rubber or leather gloves (not fabric ones that will allow the irritant to penetrate), and at first work on just a small part of the plant until you know whether you are likely to react badly. It is advisable not to burn the prunings as the smoke can carry droplets of poison. Regard all parts of the plant as toxic.

RIBES
FLOWERING CURRANT

Deciduous ribes, such as the flowering currant, *R. sanguineum*, benefit from annual pruning to keep them compact and with plenty of flowers. Cut out one stem in three (Technique 5) as soon as possible after flowering. The evergreen species such as *R. laurifolium* need no routine pruning.

Ribes sanguineum

ROBINIA

Robinias are summer-flowering trees that thrive in poor dry soils. They often develop spines. Their wood tends to be brittle and prone to wind damage, so make sure only one main shoot develops and remove any competitor that could form a forked trunk, a weak and vulnerable point. Pruning such as this is best done in mid- or late summer if at all possible, to reduce the risk of problems from bleeding.

New shoots are freely produced from the base of species such as the false acacia or black locust, *R. pseudoacacia*, and the popular golden variety, 'Frisia', and they will regenerate readily if pruned hard.

The mop-head acacia, *R. pseudoacacia* 'Inermis' (also found under its more correct name of 'Umbraculifera'), sometimes produces strong shoots from below the graft line, which is situated just beneath the head of foliage. Prune these back flush with the trunk before they have a chance to spoil the tree by destroying its mop-headed character.

After planting For a clear stem, see page 167. For varieties with a columnar habit, such as *R. pseudoacacia* 'Pyramidalis', the shape is improved if the sideshoots along the lower part of the stem are retained.

Robinia pseudoacacia has foliage that looks particularly attractive if the tree is pruned to produce a compact, dense head. Between late winter and mid-spring prune all the previous year's growth by two-thirds (thin, weak shoots can be cut back harder). If you want to keep the plant fairly small and compact, this pruning can be repeated annually. The mop-head acacia, *R. pseudoacacia* 'Inermis', forms a close, compact head naturally.

ROMNEYA
TREE POPPY

There are only a couple of species, of which *R. coulteri* is the better known. These lovely plants are too tender to grow outdoors in cold areas, but where conditions suit they spread by means of underground stems.

Except in the mildest areas the top growth will be killed during winter, but, as romneyas flower on new shoots readily produced from the base, this is not too much of a problem. Cut back the previous year's shoots to ground level (Technique 6) in mid-spring.

Where conditions are favourable romneyas can be allowed to form a framework of shoots to give the shrub greater height. In this situation prune out one-third of the stems (Technique 5) each spring.

After planting Cut back all the previous season's growth to within 2.5–5cm (1–2in) of the ground as soon as new growth is noticed.

Romneya coulteri

ROSA

ROSE

There are many different ways to prune roses and enthusiasts have their own preferences. However, if you have a lot of roses and want to save time pruning simply go over them with a hedgetrimmer.

Pruning trials organised by *Gardening Which?* in conjunction with the Royal National Rose Society have shown that rough pruning with secateurs or a hedgetrimmer can produce results just as good as, or better than, traditional methods. Cluster-flowered (floribunda) roses produced more and better-quality flowers in beds when pruned roughly with secateurs or with a hedgetrimmer than those pruned carefully with secateurs, while the blooms of large-flowered (hybrid tea) varieties were equally good with both methods. And the number of shoots dying back was unaffected by the fact that the hedgetrimmer method leaves a lot of ragged cuts and ripped shoots (possibly because modern varieties are vigorous and not very susceptible to this problem). At the time of writing the trials have been running for four years and show no adverse response to the 'rough and ready' method.

The long-term effects have yet to be assessed, and it is possible that the more open-centred plant produced by traditional pruning means the plants are less prone to diseases. But if you want to save time the hedgetrimmer technique is worth trying.

The majority of garden rose varieties are grafted or budded on to a vigorous-growing, wild rose rootstock. If shoots grow from low down, beneath the budding or grafting point (which shows as a swelling at ground level, or at the top of the main stem on a standard rose), they are probably from the rootstock. If you allow these to remain they can become dominant.

Remove a base shoot as soon as it is noticed. Trace it back to its point of origin, even if this means removing

Basal shoots or suckers should be removed

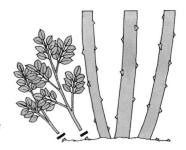

The leaves on suckers usually have seven leaflets instead of five

some soil, then, wearing thick leather gloves, pull it off (if you cut it off at ground level more shoots will be produced). Shoots that appear on the stem of a standard rose can usually be rubbed off with the fingers if you act as soon as they are noticed.

When to prune Rose pruning can usually be done whenever it is convenient, between autumn and when the leaves emerge in spring.

If you prune in the autumn, diseased shoots and shoots from the base are easier to recognise, less diseased material is likely to be carried over the winter, wind is less likely to cause damage (wind rock), and the beds look neater if you underplant with bulbs and spring bedding plants.

If you wait until spring the danger of frost damage to newly pruned shoots is reduced, and you may enjoy the attractive hips of some rose species for longer.

A good compromise is to prune in late winter and early spring.

These roses were part of the Gardening Which? *trials. The roses on the left were cut with a hedgetrimmer, the centre roses by traditional methods and the roses on the right were rough pruned with secateurs.*

How to prune cluster-flowered and large-flowered roses Large-flowered (hybrid tea) and cluster-flowered (floribunda) roses are sometimes pruned in slightly different ways, but both will respond well to the method described below. You can simplify things even more by using the rough pruning method referred to above.

Some gardeners prune in the autumn, others spring. A compromise is to reduce the longest shoots of vigorous plants in the autumn to reduce what is known as wind rock, which may loosen and damage the roots, then complete the pruning in spring when it is easier to see which shoots have succumbed to dieback.

Shorten the shoots by cutting them back by about one-third to half of their original length (to leave the bush half to two-thirds its original height).

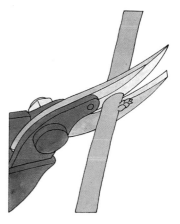

If pruning early, before the buds are expanding, the pruning point is more difficult to see. This shoot is being pruned above a bud that has started to develop, but the dormant buds can be seen just above the scars left by the old leaves.

Start by removing any dead or diseased shoots by cutting back to healthy wood.

Prune back shoots by about a third to half of their original length, cutting just above an outward-facing bud to keep an open centre and attractive shape.

Prune cluster-flowered (floribunda) roses and large-flowered (hybrid tea) roses to an even height, about 45cm (18in), as shown here. But cut back any very weak, thin shoots further than strong ones, to stimulate growth.

If pruning a cluster-flowered (floribunda) rose to extend the flowering season, leave some shoots unpruned to flower early, but be sure to prune these shoots the following year.

How to prune shrub roses Shrub roses, which include species of wild rose, modern shrub roses and old-fashioned varieties, often make large bushes. Unlike large-flowered (hybrid tea) and cluster-flowered (floribunda) roses, they usually bloom over a much shorter period.

Shrub roses may not require regular pruning, but established shrub roses generally benefit from annual pruning to prevent them becoming too large and congested.

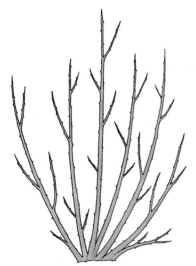

A shrub rose of this size will require pruning to prevent the shoots becoming too congested and woody.

Cut back new shoots that grow from the base by half. If the plant is old and

large with few new basal shoots, concentrate on reducing the height of the plant by about a quarter. Then shorten small sideshoots that have flowered to a few buds.

If there is a lot of old and congested wood that has been flowering poorly, cut some of this out from the base. You will need to use long-handled pruners.

How to prune standard roses Prune ordinary standards, whether they have large-flowered (hybrid tea) or cluster-flowered (floribunda) blooms, during the dormant season.

Do not prune too hard, otherwise over-vigorous shoots will be stimulated and spoil the shape.

Remove any dead or diseased wood

first, then cut back the summer's growth to create a shape that is as even as possible, cutting to a bud, usually upward or outward-facing, that will shoot in the appropriate direction.

Weeping standard rose

How to prune weeping standards These sometimes have their shoots trained over an umbrella framework. Prune in summer or autumn (once the flowering display is over). Cut back each shoot that has flowered to a point where a vigorous new shoot is ready to replace it (the position of this will depend on the variety and the plant). If no new replacement shoot has grown, leave the old one unpruned apart from cutting back the sideshoots to two or three buds.

In early spring cut the tips off of the longest new shoots, to produce an attractive even cascade.

How to prune ground-cover roses

There are two types of ground-cover rose: those that are prostrate and creep along the ground with horizontal shoots, and the arching or bushy growers that may be as much as 90cm (36in) high but with a considerably wider spread.

Prostrate ground-cover roses require little or no pruning. Just remove dead or diseased shoots and cut them back if they become invasive. Excessive pruning will produce vigorous growth at the expense of the plant's flowers.

Bushy types benefit from pruning. Cut back any very old shoots that are not flowering well, and shorten any branches that tend to grow vertically. Otherwise just remove dead or diseased shoots.

Ground-cover roses

How to prune climbers and ramblers

Rambler roses grow plenty of new shoots from ground level each year. Climbers tend to produce new growth from an existing framework of branches. There are, however, climbing roses that do not fit neatly into either of these two categories. Pruning is also affected by flowering: repeat-flowering climbers should be treated in a different way from those that flower only once a year.

WHICH GROUP?

Study the type of growth your rose makes, and when it flowers, then try to place it in one of these four groups:

1 Is it a very vigorous species or species hybrid rose, putting on more than 3m (10ft) of growth in a year when established, and flowering once in early or mid-summer?
Yes see **Group A**
No go to question 2

2 Does it produce most of its new shoots, which are vigorous and flexible, from the *base* each year?
Yes see **Group B**
No go to question 3

3 Does it flower just once, on old wood?
Yes see **Group C**
No see **Group D**

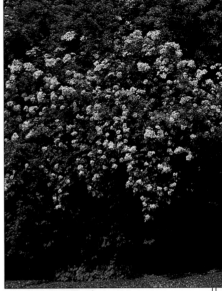

Rosa 'Wedding Day'

GROUP A Climbing wild roses

This group comprises climbing wild species and their hybrids, such as *R. filipes* 'Kiftsgate' and *R.* 'Wedding Day'. They produce large sprays of scented flowers on old wood.

These roses are too vigorous to restrain by pruning, and they are usually grown up a substantial support, such as a large tree.

No regular pruning is required. Just remove any dead wood in early spring, or after flowering. If the rose is trained along ropes between poles, you may need to cut out some of the old shoots from time to time to restrict the plants growth.

GROUP B Rambling roses

Ramblers can grow vigorously but they produce new stems from the base each year and do not become uncontrollably tall. They flower once in mid- or late summer, and usually have masses of small blooms in large trusses.

As they flower on shoots produced the previous year, prune as soon as flowering is over. You will have to modify the amount of old wood that you cut out to balance the new growth available to replace it. This will vary with variety and season. As a general rule, cut out an old shoot only if there is a new one to replace it.

Prune old shoots that have flowered, provided there are enough new ones to replace them. Then tie in the new shoots, which will flower the following year.

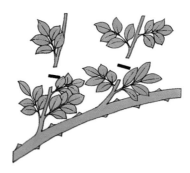

Some varieties do not produce sufficient replacement shoots to justify cutting out all the flowered wood. Retain the strongest old shoots but prune the sideshoots to two or three leaves from their base.

Start by cutting back close to the ground all the spindly, dead or damaged branches.

Rosa 'Kew Rambler'

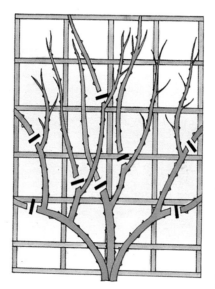

Some ramblers do not produce many new shoots from the base. If they arise some way up the old stem, cut back to that point, and not to the ground.

Rosa 'Albertine'

PATIO AND MINIATURE ROSES

'Patio rose' is a term generally used to describe compact, cluster-flowered varieties under 75cm (30in) tall that produce a mass of flowers over a long period. Prune them like ordinary cluster-flowered (floribunda) roses.

Miniature roses can also be pruned on the same principles as cluster-flowered roses, but pruning is less important and they will tolerate a simpler approach. Remove dead flowers as they fade, and in spring cut back any stems that have died or gone brown, to a point where the shoot is unaffected. If the bush begins to grow too large, just cut all the shoots back by half in late spring.

GROUP C Once-flowering climbers

Climbers develop a permanent framework of old, woody stems and do not often produce new growth from the base. They have larger flowers than ramblers, produced on old wood.

Prune during the summer after flowering is over.

A few once-flowering varieties, such as 'Climbing Allgold' and 'Meg' should be pruned in the same way as Group D, repeat-flowering types (see below), because they also flower on new wood.

Shorten sideshoots on remaining old wood to two or three buds.

If vigorous young shoots are produced higher up the plant, cut back flowered growth to just above them.

Remove a proportion of the oldest wood, cutting it to the base if there is a convenient new basal shoot to replace it, or to within about 30–45cm (12–18in) of the base if the replacement shoot starts higher up the stem.

Mme. Gregoire Staechelin

GROUP D Repeat-flowering climbers

Mostly these have large flowers and bloom from mid-summer to mid-autumn. They are sometimes described as recurrent, remontant or perpetual-flowering roses. They are generally less vigorous than the other climbing types, and once established produce relatively few new branches. They flower on new wood.

Little pruning is required, but ideally it should be done in two stages: summer and winter.

If possible, deadhead once the flowers fade, cutting back to the nearest leaf (this may not be practical on large climbers). In winter, prune as shown below.

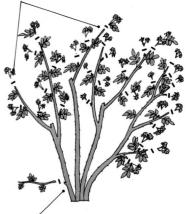

Shorten the sideshoots that flowered during the summer to two or three buds.

Between mid-autumn and early spring, cut out any dead or very weak short, thin shoots, and tie in new ones.

How to prune pillar roses Pillar roses are short climbers that do not normally grow much taller than 2.7m (9ft), and as the name suggests are usually grown up a pillar support. Prune as Group D, but you will probably have to cut back some of the main stems and sideshoots simply to keep the plant compact around its support.

ROSMARINUS

ROSEMARY

Most rosemaries (varieties of *R. officinalis*) need regular pruning so that they do not become woody and unattractive. Creeping or ground-hugging varieties do not need any routine pruning.

To encourage compact plants with plenty of young foliage, cut back the previous year's growth to within 5–10cm (2–4in) of the ground (Technique 9) as new growth begins in spring, on the other hand if you want larger plants cut back to within 5–10cm (2–4in) of a taller framework of old woody stems which will give you the required height.

The variety 'Miss Jessopp's Upright' (syn. *R. officinalis* 'Fastigiatus') is tall, narrow and upright, and you may spoil its character if you prune it back close to the ground each year – just reduce new shoots by half their length after flowering. This technique can also be used for other varieties if you want a large bushy plant up to 1.8m (6ft) high and almost as much across.

Old, neglected specimens will usually develop fresh growth if cut back severely. But as rosemary is easy to propagate from cuttings taken in summer, it is best to start again with a new plant that you can prune regularly from an early stage.

Rosemary can also be used for hedging ('Miss Jessopp's Upright' is a popular choice). Trim lightly with shears each spring after flowering .

After planting If planting in spring, cut back the previous year's growth to within 2.5–5cm (1–2in) of the ground, when you can see new shoots emerging from near the base. If planted at any other time of the year, wait until the following spring before cutting back.

RUBUS

Among this large group of shrubs are some that produce bramble-like canes from the ground each year, and some with more bushy growth and attractive flowers. Some rubus are very prickly: where you have to work close within the plant gloves are essential for comfort and eye protection is a worthwhile precaution. Recommended pruning varies according to the characteristics of the plant, but you should be able to place yours within one of the following groups.

The white-washed bramble, *Rubus cockburnianus*, is grown for its decorative stems; they have an attractive white bloom, which is conspicuous in winter. The bloom is best on the youngest stems, and because the flowers are of no decorative value cut all the old shoots down to ground level (Technique 6) in

Rosmarinus brevifolia

Rubus spectabilis

Rubus phoenicolasius

early spring. Others that are treated this way, and which also have white stems, are *R. biflorus* and *R. thibetanus*.

For flowering bushy species such as *R. odoratus* and *R. tridel* cut out one stem in three (Technique 5) during mid-summer.

Fruiting species such as raspberries and blackberries are dealt with in Chapter Six (see page 221–2). But the Japanese wineberry, *R. phoenicolasius*, is sometimes grown more for its pale green attractive leaves and bristly red stems than its fruit. It needs the support of a wall or fence, and is pruned by cutting the stems that have fruited down to ground level. Tie in any new shoots to supporting wires at the same time.

Ground-huggers such as *R. tricolor* require little in the way of pruning except to remove any damaged stems or restrict growth if the plant exceeds its allotted space. Do this in early spring.

After planting Prune *R. tricolor* after planting in spring by shortening the previous season's growth by one-third. If planting at any other time, do this the following spring.

Rubus cockburnianus

RUSCUS

BUTCHER'S BROOM

These easy-going, small, evergreen shrubs eventually spread to form thickets. The 'leaves' are, in fact, flattened stems which carry bright red berries. Ruscus require little in the way of routine pruning, but old shoots sometimes look unattractive and it is worth cutting out the worst of them in early spring.

Ruscus aculeatus 'Sparkler'

RUTA

RUE

Ruta graveolens, and its varieties, is the species most likely to be grown. Although evergreen, rue looks almost like a herbaceous plant, but some woody growth is produced.

Although pruning is not essential the plant will look more attractive if cut back annually. Prune the previous year's shoots to within 5–10cm (2–4in) of the ground (Technique 9) as soon as new growth can be seen at the base in spring. This will encourage brightly coloured new foliage, but if you prefer a taller plant cut back to within 5–10cm (2–4in) of a larger framework of old wood.

Health warning Despite having been popular as a culinary herb, rue can cause a severe allergic skin reaction, especially if the skin is exposed to sunlight. Wear gloves, try to keep the sap off your skin and wash carefully afterwards. Keep children away from recently pruned plants until the cuts have dried and dispose of prunings out of their reach.

After planting Cut back the previous season's growth to within 2.5–5cm (1–2in) of the ground, once new shoots can be seen growing from near the base. If planting at any other time than spring, wait until the following spring to do this.

Ruta graveolens

S

SALIX

WILLOW

This large genus includes species of all shapes and sizes, from those that form tiny ground-hugging shrubs to large spreading trees. Although many can be left to grow freely, others can be improved by judicious pruning. Among those that benefit most from regular pruning are those grown for their attractive winter stems, and indeed, pruning is essential to keep their size within bounds.

Prune the red-stemmed willow, *S. alba* 'Chermesina' (syn. 'Britzensis'), and other willows with ornamental stems such as *S. irrorata*, in spring. Leave the job until the new buds are about to break if you want to enjoy the coloured stems for as long as possible. Cut back all the stems to a short framework of shoots (Technique 7) every spring or every second year. Pruned in this way the plants will be suitable for growing in a border, and will resemble the coloured-stemmed dogwoods (*Cornus*).

Solitary specimens and those plants growing by water look more striking if pruned back to a short stump, about 60–90cm (24–36in) tall, a form of pollarding. If starting from scratch, prune the young tree down to the required height in early spring. This will induce plenty of shoots to grow, but remove those that grow from close to the base to encourage a clear stem. Then each year cut all the previous year's shoots back to within 2.5–5cm (1–2in) of this stump. Many other willows can be pollarded in this way

Salix lanata

(see also page 171), usually on taller stems. Plants like the goat or pussy willow, S. caprea, should not be pruned in this way, or their attractive catkins will be lost.

Although the corkscrew willow, S. matsudana 'Tortuosa', normally requires no routine pruning, you can remove some of the branches or prune them to improve the winter profile of the tree. If you cut it back severely the tree should quickly recover and produce new growth.

The weeping willows, such as the golden S. × chrysocoma, will form large trees which need no routine pruning unless you want to control their size, in which case they can be pruned back hard in spring. However, there is no point in trying to control very large species such as the true weeping willow, S. babylonica, growing in an unsuitable position. If one is causing a problem, consult a tree surgeon.

The small weeping Kilmarnock willow, S. caprea 'Pendula', is a grafted plant that seldom grows higher than 3m (10ft); no routine pruning is required to keep it compact, but you may want to thin or shorten the shoots if they have become congested on an old specimen.

Shrubby willows such as S. helvetica and the woolly willow, S. lanata, can be clipped to shape (Technique 1) in mid-spring if you want a tidier plant.

Salix integra 'Hakuro-nishiki'

Salix alba 'Vitellina'

Dwarf willows, like S. × boydii, will require pruning only if there is a specific problem such as a damaged stem or the spread of the plant needs to be restricted.

Salix integra 'Hakuro-nishiki' is a shrubby plant grown for its attractive variegated foliage. To improve the foliage, cut the previous year's growth back by two-thirds annually early in the spring.

After planting For better foliage and to restrict the size of the tree in the early years, prune back the previous year's shoots on the golden weeping willow, S. × chrysocoma, by two-thirds (cut back thin, weak ones even harder) if planting between late winter and mid-spring. If planting at any other time, wait until the following year before pruning.

If growing the white willow, *Salix alba*, as a tree form with a clear stem, see page 167 for initial training.

If growing it as a compact plant hard-pruned regularly for its colourful stems, prune all the previous year's shoots to within 5cm (2in) of the old wood. Do this in early or mid-spring; wait until the following spring if planting at any other time. Varieties usually treated this way include the silver, scarlet and golden willows, respectively S. alba 'Argentea', 'Chermesina' and vitellina.

Other willows that benefit from the same hard initial spring pruning include S. caprea (but not S. caprea 'Pendula'); grey sallow, S. cinerea; violet willow, S. daphnoides; coyote willow, S. exigua; hoary willow, S. incana; and S. irrorata.

To improve the shape of shrubby willows such as S. integra 'Hakuro-nishiki', S. hastata 'Wehrhahnii', S. helvetica and S. lanata, shorten the previous year's growth by one-third after planting in spring. If planting at any other time, wait until the following spring before pruning.

SALVIA

Shrubby salvias benefit from regular pruning. Sage, S. officinalis, is the species usually grown, generally in one of its variegated or purple-leaved varieties. It makes an attractive plant when young, but unless pruned regularly will become straggly with bare patches with age.

To encourage dense and healthy foliage, cut back all the stems to within 5–10cm (2–4in) of the ground once you can see new shoots beginning to grow from near the base in spring. Old plants may not respond well to this treatment if they have not been pruned routinely, but they can be cut back to within 5–10cm (2–4in) of a larger framework of old shoots to make them more compact.

After planting If planting in spring, cut back all the previous year's growth to within 2.5–5cm (1–2in) of the ground if new shoots can be seen growing from near the base. If planting at any other time, wait until the following spring.

Salvia officinalis 'Icterina'

SAMBUCUS

ELDER

All elders are improved by routine pruning to encourage a better-looking plant with a good display of flowers, fruits and foliage.

If you want to encourage flowering and fruiting cut out one stem in three (Technique 5) in mid-spring.

Those grown for their foliage, such as *S. racemosa* 'Plumosa Aurea', *S. nigra* 'Laciniata' and *S. nigra* 'Purpurea', will be more compact with bigger leaves if the whole plant is pruned hard annually. Cut all the shoots back to 2.5–5cm (1–2in) from

Sambucus racemosa 'Plumosa Aurea'

the basal framework of old wood (Technique 7) in mid-spring.

After planting Cut back the previous year's growth to within 5cm (2in) of the old wood, in early spring before growth emerges. If planting at any other time, wait until the following spring before pruning.

SANTOLINA

COTTON LAVENDER

The species most often grown is *S. chamaecyparissus* (syn. *S. incana*), but all these evergreen shrubs can be treated in the same way. Regular pruning is necessary to produce dense plants with attractive foliage. Left unpruned, the plant will become tall and straggly, and the shape spoilt where snow or wind has produced open areas within the plant.

Cut the shoots back to 5–10cm (2–4in) from the ground once you can see new shoots growing from near the base (Technique 9) in mid-spring. For the best foliage on the most compact plants, do this every year. However, it will take some months for the plants to regrow to a height close to that of an unpruned plant and you may prefer to prune less drastically most years, in which case cut back to within a few inches of a larger permanent framework of shoots. If the plant becomes too straggly after a few years, try pruning back hard to within 5–10cm (2–4in) of the ground: it will usually reshoot from the old wood.

Santolinas have small yellow flowers, but if you grow the plant mainly for foliage effect clip the developing flower stems off with shears before they spoil the shape of the plant.

Cotton lavender is sometimes used for a low hedge, perhaps in a knot garden or round a herb bed. Clip it with shears in early spring and again in the summer if flowers appear.

After planting Prune all the shoots back to within 2.5–5cm (1–2in) of the ground as soon as you can see new growth near the base in spring. If planting at any other time of the year, wait until the following spring before cutting back.

SARCOCOCCA

CHRISTMAS BOX, SWEET BOX

These compact, winter-flowering shrubs are naturally dense, so there is no need to remove any of the crowded shoots and no routine pruning is required. In fact, these neat evergreens are best left untouched unless there is a specific problem such as dead or damaged growth after a particularly harsh winter, in which case deal with it in late spring.

Sarcococca

SASA

BAMBOO

These broad-leaved bamboos need no routine pruning unless the clump becomes very congested. If this happens, cut out some of the old, dead canes in mid- or late spring.

SCHISANDRA

The best way to prune these climbers depends on the method of training.

If grown up a wigwam of poles or a tripod, the stems will cascade down once they reach the top of the support. In winter, cut out the oldest stems where there are young shoots to take their place. If the plant has become

Schisandra rubriflora

Santolina chamaecyparissus

very congested, remove some of the young shoots too.

If the plant has been trained against a wall, cut out the oldest and weakest stems that have reached the top of the wall and are now cascading forward. Do this during winter or in early spring before new shoots start to grow.

SCHIZOPHRAGMA

These climbing plants attach themselves to their support by aerial roots, like ivy, and if growing up a tree trunk require no routine pruning.

To improve the appearance, remove old flower heads and any dead or surplus growth from a wall-trained plant, or one growing over a pergola, in the autumn.

SCIADOPITYS

This slow-growing tree looks best with a single central leading shoot. Established trees need no routine pruning, but watch for shoots competing with the main stem while the tree is young. These spoil the tree's shape if not pruned out promptly.

After planting Leave any sideshoots that are growing from the main stem as the tree is particularly attractive with branches down to the ground. If there is any sign of a rival to the leading shoot, cut this out promptly.

For pruning conifers for specific problems, see page 176.

Sciadopitys verticillata

SEMIARUNDINARIA

BAMBOO

Like most bamboos this needs no routine pruning, but if the clump becomes very congested in time, carefully cut out the old, dead canes in mid- or late spring.

Semiarundinaria fastuosa

SENECIO

The shrubby species grown for their silver foliage, such as S. *greyi*, S. *laxifolius*, S. *monroi*, and S. 'Sunshine', benefit from regular pruning, though not necessarily annually, to stimulate plenty of attractive foliage rather than flowers and to maintain compact plants. Cut back the stems to within 5–10cm (2–4in) of the ground in spring as soon as shoots can be seen growing from near the base. This drastic treatment is only likely to be successful with plants pruned hard annually from an early age. If there are no new shoots near the base, or if you want a taller plant, cut the previous year's shoots back to 5–10cm (2–4in) of a taller framework of old wood.

A neglected senecio, or one that has been damaged during a harsh winter, can sometimes be rejuvenated by cutting back very hard. To do this, prune to within 5–10cm (2–4in) of the ground in spring, then water and feed well. The plant will then probably recover.

After planting Cut back all shoots to within 2.5–5cm (1–2in) of the ground in spring, as soon as new growth appears at the base of the plant. If planting at any other time of the year, wait until the following spring before pruning.

SEQUOIA

COAST REDWOOD

The only species is S. *sempervirens*, which needs little attention once established. If shoots appear around

Senecio 'Dunedin Hybrid'

Sequoia sempervirens

the base of the trunk remove these in autumn or winter.

The main shoot on a young tree is vulnerable to frost damage, and competing shoots sometimes develop. Make sure you allow only one main shoot to develop otherwise the characteristic conical shape of the tree will be spoilt.

These are large trees, suitable only for the largest gardens, and pruning a well-established specimen needs the services of a professional tree surgeon.

For pruning conifers for specific problems, see page 176.

SEQUOIADENDRON

WELLINGTONIA

There is only one species, S. giganteum. Follow the advice given for sequoia (see previous entry).

Sequoiadendron giganteum

SINARUNDINARIA

BAMBOO

No routine pruning is required, but if the clump becomes overcrowded in time cut out the old, dead canes in mid- or late spring.

Sinarundinaria 'Murielae'

SKIMMIA

The majority of these bushy evergreens produce their male and female flowers on different plants. In order to induce berrying you must have plants with female flowers and at least one with male flowers for pollination purposes. The dead flower heads from male varieties should be removed to encourage more flowers the following year, but do not do this if the plant is a female, otherwise you will remove the developing berries. Apart from this no routine pruning is required. If the bush becomes too large, try cutting it back in spring close to the ground – it should grow easily from the base.

Skimmia japonica 'Nymans'

SOLANUM

The Chilean potato tree (S. crispum), can be grown as a free-standing shrub in mild areas, in which case it will need no routine pruning. However, in most areas it is best trained against a wall. Tie in the young shoots each autumn, then in spring cut out thin, weak shoots along with any that are damaged by frost.

Once the shrub has filled its allotted space, prune the previous year's shoots back to about 15cm (6in) from the old stems to keep the plant within the allotted space.

After planting To encourage good branching from the base of the plant, shorten all the previous year's shoots by one-third in spring. If planting at any other time, wait until the following year before doing this.

Solanum crispum 'Glasnevin'

SOPHORA

The Japanese pagoda tree. *S. japonica*, and kowhai, *S. microphylla*, form trees and *S. tetraptera* a large shrub.

They need a sheltered position in a mild area to do well, need no routine

Sophora microphylla .

pruning and cannot be successfully cut back to fit a restricted space.

After planting For how to train *S. japonica* with a clear main stem of about 1.8–2.4m (6–8ft), see page 167.

SORBARIA

Sorbarias respond well to regular pruning. To encourage new growth, cut out one stem in three (Technique 5) between late winter and mid-spring.

The tree spiraea, *S. arborea* (syn. *S. kirilowii*), and several other species, produce large numbers of shoots from ground level. Unless these are removed from around the edge of the plant it will colonise a large area. Saw them off while they are still young, or if not too large, chop them off with a spade before they encroach beyond their allotted space.

Sobaria sorbifolia

After planting To get the plants off to a good start, cut back the previous year's growth to within 5cm (2in) of old wood, in early or mid-spring. If planting at any other time, wait until the following spring before cutting them back.

SORBUS

Most sorbus are trees, such as the mountain ash or rowan, *S. aucuparia*, and whitebeam, *S. aria*, but there are also shrubby species such as the creeping mountain ash, *S. reducta*, which is a low thicket-forming plant.

A young whitebeam can be kept relatively compact with a dense head of foliage by pruning the previous year's growth by at least two-thirds between late winter and mid-spring.

Otherwise sorbus need no routine pruning. Any dead or damaged branches should be removed during mid-spring.

After planting See page 167 for the formative pruning of tree forms such as *S. aria*, *S. aucuparia*, and *S. hupehensis* with a clear trunk.

Once a head has formed at the appropriate height, prune whitebeam (*S. aria*) by cutting the previous year's shoots back by two-thirds (cut very thin and weak shoots back further) in spring. This will ensure that the tree develops a dense head of attractive foliage.

SPARTIUM

SPANISH BROOM

There is only one species, *S. junceum*, which makes a large and spectacular shrub. Mature plants are best left alone but if you have to restrict size, do not cut into wood more than a year old.

Sorbus aucuparia 'Matsumarana' *in autumn colour*

To encourage bushy growth during the plant's early years, cut back the previous year's stems by about half their length. On an old bush cut back to within 2.5–5cm (1–2in) of the old wood just as the new growth starts to show in the spring.

After planting To induce bushiness from an early stage, shorten the previous year's stems by one-third in spring. If planting at any other time of the year, wait until the following spring before pruning.

Spartium junceum

SPIRAEA

Spiraeas vary in the way they grow and flower, so decide which group your plant belongs to before pruning.

Spring-flowering species These bloom on old branches and include bridal wreath, S. × *arguta* and S. *thunbergii*. Cut out one stem in three (Technique 5) after flowering.

Summer-flowering species that bloom on old branches These include

S. *nipponica* 'Snowmound' and S. × *vanhouttei*. Routine pruning is not essential for good growth, but to keep the plant within bounds and to improve overall appearance, cut out one stem in three (Technique 5) after flowering is finished.

Summer-flowering species that bloom on the current year's growth These include S. × *bumalda* and S. *japonica* 'Shirobana'. Most plants in this group can simply have one-third of their stems removed as suggested for the other groups, but slightly more compact plants, such as varieties of S. × *bumalda*, and S. *japonica* 'Shirobana', can be cut down to within 5–10cm (2–4in) of the ground (Technique 6) during early or mid-spring. It is usually possible do this with shears.

Special cases *Spiraea douglasii* and S. *menziesii* are thicket-forming shrubs. Leave them unpruned to form large thickets. Alternatively, for a smaller clump, cut them to just above the ground (Technique 6) in early spring. Don't be surprised if they flower a little later than normal.

STACHYURUS

The two species commonly grown, S. *chinensis* and S. *praecox*, readily produce vigorous young shoots from the base. Although routine pruning is not essential, once a plant has reached its expected size it is worth removing the oldest third of the shoots (Technique 5) annually, or every second year, in mid-spring. This will encourage new growth.

Stachyurus chinensis

Spiraea thunbergii

STAPHYLEA

BLADDER-NUT

Normally these hardy shrubs need no routine pruning. However, it may be necessary to deal with shoots growing from the ground on species such as *S. colchica* and *S. trifolia*. These sometimes come up some distance from the plant, and should be dug up. Remove some of the shoots if a plant becomes very congested.

Staphylea colchica

STEPHANANDRA

The species most likely to be grown are *S. incisa* and *S. tanakae*, shrubs grown mainly for their foliage and attractive brown winter stems. Regular pruning will ensure that they produce plenty of brightly coloured new shoots and healthy leaves.

Cut out one-third of the stems in mid- or late summer, after flowering. To improve the foliage, you can cut *S. incisa* back almost to ground level after flowering, but you should also mulch and water the plants well to stimulate new growth. The reason for pruning after flowering is to expose the new shoots to plenty of light and air, which enhances the colour of the shoots.

STEWARTIA

The name of these lovely late-flowering small trees is sometimes spelt *Stuartia*.

The lower branches are sometimes removed to show off the attractive trunk, but these should not be removed from young plants. Specimens that branch low down are often very pleasing, so allow the tree to grow naturally for as long as possible, and prune in spring only if there is a specific reason, such as a dead or damaged branch.

Stewartia pseudocamellia

STRANVAESIA

The species usually grown is *S. davidiana* (now more correctly *Photinia davidiana*). Routine pruning is not necessary, but cutting out one stem in three (Technique 5) in mid-summer will encourage new leafy shoots from the base and can improve the overall appearance of this shrub.

After planting To encourage a shapely plant, shorten all the existing shoots by one-third in spring. If planting at any other time, wait until the following spring before doing this.

Stranvaesia davidiana

STYRAX

The Japanese snowbell, *S. japonica*, develops into a small tree. It has horizontal branches with twiggy shoots, but these are part of its character. No routine pruning is necessary for this or other species that are sometimes grown, unless any damaged growth needs to be removed in spring.

Styrax hemsleyana

SYMPHORICARPOS

SNOWBERRY

Most of these hardy shrubs bear white berries which remain on the plant for several months. To encourage the growth of new shoots, cut out one stem in three in mid-summer (Technique 5).

Some species, such as *S. albus*, eventually form thickets and it is difficult to restrict their spread. Rather than attempt to control by pruning, plant them where there is a natural constraint to their spread, such as a concrete path.

Snowberries are often grown as informal hedges (see page 186).

If a snowberry is neglected it can become an impenetrable mass of stems that are difficult to prune. Try cutting back to just above the ground in spring. New shoots will usually be produced that will be easier to prune routinely in future, but if the clump is very large it may be best to dig it up and replant some smaller pieces.

Symphoricarpos albus

SYRINGA

LILAC

Lilacs benefit from routine pruning. Although some of the species have a naturally low, bushy habit, the popular *S. vulgaris* varieties grow tall and leggy if pruning is neglected, and they also need sufficient space and light for the shrub to develop without competition from other plants.

To maintain an attractive overall appearance, cut out very old or very weak stems in winter. Aim to remove about a quarter of the old or weak stems each year on mature plants.

Careful deadheading will improve flowering the following year. As soon as flowering is over, cut the dead blooms back to the first pair of leaves below the flower head. Do not cut back further or you risk removing the buds from which the new flowering shoots will be produced.

The bushier species, such as *S. × josiflexa* 'Bellicent' and *S. microphylla*, require only one-third of the oldest stems removing close to the base after flowering, starting when they are about five years old. Even this may not be necessary if the plants remain compact and flower freely.

Some lilacs are grown on their own roots but others are grafted on to a rootstock of *S. vulgaris* or privet (*Ligustrum vulgaris* or *L. ovalifolium*). Shoots from the rootstock are sometimes produced around the base

Syringa vulgaris

Syringa vulgaris 'Jeanne d'Arc'

of the plant. Remove these while they are still small, tracing them back to their point of origin if possible, otherwise they will ruin the shrub.

In time lilacs, especially varieties of S. *vulgaris*, become very large, often with the flowers much higher than is desirable. These old, neglected plants can often be rejuvenated by sawing the plant down to stumps 30–90cm (12–36in) high. New growth will be produced even from this old wood, but do not expect a good show of flowers for two or three years.

TAMARIX

TAMARISK

These feathery shrubs grow well by the seaside and T. *pentandra* can be used as a hedge (see page 186). When grown as a shrub, regular pruning, although not essential, will improve the overall appearance of tamarisks.

For summer-flowering species such as T. *pentandra* which bloom on the current year's growth, cut back the previous year's growth hard in mid-spring. (Technique 8), taking the shoots back to within 5–7.5cm (2–3in) of the old wood. If not pruned they become sparse at the base.

For taller shrubs with less compact growth cut the previous season's growth by between a half and two-thirds at some stage between mid-autumn and late winter.

For spring-flowering species such as T. *parviflora* and T. *tetrandra* which flower on the previous season's

Tamarix

growth, cut back the current year's growth in mid-summer to produce compact plants.

For taller shrubs with less compact growth, and possibly more blossom, prune back the previous season's growth by between a half and two-thirds after flowering.

After planting For both types of tamarisk, cut back the previous season's shoots to within 5cm (2in) of the old wood, in early or mid-spring before new growth emerges. If planting at any other time, wait until the following spring before pruning.

TAXODIUM

SWAMP CYPRESS

No routine pruning is required. If two main shoots develop, however, reduce to one as soon as possible.

For advice on pruning conifers for specific problems, see page 176.

Taxodium distichum

TAXUS

YEW

Yew is one of the finest plants for a hedge, see page 186, or as a topiary specimen. However, when grown as a tree, no routine pruning is required. Slow-growing and dwarf varieties also need no routine pruning.

For general advice on pruning conifers for problems, see page 176.

Taxus baccata 'Standishii'

TEUCRIUM

The shrubby germander, *T. fruticans*, will be improved if the previous year's growth is shortened by two-thirds to three-quarters in mid-spring, although this is not essential. If you have a wall-trained specimen, remove any frost-damaged tips in mid-spring, then shorten all shoots by about half to limit the plant's spread.

Teucrium chamaedrys is a low, spreading shrub that forms a mat of shoots useful for ground cover. It can be clipped back in spring (with shears

if the area is large) if you want to tidy up its appearance.

After planting To stimulate bushy growth, prune the previous season's growth by one-third in spring. If planting at any other time, wait until the following spring.

THUJA

ARBOR-VITAE

Like many conifers, *Thuja* has numerous dwarf varieties as well as large trees, but none requires routine pruning. It can also be grown as a hedge, see page 186. These plants are best grown with branches down to the ground, so do not remove sideshoots on a young plant.

For some general advice on how to prune conifers for specific problems, see page 176.

Thuja plicata

THUJOPSIS

The species most commonly seen, *T. dolabrata*, naturally makes a bushy conifer without requiring any routine pruning.

For advice on pruning conifers for specific problems, see page 176.

TILIA

LIME, LINDEN

Limes respond well to very hard pruning, and even if major branches are cut back new ones will grow during the following years.

Common problems with limes include clusters of shoots growing from the trunk or branches as a result of wounding. Unwanted shoots may also grow around the base of the plant. These should be cut out while the plant is dormant during winter or early spring.

If you have to remove a large branch, mid- or late summer is the best time as bleeding is less likely to be

Tilia 'Petiolaris'

a problem and the wound should heal more rapidly.

Although established lime trees can be left to grow naturally, young limes are easily trained. In very large gardens avenues of limes are sometimes pleached (trained into a type of aerial hedge on clear trunks), or pollarded (see page 171) every year or two.

After planting Limes can be grown with a clear trunk or with branches down to the ground. For a clear trunk, see page 171.

TRACHELOSPERMUM

These evergreen climbers do best in a mild climate, and flourish where conditions suit. In such situations the appearance of the plants is improved by annual pruning in early or mid-spring. After cutting out any dead or damaged shoots, remove as many of the very vigorous shoots as necessary to restrict growth.

Trachelospermum jasminoides 'Variegatum'

TRACHYCARPUS

CHUSAN PALM, FAN PALM

Trachycarpus fortunei is the only palm tree hardy enough to grow outdoors in Britain and needs a sheltered, sunny spot. No pruning is necessary except to remove any damaged leaves in spring to improve its appearance.

Trachycarpus fortunei and *Cordyline australis*

TSUGA
HEMLOCK

Some species, such as Western hemlock, *T. heterophylla*, will tolerate clipping and are sometimes used for hedges (see pages 186), but specimen trees and the dwarf varieties need no routine pruning. They are best left with branches to the ground, so do not remove the lower sideshoots from a young plant.

For advice on pruning conifers for specific problems, see page 176.

Tsuga heterophylla

ULEX
GORSE

Gorse will naturally form a spreading, very prickly shrub. If you have plenty of space, no pruning is normally required. But to reduce the shrub's overall size, some routine pruning will be necessary.

Gorse will make an attractive compact shrub if trimmed with shears (Technique 1) or cut back hard with secateurs, in early summer, annually if necessary, or every two or three years for a larger plant.

A tall, leggy plant can be revitalised if cut back to within 15cm (6in) of the ground in early spring to induce new growth from the base.

Ulex europaeus 'Plenus'

ULMUS
ELM

Although most elms form large trees and need plenty of space to look their best, there are species and varieties of modest size. They require no routine pruning, although some species, such as *U. × hollandica* and *U. procera*, produce shoots from the base which should be removed while the plant is dormant in winter or early spring. This is not necessary with narrow, upright varieties such as the one illustrated.

Ulmus × hollandica 'Wredei'

V

VACCINIUM

Vacciniums vary considerably in size
and form and normally they do not
require routine pruning. However, if a
bush becomes very congested remove
some of the branches occasionally.
There is likely to be strong growth to
cut back to, even from old wood.
Prune deciduous species during the
winter, evergreens in the spring.

Some species, such as *V. vitis-idaea*,
often produce strong shoots from the
ground or at the base of the plant. This
is normal and such shoots should be
allowed to grow.

Vaccinium ovatum

VIBURNUM

Many viburnums benefit from periodic
pruning to stimulate new growth and
to prevent the shrub becoming too
large or congested.

Scented viburnums that flower in
spring, such as *V.* × *burkwoodii*, *V.* ×

Viburnum rhytidophyllum

carlcephalum, and *V. carlesii* need no
routine pruning unless there is a
specific problem, such as damaged or
congested growth, in which case prune
in early summer.

The Japanese snowball, *V. plicatum*,
should not be pruned unless there is a
specific problem otherwise the
appearance of the tiered branches may
suffer. If a damaged branch needs to
be removed, do this in mid-spring.

Winter-flowering evergreens, such as
laurustinus (*V. tinus*) need no routine
pruning, but if you want a more formal
outline trim the plant to shape
(Technique 1) in late winter or early
spring, using secateurs not shears. For
a compact bush, cut out one stem in
three (Technique 5) after flowering. A
neglected specimen can be cut back
hard (see page 160).

**Species grown primarily for their
fruit**, such as *V. betulifolium*, and
winter-flowering deciduous species
such as *V.* × *bodnantense* and *V. farreri*
(syn. *V. fragrans*) do not require
annual pruning, but cut out one stem
in three (Technique 5) on mature
plants in the spring of every second or
third year.

Large-leaved evergreen species such
as *V. buddleifolium*, *V. henryi* and *V.
rhytidophyllum* do not need annual
pruning, but to encourage new growth
and revitalise a mature plant, cut out
one stem in three (Technique 5) about
every five years in mid-summer.

Other viburnums *Viburnum davidii*
can be left unpruned or clipped back
to size using secateurs, not shears, in
mid-spring.

The wayfaring tree, *V. lantana*, and

guelder rose, *V. opulus*, can be left unpruned to grow naturally. To keep a mature bush compact and vigorous by encouraging new growth from the base, cut out one stem in three on mature plants (Technique 5), in early summer every three to five years. Any damaged or dead growth should be removed in mid-spring.

Rejuvenating a neglected viburnum
Most viburnums will shoot freely from the base or from older branches, and if a neglected plant has to be pruned severely it will usually re-grow. *V. tinus* responds particularly well to hard pruning if it becomes necessary, and will usually re-grow even if cut down to within about 30cm (12in) of the ground in late spring, a useful technique for a very large or neglected specimen that would otherwise have to be removed.

Viburnum plicatum 'Pink Beauty'

VINCA
PERIWINKLE

The hardy vincas are ideal plants to grow as ground cover in an informal part of the garden. Although pruning is not essential, the cover will be denser and the flowering better if all the shoots on well established plants are cut back to just above ground level annually (Technique 6) in early or mid-spring. This will also prevent the plants becoming overgrown or straggly. Use shears or a nylon line trimmer rather than secateurs if you have a number of plants.

Vinca minor 'Aureovariegata'

VITIS

Vines, such as *Vitis coignetiae*, growing through a tree or over a large pergola where space is relatively unrestricted, need no routine pruning unless they outgrow their allotted space. If this happens remove some of the oldest shoots and shorten young ones. This is best done while the plant is dormant during the winter, but if the vigorous shoots become a nuisance, perhaps near a path, further pruning may be necessary during the summer.

Ornamental vines growing in a restricted space need to be pruned back to a framework of old branches in early or mid-winter. Cut the shoots produced during the previous summer back to one or two buds from the old stem. As these grow they can be trained to wires against a wall, or over an arch, trellis or pergola.

If space is very restricted and the young growth is too vigorous, cut the new shoots back to five or six leaves in mid-summer as the wood begins to harden and ripen at the base.

Terrace with Vitis coignetiae in background

WEIGELA

Weigelas flower on shoots produced the previous year. To encourage new shoots and plenty of flowers for future years, cut out one stem in three (Technique 5) in mid-summer. This will also prevent the shrub becoming woody. Weigelas respond well to being cut back hard.

Weigela 'Bristol Ruby'

WISTERIA

Wisterias look best trained against a wall along horizontal wires, so that it is easier to control their vigorous growth. Regular pruning is also important for controlled growth and prolific

Wisteria sinensis

flowering. Once a wisteria has been planted for three years, prune it in summer and again in winter.

In mid- or late summer, cut back the young, whip-like shoots to within five to seven leaves from the main branch to limit the overall size and spread of the plant. Then in the winter cut these shoots back further to two buds from the base of the previous year's growth.

Wisterias can be grown as free-standing shrubs, but follow the summer and winter pruning advice to keep them relatively compact They can also be trained as standards.

After planting Plant against a wall with horizontal support wires fixed 30–45cm (12–18in) apart, in winter or early spring. Select the strongest shoot, tie it to a supporting cane, and cut it off just above a bud about 75–90cm (30–36in) from the ground. Remove any other shoots.

During the first summer new shoots will grow. Train the top shoot vertically, but tie in any lower shoots to the wires at an angle of about 45 degrees (if any shoots grow from the base, below the wires, cut these off).

In late or mid-winter, untie the sideshoots and shorten each one by about one-third of its length. Re-tie them horizontally to the wires. Then shorten the vertical leading shoot so that it is about 75cm (30in) above the highest sideshoot.

The following summer, train the topmost new shoot vertically, and tie in new sideshoots that grow from the main stem, at an angle of about 45 degrees. In late summer cut back new shoots from the horizontally trained branches to within 15–23cm (6–9in) of the branch. If too many new sideshoots have been produced, cut out the surplus ones so that the framework of sideshoots does not become too congested.

Wisteria sinensis

Follow the same pruning method as the previous winter: re-tie the angled branches horizontally to the wires, and shorten the summer's growth on all the horizontal shoots by about one-third. Cut back the vertical leading shoot to a point about 75cm (30in) above the highest of the horizontal branches.

After the following summer, carry out the pruning suggested above.

Training a standard You may be able to buy a wisteria already trained as a standard, but you are more likely to have to train your own.

Plant while dormant in late winter or early spring and choose the strongest shoot to train upright against a support. Remove all the sideshoots.

In the second winter, prune off any sideshoots, and cut the top off the leading shoot at the height you want the head to form.

In the third winter, shorten the new shoots to between one-third and half of their original length.

Routine pruning of a standard Once a framework of branches has been formed, prune annually during the summer. Cut back sideshoots that have grown, to a bud 5–7.5cm (2–3in) from the main branch. The framework branches will also have grown longer, so prune these back to a length that you find visually attractive.

XANTHOCERAS

YELLOW-HORN

Xanthoceras sorbifolium makes a large shrub or small tree. No routine pruning is required, but remove any damaged or diseased branches in mid-spring. It will produce new shoots freely from old wood.

Xanthoceras sorbifolium

XANTHORHIZA

Xanthorhiza simplicissima is a small shrub that eventually forms a thicket, slowly spreading by underground stems. As it cannot be controlled satisfactorily by pruning, no routine attention is necessary.

Y

YUCCA

Yuccas consist of rosettes of sword-shaped leaves on a woody stem; in some species this stem barely rises above ground level. To improve their appearance, remove dead or damaged leaves in mid-spring. Watch out for the needle-like spines on leaf tips. Rough leaf edges can also cut.

Yucca filamentosa

Z

ZANTHOXYLUM

These spiny shrubs or small trees need no routine pruning, except sometimes to remove any build-up of dead wood.

Zanthoxylum simulans

ZELKOVA

For a particularly attractive tree, it is worth training *Z. carpinifolia* with a single main shoot to produce a clear trunk of about 1.8–2.4m (6–8ft). Left untrained, it will probably develop densely packed branches down to ground level. Established trees need no routine pruning.

Zelkova serrata

ZENOBIA

Zenobia pulverulenta is a rather untidy-looking shrub. Remove dead flowers, along with any weak growth, to a point above a strong shoot in late summer. This will encourage the plant to put more energy into producing vigorous shoots and better flowers the following year and prevent it getting untidy.

An old overgrown shrub can usually be improved by hard pruning.

Zenobia pulverulenta

PRUNING AND TRAINING TREES

INCLUDING
WALL SHRUBS

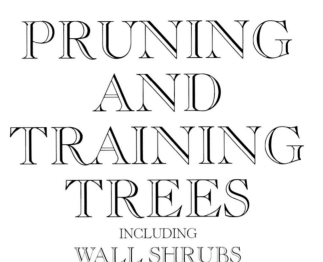

Careful formative pruning of a young tree will contribute to its ultimate shape and size and will often help to avoid the need for more drastic surgery later. Mature trees need minimal pruning, and any major pruning on a large tree is a job best tackled by a tree surgeon.

Many conifers develop a neat formal outline without intervention and are easily spoilt by overzealous pruning. Problems such as overhanging branches, or foliage that is turning brown are dealt with here.

Initial training for wall shrubs, such as fixing into a wall, and maintenance pruning, is also dealt with in this chapter.

For advice on a specific tree, consult the appropriate entry in the A–Z directory.

CHAPTER

4

PRUNING AND TRAINING TREES

INCLUDING

WALL SHRUBS

MATURE TREES normally require pruning only if a branch becomes diseased or damaged, or they outgrow their space. Pruning can be vital in the formative years, however, and initial training will help to establish the shape and form of the mature tree.

Early pruning will determine whether the snowy mespilus (*Amelanchier lamarckii*, *A. canadensis*) grows as a tree with a single trunk (see right) or as a large shrub with multiple stems. There are many other trees whose shape is affected by formative pruning, including eucalyptus, which can be grown as a single or multi-trunked tree or as a coppiced shrub.

The aim of formative pruning is to develop a framework of strong branches and an attractive well-balanced shape If trees are well shaped drastic surgery is less likely to be needed later.

A container-grown plant from a garden centre will probably be about 1.8m (6ft) tall with a number of small branches quite low down, and will require appropriate pruning according to the type of tree you want to produce – a standard tree, or one with side growths, known as a feathered tree, and so on. Larger, more mature specimens, for which preliminary training should have been done, are available from specialist nurseries.

Malus 'Red Jade'

Amelanchier lamarckii grown as a tree

MAIDENS

Specialist tree suppliers may sell maidens or whips (see *Glossary*), which are young trees usually less than 1.5m (5ft) tall. More formative training will be necessary than if you buy an older tree.

Starting at ground level and working up, remove two-thirds of the sideshoots from feathered whips, or from maidens when they start to produce sideshoots, but leave any rosettes of leaves without shoots. Support the tree with a cane to keep it upright.

In the second year you need to deal with sideshoots produced since the initial pruning. Again remove sideshoots from the base up, leaving just the top third to grow for another year. From then on prune according to the shape you require.

(See also Chapter Six: *Pruning and training fruit*.)

Amelanchier lamarckii

STANDARDS

MOST TREES are grown as standards, with a clear trunk. The height of clear trunk below the first branch varies as follows:

Half standard: 1.2–1.5m (4–5ft)
Light standard: 1.5–1.8m (5–6ft)
Standard: At least 1.8m (6ft)

All standards start off as 'central leaders' with a dominant main central trunk but sideshoots will soon grow. For smaller trees such as ornamental cherries, crab apples (*Malus*) and rowans (*Sorbus aucuparia*) a branching head or dense framework of branches should be allowed to develop as this helps to restrict the height of the tree. With a branching head branches are usually evenly spaced around the trunk and are more likely to be set at right angles, with fewer weak junctions where there is a narrow crotch or angle which may be prone to splitting in a severe gale. Pruning for a branching head should begin while the tree is still young.

Most tall trees, such as liquidambers

Malus 'Laxton's Red', standard with a branching head

and liriodendrons are allowed to retain a dominant central leader or main stem, and need training when young to produce a clear stem.

Acer platanoides 'Drummondii'

Liriodendron tulipifera, a tall central leader tree

FORMATIVE PRUNING

For a clear stem remove any sideshoots from below the height at which you want the branches of the crown or head to form.

Sometimes clusters of leaves grow that do not attempt to form a shoot and these can be retained as they have a strengthening effect on the main stem.

A single dominant main stem normally forms without intervention, but if a competing dominant shoot appears, cut it out promptly.

If the tree is still very small remove branches from the bottom two-thirds of the stem in two stages. During the summer cut back any new shoots that grow low down to about 10–12.5cm (4–5in), once they reach about 30cm (12in) long. When the tree is dormant, cut all these shoots back cleanly, flush with the main stem. Continue the process until the clear stem is the required height.

Trees best grown with a branching head will have a main central stem initially. This should be cut out when it grows to about 60cm (2ft) above the final height of the clear stem that will form the trunk. This stimulates multiple branching.

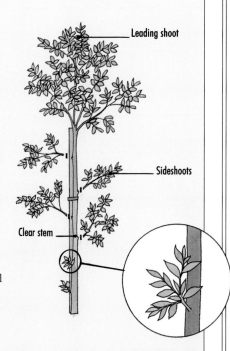

Leading shoot

Sideshoots

Clear stem

FEATHERED TREES

A FEATHERED TREE has a prominent leading shoot that follows a straight line up through the tree, but unlike a standard it has sideshoots almost to ground level. This feathered effect is sometimes desirable. Trees such as catalpas and birches (*Betula* spp.) can look attractive with low branches; fastigiate trees (those with narrow, upright growth), such as *Prunus* 'Amanogawa' *Fagus sylvatica* 'Dawyck' (syn. 'Fastigiata'), and Lombardy poplar (*Populus nigra* 'Italica') look best with plenty of low branches.

A feathered tree can be made into a standard by removing the lower shoots, but this is always best done at an early stage.

Betula showing low branching

A feathered populus × candicans 'Aurora' with low branches instead of a clear stem

Fastigiate trees such as this populus nigra 'Italica' are usually left feathered

FORMATIVE PRUNING

A feathered tree requires minimal training. After planting, cut back the sideshoots once to within 5–10cm (2–4in) of the main stem when the plant is dormant. Occasionally it is worth thinning out some of these sideshoots again later, especially low and weak ones, if the branches have become crowded.

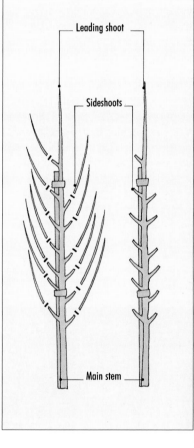

Leading shoot

Sideshoots

Main stem

BUSH AND MULTI-STEMMED TREES

Bush trees

Bush trees are like short standards, with a trunk of about 30–75cm (12–30in). Amelanchiers, *Catalpa bignonioides* 'Aurea' and *Parrotia persica*, can look attractive in this form.

Catalpa bignonioides

FORMATIVE PRUNING

Generally this form is suitable only for small trees which have a naturally bushy habit with a central leader that soon breaks up to form a head. Apart from creating a clear stem to a height of 30–75cm (12–30in), in the same way as described for standard trees, further formative pruning is not normally necessary as these trees tend to branch naturally instead of forming a dominant central leader. Hard pruning will encourage further branching if this is necessary.

Multi-stemmed trees

Although most species look more natural with a single stem, some trees tend to form multiple stems. Trees that have this attractive natural habit include hazel (*Corylus avellana*), stewartias, and the corkscrew willow.

Birches and eucalyptus sometimes form multiple stems, and these can be left to create a more spreading effect which resembles a copse of several closely planted trees. Other species that look good as multi-stemmed trees include *Acer capillipes* and *A. grosseri* var. *hersii*.

FORMATIVE PRUNING

Multi-stemmed trees may be available from garden centres, but they are not common. You can produce your own by starting with a very young tree, ideally one with only one straight shoot and no branches. This is called a maiden. Prune this back hard, then allow two or three shoots to grow.

Eucalyptus gunnii

WEEPING TREES

WEEPING TREES require a clear stem with plenty of height so that the pendulous branches can hang without touching the ground.

Some weeping trees are created by grafting, and the height will have been determined by the nursery. Some very dwarf weeping trees are created by grafting a low, spreading variety on to a tall stem of an upright kind. *Cotoneaster* 'Hybridus Pendulus' is treated in this way. *Salix subopposita* is a dwarf willow occasionally grafted on a tall stem to make a weeping tree.

The only routine pruning required for a weeping tree is to thin out overcrowded shoots and to remove any badly crossing branches and, of course, any dead or diseased sections.

Betula pendula 'Youngii'

FORMATIVE TRAINING

Any initial training will probably have been done before you buy the tree. During the first few years after planting, however, some formative pruning may be beneficial.

For a mushroom shape, cut out any inward-facing sideshoots that would spoil the effect. If the branches are uneven, trim them to approximately the same length so that the tree looks more balanced.

Weeping trees with a central leader, such as weeping hollies, rarely require pruning. If a split leader forms, prune out one to leave the better-placed shoot to form a single leader. If you need to control the height, cut out the central leader just above a branch and prune out any new leaders that form subsequently, taking them back to their point of origin.

Spreading, bushy trees, such as *Pyrus salicifolia* 'Pendula', may need sideshoots removing from the main stem if you want a clear trunk. Once the tree reaches the desired height, cut any upward-growing stems back to their point of origin every two or three years.

POLLARDING

This drastic form of pruning destroys the tree's natural shape but can create a dramatic effect in an appropriate setting. For example, some willows, such as *Salix alba* 'Chermesina' (syn. 'Britzensis'), can be pollarded for ornamental effect, producing their young, coloured stems on a stump about 1.2–1.8m (4–6ft) tall.

The technique is also used to restrict the growth of trees that have become too large, where a normal framework of branches is a hazard to traffic, for instance (see page 172).

Traditionally pollarding was used as a way of obtaining firewood, and willows were pollarded to stimulate the production of young growth (withies) for basketry.

The trees are normally cut back at 2.4–3.6m (8–12ft), and the branches which form the main framework are cut back at 60cm–1.5m (2–5ft). From then on the shoots are pruned back to these branches every year.

Salix alba 'Chermesina', after pollarding

Pollarded lime tree

Pollarded salix

CUTTING BACK A LARGE TREE

Mature trees sometimes outgrow their space or begin to succumb to diseases. A tree surgeon should be able to advise on whether the tree can be improved safely or whether it is posing a hazard and should be felled.

Generally, limiting the size of a mature tree is a job for a properly qualified and insured tree surgeon as the techniques involve the use of a chain saw and special equipment for working safely in the tree.

The main ways to restrict the size of a tree are shown here.

Crown thinning may help if the tree is healthy and attractive but simply casts too much shade. This calls for great skill to avoid spoiling the shape of the tree, however, and usually no more than 30 per cent of the branches are removed, starting with those that are crossing, weak or dying. This technique is usually restricted to deciduous trees.

Crown reduction helps to reduce the density of the head, making a weakened tree less vulnerable to gale damage, and allowing in more light which may improve its growth. It can also benefit a tree with uneven or lop-sided growth. The crown is reduced by cutting back the longest branches to well placed side branches, and is done throughout the tree.

Crown lifting for a large tree, sometimes called crown raising, is useful if low branches are a nuisance, either because they cause an obstruction or cast too much shade for plants to grow beneath it. The lowest branches are removed to produce a taller clear trunk.

Pollarding a large tree (sometimes called topping or lopping), can be carried out on trees that are overhanging a road or drive, or beginning to overhang the house. The branches are cut back drastically close to the main trunk. This leaves large wounds on a large tree pollarded simply to restrict size, and can produce a mis-shapen tree as new shoots grow. Pollarding is sometimes done regularly for ornamental reasons (see page 171), using the same basic technique to produce very attractive trees.

Cutting large branches

Once cut half way through, the weight of a large branch may cause it to fall and tear the wood, making the wound difficult to heal. Where this is likely to happen, remove the branch by making three cuts – the first two to remove the branch without damage to the part you want to retain, and the third to cut off the stub cleanly.

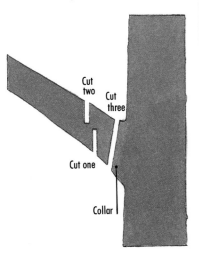

Cut off a large, heavy branch about 30cm (12in) from the trunk (if it is very long, remove it in several sections). The branch should not be cut too close to the trunk as the size of the wound will be larger and more difficult to heal. Avoid cutting into the branch collar. Make an upward cut first, as shown, to reduce the risk of tearing, then a second cut downwards to remove the branch. A third cut removes the outstanding stub. If the branch is larger than 10cm (4in) in diameter, paint the edge with a wound paint, but leave the centre exposed (see box opposite).

On a small wound a pruning knife can be used to trim rough wood, but on a large one you may find a wood rasp easier to use. A knife can be used to trim live bark for a smooth finish.

Root pruning

Root pruning used to be a popular way of controlling the size of fruit trees, but with modern dwarfing rootstocks it should not be necessary. Ornamentals are seldom root-pruned, but if you have inherited a tree that is simply too large to contain by normal pruning, you may want to try this technique.

Dig out a circular trench 45–60cm (18–24in) deep, its outer edge at about the same distance from the trunk as the outer limit of the branches. Saw through the thick roots, but leave the smaller ones uncut. Replace the soil.

Bark ringing

Like root pruning, this is used to check the growth of over-vigorous and unproductive fruit trees (usually apple or pear – don't use the method for stone fruits, such as plums and cherries, because it increases the risk of silver-leaf infection).

To 'ring' a tree, remove a very narrow ring of bark down to the hard wood, at blossom time, about 60cm (24in) above soil level. Immediately cover the wound with adhesive tape, so that it bridges the gap but does not actually touch the wound (the object of taping is to prevent the wound drying out and to reduce the risk of infection). The tape should be removed in the autumn.

It should always be done with care and never remove a strip wider than 6mm (¼in).

Full ring

WOUND PAINTS

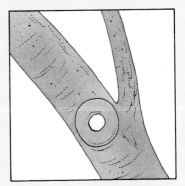

Wound paint on large cut

Wound paints, available from garden centres, are intended to seal large pruning wounds to reduce the risk of infection. However, painting the whole surface with a normal wound paint, such as one based on bitumen, could actually trap spores of wood-rotting bacteria or fungi under the seal.

To seal large pruning cuts on most trees and shrubs, trim off any jagged edges with a pruning knife, then paint a ring of sealant around the outside of the wound, *but leave the centre untreated*. This will prevent the actively growing cells under the bark (the cambium layer) from drying out without sealing in harmful disease spores over the greater part of the wound.

The exceptions are fruit trees such as apples, cherries, peaches, pears, plums, and their ornamental relatives, as these are prone to diseases that develop on freshly cut surfaces. In these cases, it is best to seal the wound completely. Serious diseases such as silver leaf and bacterial canker are potential risks if the wound is not sealed, and this outweighs the risk of sealing in a few less serious diseases that may affect only the one branch if they develop.

WALL SHRUBS

SOME TREES, such as Magnolia grandiflora, and many shrubs, produce very attractive clothing for walls as well as benefitting from the increased warmth and shelter. However they need regular pruning and training if they are to remain within bounds and give an attractive display.

One of the easiest and most unobtrusive methods of supporting them is with wire stretched between vine eyes or screw eyes. If using screw eyes, drill holes in the wall, fit wall plugs, then screw in the eyes. Avoid drilling and plugging lime-based mortar in very old walls because it is weaker than modern mortar. Non-screw vine eyes can be knocked into a wooden fence support, but not into a brick or masonry wall. Wire spaced 30–40cm (12–16in) apart is suitable for most wall shrubs. If you prefer to fix a trellis, make sure there is a gap of 5cm (2in) between the wall and the trellis by screwing battens to the wall first.

After pruning, space the young shoots out to fill gaps or extend the area covered, and secure them with garden twine or proprietary ties. Whichever you use, check all ties at least once a year to make sure they are not biting into the stems. Loosen them or remove them completely if the branch is firm enough.

For more about training fruit on walls, see Chapter Six (see box opposite).

Chaenomeles speciosa 'Moerloosii'

Maintenance Pruning

For most wall shrubs you can use the pruning methods recommended for free-standing shrubs. If branches have been tied to the wire you may have to untie them first and retie them again after pruning, spacing the shoots out to produce even cover.

In mid-summer, tie in new shoots produced in spring and early summer, to keep the plant neat and tidy.

Many shrubs, such as pittosporum and *Euonymus fortunei*, trained against a wall require no more than clipping to shape and size, like a hedge. Even shrubs that normally have their sideshoots reduced by two-thirds to encourage more flowers the following year can be trimmed with shears if they are small-leaved and twiggy.

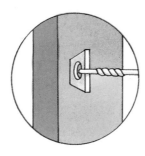

Vine eyes are knocked into a fence post with a hammer

Space wires 30–40cm (12–16in) apart

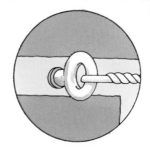

Screw eyes are screwed into the wall after drilling and plugging

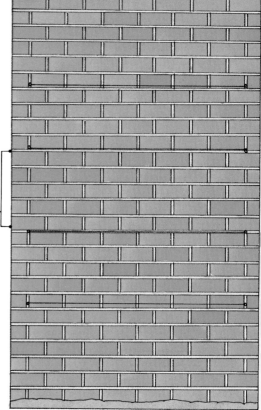

Some wall shrubs, such as *Forsythia suspensa* and *Cytisus battandieri* need pruning to keep them compact against the wall. After removing dead, diseased or damaged branches, cut back any shoots that are growing away from or directly towards the wall. Make sure the others are tied in well to cover gaps, and tie in new shoots during the summer if necessary.

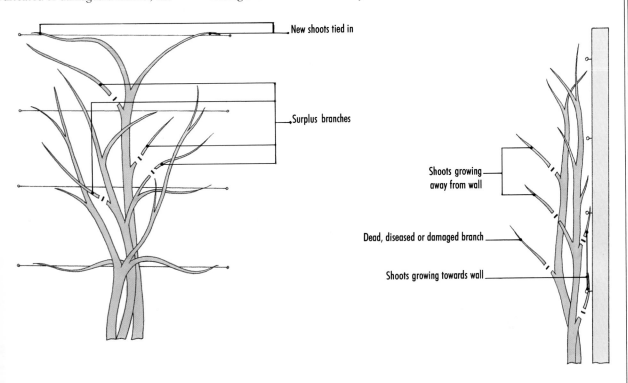

New shoots tied in

Surplus branches

Shoots growing away from wall

Dead, diseased or damaged branch

Shoots growing towards wall

ESPALIER TRAINING

Espalier training can be used for ornamental plants as well as fruits such as apples and pears (see pages 193 and 208). Pyracanthas and wisterias look particularly attractive trained in this way.

Fix horizontal training wires to the wall about 30cm (12in) apart. Most of the training is done in late spring and early summer by tying in flexible shoots to the wires and pinching back long shoots as they arise.

Ornamental shrubs can be trained as espaliers. Pyracanthus are particularly amenable to this treatment.

CONIFERS

CONIFERS REQUIRE little training and practically no pruning except when grown as a hedge. Although very diverse in shape and size they usually develop an attractive shape without intervention.

Those with an upright, cone-shaped outline should never have the main shoot removed or else the tree's natural shape is likely to be destroyed. If the main shoot is damaged or accidentally removed, choose a shoot close to the top and tie this to an upright stake. This should become the new leading shoot.

If a conical tree that normally has only one main shoot develops a competing leader, cut out the weaker of the two as soon as possible. This will ensure that the tree retains its natural shape. Do not do this to trees that normally develop multiple leaders.

Some conifers, especially those with pendulous growth such as *Cedrus libani* var. *atlantica* 'Glauca Pendula', must be staked when young and the growth trained upwards to prevent prostrate growth.

Other conifers, such as yews (*Taxus*) and junipers (*Juniperus*), usually have several main shoots instead of just one dominant one. You do not need to reduce any of these multiple shoots.

If prostrate conifers produce upright shoots, remove these at their point of origin.

With few exceptions, such as yew and Western red cedar, conifers do not grow well from old wood. If you cut back into mature wood new shoots will rarely develop and you will be left with bare stubs. Therefore only cut conifers back to live, visible buds. Do not cut back into old wood: cut off damaged or misplaced branches completely rather than leave a stub.

Once lower limbs have died because of too much shade, or for some other reason, pruning is unlikely to produce replacement growth.

If pruning is required to control spread, it should be done in spring or early summer by reducing the length of the thin new growth. This can often be done simply by pinching out the new growth between finger and thumb.

Conifers that produce tight growth in a formal shape such as cone, ball, or column, can be clipped regularly to retard growth and prevent them growing too large. This may also improve their shape.

Pines (*Pinus*), firs (*Abies*), and spruces (*Picea*) produce new growth in 'candles' and by pinching these back in spring before the needles have expanded you can influence the spread and growth. To extend the height or spread of a branch, remove all but the longest candle, but if you want to promote dense, bushy growth shorten all the candles by a half to two-thirds. This technique is not practical on large trees, but can be useful on young ones.

Changing foliage

The foliage of many seedling conifers looks markedly different from that of the adult plant. This is common in the cypresses (*Chamaecyparis*), which may have juvenile needles but scale-like adult foliage.

Usually seedlings grow out of their juvenile foliage, but some dwarf conifers including varieties of the Sawara cypress (*Chamaecyparis pisifera*) retain their more feathery-looking young form.

Sometimes varieties which retain their juvenile foliage will produce shoots showing the coarser adult form. Cut these back to their source as soon as you notice them as they will spoil the appearance of the plant.

Removing adult foliage from juvenile foliage conifer

Pinus pumila showing 'candles'

Overgrown conifers

Prostrate conifers sometimes outgrow
their allotted space, and may start to
smother nearby plants or overhang a
path. They can usually be restrained
by cutting out the overhanging
branches. Take them back to a point
beneath an overlapping branch so that
no ugly stump is visible.

Cutting back overhanging conifer

Over-large trees

Many conifers grow too large for a
small garden, and fast-growing species
sometimes take their owners by
surprise.

   The best solution is to replace the
tree with one that is more appropriate.
If you have a large-growing conifer
that you do not want to remove, try
topping it at an appropriate height,
then clip it to a shape like that of the
one illustrated. This technique is most
appropriate for trees that are still fairly
young and well clothed to the base.
Species used as hedging plants are the
most likely to respond well to this
treatment.

This Cupressus macrocarpa 'Lutea' was topped and clipped because it grew too large for the site

Brown foliage

The cause of brown foliage may be
disease and in many cases you will
have to remove the plant. But hedges
and dwarf conifers exposed to strong
winds in a harsh winter, or to periods
of summer drought, sometimes look as
though they are dying, but recover
once new growth starts.

   If you think the problem is caused
by the weather, do not prune out
affected branches unless you know the
plant is likely to shoot easily from old
wood (see A–Z), as is the case with
yew. Wait to see whether the new
growth will hide the damaged area.

Brown foliage caused by drought and wind

MAINTAINING HEDGES

Pruning at the right time of year can ensure a strong, neat, attractive hedge with the minimum of effort. This chapter looks at ways of maintaining all styles of hedge with useful tips such as how to save pruning time by making sure the hedge is not unnecessarily high or wide.

The Table on page 186 is a guide to when and how to trim your hedge and will give you an idea of how much work might be involved if you are intending to plant a new hedge. When establishing a new hedge follow the after-planting advice to produce bushy plants with shoots down to the ground.

Informal flowering hedges also respond well to careful pruning, and again the Table on page 186 will give you the best time to prune for maximum flowers.

5

MAINTAINING HEDGES

MOST HEDGES require regular pruning if they are not to look neglected and outgrow their allotted space. Those with large leaves, such as cherry laurel (*Prunus laurocerasus*) and spotted laurel (*Aucuba japonica* varieties) are best pruned with secateurs, otherwise the cut leaves can look unsightly when they die and start to turn brown. Most hedges, however, can be trimmed with shears or a powered hedgetrimmer.

Formal hedges are closely and neatly trimmed to a crisp outline; informal ones are left to grow more naturally without such a tidy profile. Formal hedges generally respond best to tight clipping with shears or a hedgetrimmer. Informal hedges require less frequent pruning, but are usually unsuitable for a boundary adjoining a footpath as shoots may overhang the path.

Many informal hedges are made up of plants with attractive flowers. If such hedges are clipped back hard like a formal hedge, most of the flowers will usually be removed. Because informal hedges are usually allowed to grow longer shoots, which may also be thicker than those of a formal hedge, secateurs are often more appropriate than shears for pruning them.

Choosing the right time to prune is important for most hedges. For flowering hedges like forsythia that bloom on year-old wood, timing is crucial and will affect the amount of flowers they carry (see page 186).

The height and the width across the top of a hedge will significantly affect the time taken. Worthwhile savings

can often be made by lowering the height, and it is often possible to reduce the size of an established hedge that has grown too large (see Improving an old hedge, page 184). Most plants have an optimum height when grown as a hedge, and the table on page 186 indicates the best height range for some of the most common hedging plants.

Beginning a hedge

Pruning starts straight after the hedge is planted. Cut back vigorous deciduous plants, such as hawthorn and the semi-evergreen privet, to 15cm (6in). Evergreens such as box and shrubby honeysuckle are best planted in spring and at that time should be cut back by about a third. Reduce the height of flowering shrubs by about a third after planting.

If you neglect this very early pruning the hedge will grow away at the tips and may never thicken up at the base.

For a formal hedge, trim back the new shoots by half in early summer, to stimulate branching at the base of the hedge. Trim all the new growth back by half again in the autumn, and at this point start to shape the hedge by tapering the sides and making the top flat or rounded. The following summer, trim the new sideshoots by half and continue the shaping. Trim the top level in the winter. For informal flowering hedges reduce the main shoots by a third in the second winter, then follow the advice for the particular species (see page 186).

Exceptions to the advice given above are conifers, large-leaved evergreens such as laurel, or aucuba, and slow-growing deciduous plants like beech and hornbeam. Cut back sideshoots by a quarter to a third after planting, and do the same again to new growth the next summer, but allow the leading shoot to grow intact until the desired height is reached.

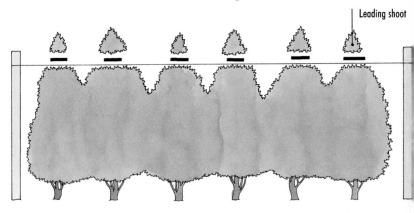

Leading shoot

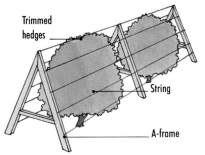

Trimmed hedges

String

A-frame

Start to shape a hedge while it is still young. To create a tapering hedge, make a set of A-frames from scrap wood to which you can attach strings. Set the frames in the hedge, attach and tauten strings, and trim to this outline.

SHAPING A HEDGE

THE MAJORITY of formal hedges are grown with a flat top and vertical sides. For a low box hedge that forms part of a knot garden or parterre this is entirely appropriate, but for taller conventional boundary hedges this is not the ideal shape for a well-clothed plant.

The best shape for a formal hedge is one that tapers towards the top, so that plenty of light reaches most parts of the plant. This also means that heavy snow is less likely to settle than on a broad, flat top and thus less likely to spoil the shape of the hedge by bending or breaking the branches. A tapering shape also makes a wide hedge easier to cut across the top.

The least satisfactory shape is one that narrows at the bottom. Poor light, and more competition from weeds generally results in a bare or sparsely clothed base.

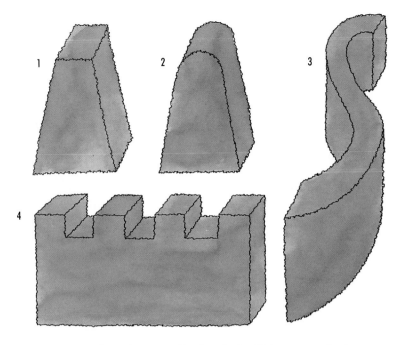

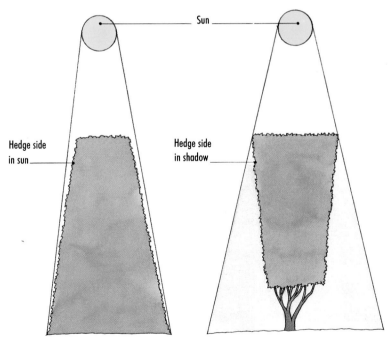

1 and 2 are typical hedge shapes. The serpentine (3) and castellated top (4) shapes are examples of the more imaginative ways a formal hedge can be shaped.

Holly hedge

RESHAPING AN ESTABLISHED HEDGE

IT IS BEST to begin shaping a hedge at an early stage, but a taper can often be achieved on an established hedge provided the plants will tolerate drastic cutting. Beech, privet, blackthorn and yew are among the plants that usually respond well. The best time to reshape a hedge is in winter or early spring.

Yew hedge

Make a frame to the required shape from two long timbers nailed together with a cross-piece just above the desired hedge height. Place the frame against one end of the hedge and cut the hedge back to the shape of the frame, moving it along gradually as you proceed.

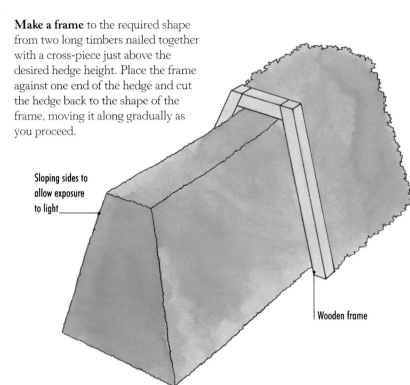

Sloping sides to allow exposure to light

Wooden frame

If it is not practical to reshape the sides because cutting into old wood may spoil the hedge, retain the straight sides but create a triangular-shaped top. Trim the sides, but let the top grow and lightly trim the 'shoulders' of the hedge as it grows.

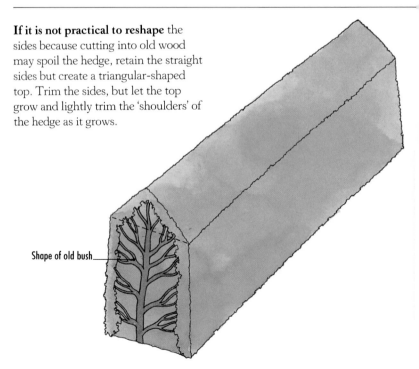

Shape of old bush

TRIMMING TECHNIQUES

AN ESTABLISHED hedge can usually be cut by eye, but if you find it difficult to keep a straight top or even sides, try cutting to a guide. To keep the line level, place a piece of wood along the top and rest a spirit-level on this. Significant rises and falls will be noticed and can be corrected as you work along the hedge.

With top and bottom lines established, it is relatively easy to trim the remainder of the uncut sides by eye.

How often a hedge needs trimming depends on the type. A closely manicured formal hedge of box or privet may need cutting every four to six weeks in summer, informal hedges usually need only an annual trim.

The best time to trim a formal hedge is when it begins to look untidy, but ideally it should be between late spring and late summer. Informal flowering shrubs should be cut at the best time to encourage more flowers: the Table on page 186 gives the most suitable trimming times for most popular hedge plants.

A neatly trimmed beech hedge

The secret of a successful curved hedge lies in the planting. Thereafter it will need careful trimming by eye.

Whenever possible trim back to a little above the previous cut, leaving about 6mm (¼in) of new growth to maintain a well-clothed and dense appearance. In time, however, it may be necessary to cut back more drastically to keep the hedge in shape.

To make easier work of collecting the clippings, lay down a sheet of polythene at the base of the hedge. Use this to gather up and carry the clippings to the compost heap (or shredder if the clippings are too woody to compost).

High hedges

Hedges taller than 1.8m (6ft) are difficult to cut. You should be able to cut the sides without much trouble, but trimming the top will require steps or a platform. Using a powered hedgetrimmer while standing on a ladder or platform is potentially hazardous.

If you have to trim a tall hedge, use two trestles or two pairs of steps and place a strong, broad plank between them. With this arrangement you do not have to keep climbing up and down so often, and are less tempted to overstretch. Make sure the trestles are safe and level; if the ground is soft rest them on planks of wood.

CHEMICAL PRUNING

If you want to reduce the frequency with which you have to clip a formal quick-growing hedge a growth regulator may be useful - though you should bear in mind the cost and time involved in spraying the hedge. Only treat hedges over three years old.

Growth regulators must always be used as the manufacturer advises. The effect is to inhibit further seasonal growth of the leading shoots. In doing this the spray not only restricts the growth of the leading shoots but also tends to stimulate side-branching to produce dense cover.

The dose varies according to the type of hedge, and not all hedging plants are suitable for treatment (the instructions on the packet will advise). Choose a calm day and protect spray drifting on to other plants (it may not kill them, but could cause foliage scorch or temporary damage).

A few long shoots may grow out from within the hedge, but these can easily be trimmed off as they appear. You can spray your side of a boundary hedge without affecting the growth on your neighbour's side.

IMPROVING AN OLD HEDGE

NEGLECTED HEDGES, or those that have simply grown too tall or been allowed to become too wide, can often be improved and brought back into shape. It will take the hedge several seasons to recover from the more drastic treatments, but you will have a better-shaped and easier-to-manage hedge afterwards.

A bare base This may be the result of poor early training, competition from weeds, or a shape that keeps the base in poor light. This can be masked by planting along the base low-growing shrubs that tolerate the dry soil and competition from the hedge. Dwarf box is a good candidate, but there are many others that you can use.

Reverting to green For a golden or variegated hedge that is reverting to green, cut back the green shoots to their point of origin, do not just clip.

Thin growth Thin growth, or new growth concentrated at the top of the hedge, may simply be a sign of starvation. Try pruning back in early spring to where the stems are starting to grow, then feed and water regularly

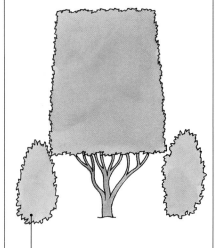

Plant hides a
bare base

for a couple of seasons to see whether there is a significant improvement. Mulching will also help.

If there are other major faults with the hedge, it may be worth cutting it back to let it rejuvenate (see A fresh start, page 185).

Gaps If one of the plants has died the gap can often be filled in over a period of years with growth from neighbouring plants. It may be possible to let some shoots grow long and weave them in to help cover the area.

Where practical, cut back the dead plant to ground level and let shoots grow in from either side. When trimming the hedge, be especially careful not to cut too far in. Alternatively, you may wish to leave the dead plant in place to maintain privacy and protection and just remove it gradually as the gap is filled up.

If the hedge is still relatively young, dig out the old plant and replace it with a new one of the same kind. Feed, water and mulch it for several years to encourage it to make plenty of new growth.

Golden privet reverting to green

Tall yew hedge shooting after hard cutting back

Too tall Most hedges will respond over a couple of seasons if cut back to the required height. Set a string line 30cm (12in) below the desired height, or insert marker canes with their tops the same distance below the target height, and cut back to this level in late winter or early spring (in late spring, just after growth has begun, in the case of evergreens). This will require long-handled pruners and possibly even a saw, rather than secateurs.

Trim new growth back to the desired height the following summer.

Too wide Insert canes in the hedge at the depth you want to cut back to (paint them a bright colour if they are difficult to see). Set them 30cm (12in) further in than the desired final width: you must cut back this extra amount to allow for new growth which you can trim later. Cut back to the markers. You may prefer to spread the work over two seasons. If doing both sides at once, complete one side before tackling the other. The best time to do this is winter or early spring (late spring for evergreens).

Trim new growth back to the desired width the following summer.

A fresh start If severe pruning combined with feeding and watering fail to improve a hedge sufficiently, you may be able to avoid the need to dig up and replant the old hedge by cutting it back completely. Cut the hedge down to about 10–15cm (4–6in) above the ground. Often the stumps will respond by throwing up plenty of new shoots the next year, and these can be shaped as a new hedge. Although the hedge will take several seasons to form a respectable barrier, this technique is quicker, cheaper and less effort than planting a new hedge.

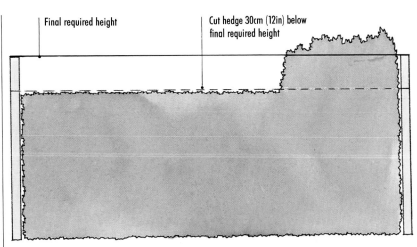

Final required height

Cut hedge 30cm (12in) below final required height

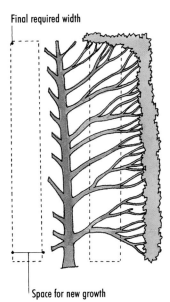

Final required width

Space for new growth

New shoots

Old hedge cut back by almost half

Conifers With the exception of yew, conifers do not usually tolerate drastic cutting back, as they do not usually re-grow readily from old wood (see Conifers, page 176).

WHEN AND HOW TO PRUNE

Plant	When to trim	Ideal height	Comments
Aucuba japonica (spotted laurel)	July, August	1.2–1.8m (4–6ft)	Prune with secateurs. Can be cut back hard with care.
Berberis darwinii	July for a formal hedge, after flowering for an informal one	1.2–1.8m (4–6ft)	If overgrown, cut back hard after flowering.
Berberis × stenophylla	After flowering	1.2–1.8m (4–6ft)	
Berberis thunbergii	Late winter for a formal hedge; after flowering for an informal hedge	0.6–1.2m (2–4ft)	
Buxus sempervirens (box) 'Suffruticosa' (dwarf box)	July, August	0.6–1.2m (2–4ft) under 60cm (12in).	Will stand hard pruning.
Camellia × williamsii	After flowering	1.2–1.8m (4–6ft)	Little regular trimming necessary, but can be pruned hard in April.
Carpinus betulus (hornbeam)	July, August	1.2–1.8m (4–6ft)	Can also be pruned hard in winter.
Chaenomeles japonica (flowering quince)	May	1.2–1.8m (4–6ft)	
Chamaecyparis lawsoniana (Lawson's cypress)	July, August	1.8–2.1m (6–7ft)	Always leave at least 7.5–10cm (3–4in) of live foliage.
Corylus avellana (hazel)	July	1.2–1.8m (4–6ft)	
Corylus maxima 'Purpurea' (purple hazel)	July	1.2–1.8m (4–6ft)	
Cotoneaster simonsii	August or winter	1.2–1.8m (4–6ft)	Easily becomes thin and untidy but can be cut back hard in winter.
Crataegus (hawthorn)	July, or June and again in August for a more solid appearance	1.2–1.8m (4–6ft)	Can be cut back hard in winter. Soon makes new growth.
× Cupressocyparis leylandii (Leyland cypress)	July, August	1.8–2.1m (6–7ft)	Do not let it get too large initially.
Cupressus macrocarpa	July, August	1.8–2.1m (6–7ft)	
Elaeagnus × ebbingei	August	1.2–1.8m (4–6ft)	Use secateurs.
Elaeagnus pungens	June to August	1.2–1.8m (4–6ft)	Use secateurs.
Escallonia macrantha	After flowering	1.2–1.8m (4–6ft)	Can be cut back hard in early or mid-spring if it becomes untidy. If frost damaged, cut back hard in June.
Euonymus japonicus (Japanese spindle)	July, August	1.2–1.8m (4–6ft)	
Fagus sylvatica (beech)	August	1.2–2.1m (4–7ft)	
Forsythia	After flowering	1.2–1.8m (4–6ft)	If summer growth becomes too long, shorten in August (but you may sacrifice some flowers).
Fuchsia magellanica	November or March, April	1.2–1.8m (4–6ft)	In cold areas where top growth has been killed, cut down to ground level. These plants re-grow very rapidly. In mild areas where top growth survives, just prune out dead or diseased wood in March.
Griselinia littoralis	July, August	1.2–1.8m (4–6ft)	For an informal outline prune with secateurs.

Plant	When to trim	Ideal height	Comments
Hebe (shrubby veronica)	August	0.6–1.2m (2–4ft)	In cold areas, wait until spring to assess winter damage.
Hippophaë rhamnoides (sea buckthorn)	July, August	1.2–1.8m (4–6ft)	As this hedge is very thorny, gloves are recommended when pruning.
Ilex (holly)	August	1.5–2.1m (5–7ft)	Use secateurs.
Lavandula (lavender)	August	0.6–0.9m (2–3ft)	Cut back close to base of current season's growth, but not into old wood. Short-lived.
Ligustrum (privet)	May to August	1–1.2m (3–4ft)	Trim monthly. Can be cut back hard in April.
Lonicera nitida (shrubby honeysuckle)	May to September	0.6–1.2m (2–4ft)	Trim monthly. Regular trimming essential. This hedge will usually re-grow if cut back hard.
Olearia × haastii (daisy bush)	After flowering	0.6–1.2m (2–4ft)	
Osmanthus × burkwoodii	July	1.2–1.8m (4–6ft)	
Philadelphus (mock orange)	After flowering	1.2–1.5m (4–5ft)	
Osmanthus delavayi	May	1.2–1.8m (4–6ft)	
Potentilla fruticosa (shrubby potentilla)	May	0.6–1.2m (2–4ft)	
Prunus cerasifera	July, August	1.2–2.1m (4–7ft)	Cut some shoots hard to base if necessary.
Prunus × cistena	June, or May and September	1.2–1.8m (4–6ft)	
Prunus laurocerasus (cherry laurel)	July, August	1.2–1.8m (4–6ft)	Use secateurs.
Prunus lusitanica (Portugal laurel)	July, August	1.2–1.8m (4–6ft)	Use secateurs.
Prunus spinosa (blackthorn)	July, August	1.2–2.1m (4–7ft)	
Pyracantha rogersiana (firethorn)	August	1.2–1.8m (4–6ft)	
Rhododendron (R. lutescens and *R. ponticum)*	After flowering	1.5–2.1m (5–7ft)	Use secateurs, and prune only to keep in bounds. Can be cut back hard in April if necessary.
Ribes sanguineum (flowering currant)	May	1–1.5m (3–5ft)	
Rosa rugosa	Winter, or early spring	1.2–1.5m (4–5ft)	Wait until hips cease to be attractive before pruning.
Symphoricarpos (snowberry)	Late winter	1.2–1.8m (4–6ft)	Remove shoots growing from around base of plant.
Tamarix pentandra (tamarisk)	June (for semi-formal shape) or March (for a less formal hedge)	1.2–1.8m (4–6ft)	
Taxus baccata (yew)	August or September	1.2–1.8m (4–6ft)	Can be cut back hard in April if necessary.
Thuja plicata (western red cedar)	August	1.2–1.8m (4–6ft)	Do not cut back into old wood without leaves.
Viburnum tinus (laurustinus)	May	1.2–1.8m (4–6ft)	Use secateurs.
Weigela	After flowering	1.2–1.5m (4–5ft)	

PRUNING AND TRAINING FRUIT

To improve the quality and yield of fruit regular pruning is essential. The pruning systems suggested here are simple to follow, easy to apply and suitable for an amateur growing fruit on a garden scale. All types of fruit are included, from apples and pears to peaches and cherries, raspberries and gooseberries to figs and outdoor grapes.

This chapter also looks at formative training of fruit. However, as this is quite a difficult skill to master, it is often preferable to buy fruit plants with the formative training already done, especially with tree fruit such as apples, pears and peaches, and this is how they are usually sold in garden centres.

This chapter deals with tree fruit first, followed by soft fruit.

6

PRUNING AND
TRAINING
FRUIT

MOST FRUIT trees and bushes benefit
from regular pruning, which helps to
increase the number of good-sized
fruits and generally makes picking
easier. Some, such as cordons and
espaliers, are intensively pruned to
restrict growth and keep the trees
compact and suitable for a small
garden.

There are fashions and personal
preferences in the way certain fruits
are pruned and there are many
variations on the methods suggested
here. The pruning systems selected are
those that are simple to follow, easy to
apply, and suitable for an amateur
growing fruit on a garden scale. Other
pruning methods may be more
appropriate for commercial growers or
fruit enthusiasts.

Most tree fruit in garden centres
will already be trained into a particular
shape. Starting with your own very
young tree can be satisfying if you have
the enthusiasm and plenty of time, but
most gardeners prefer to pay more to
save several years' waiting and avoid
this more difficult training phase. If
you want to train your own trees or
bushes from cuttings or young grafted
plants, consult a specialist fruit book.

Espalier-trained apple 'Lord Lambourne'

Blackcurrant 'Ben Nevis'

Festooned plum tree

SHAPES

Tree fruit

Tree fruits dealt with below include apples and pears, peaches and plums, and more unusual fruits such as figs and mulberries. Also included here are intensively pruned forms such as cordons and espaliers, as well as bush-trained versions on dwarfing rootstocks that produce trees more shrub-like in size and shape than the tree shapes seen in traditional orchards.

Soft fruits, such as raspberries and blackcurrants, which grow on canes or compact bushes, are dealt with later in this chapter.

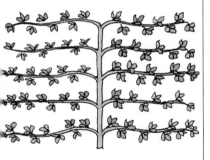

Espalier

Branches are trained horizontally to wires, usually against a wall or fence. Espaliers are more decorative than cordons and give higher yields, but they take up more space.

Step-over

Step-overs are really single-tiered espaliers, low enough to step over if you use them for an edging to a bed or fruit garden. A way to grow apples decoratively where space is very limited. See espaliers for pruning.

Cordon

Usually grown as single stems trained at an angle of 45°. Regular pruning is essential, but they are very space-saving.

Fan

Fans are decorative but training and pruning are complex. Apples, peaches and cherries are among the fruits that can be trained as fans.

Bush

The same shape as a standard tree but on a shorter stem. However, the height can still make pruning and picking difficult, and a dwarf bush on an even shorter stem may be preferable.

Dwarf pyramid

The shape resembles a Christmas tree, with the lower branches spreading wider than those above. Pruning and picking are relatively easy jobs.

Festoons

Festooning is a relatively new technique for training plums, apples and pears. It is useful for plums on 'Pixy' rootstock because the combination of dwarfing rootstock and restrictive pruning makes it possible to grow plums in gardens that might otherwise be too small.

Ballerina or flagpole apples

Ballerina apple trees grow naturally as a narrow upright column with fruit growing on short sideshoots. They need no routine pruning, and are useful if you want a no-fuss apple tree in a small garden where space is very limited.

APPLES

Size and shape

Where space is at a premium, a regularly pruned cordon, espalier, or fan is the most appropriate choice. These can be trained to wires in an open area, or against a wall or fence. Although the crop per tree is likely to be less than that of a free-standing tree, many trees can be accommodated in a limited area, and by choosing different varieties, cropping and eating can be spread over a long period.

If you have plenty of space and want a large yield, grow bush-shaped trees (see shapes on page 190). Dwarf rootstocks (see below) will keep them compact and make training and harvesting easy.

If you inherit a tree when you move into a new garden, you will have to live with the overall size and shape, but the cropping and appearance can usually be improved by suitable pruning.

Rootstocks

If you are buying a new tree, be sure to buy one grafted on to a rootstock that will produce a plant with appropriate vigour for the training method – pruning alone cannot reduce overall size. Use the following list of principal apple rootstocks as a guide when buying a tree. Do not buy the plant unless you know the number of the rootstock as well as the variety, although if you buy a tree already trained as a cordon, fan or espalier, an appropriate rootstock is likely to have been used.

M9 A very dwarfing rootstock which will produce a bush tree about 1.8–3m (6–10ft) tall. Usually starts to fruit in second or third year. Good for a dwarf pyramid or cordon, but a bush tree may need a permanent stake.

M25 Allows strong growth yet induces early fruiting. Good for half standards, but not normally used for small garden trees.

M26 A dwarfing rootstock that produces trees about 2.4m (8ft) high, which will often crop in the second or third year. Unlikely to need staking. Can be used for cordon, bush, pyramid and fan training.

M27 The one to choose for a 'miniature'. Very dwarfing, and suitable for trees in pots. Trees grafted on to this rootstock are unlikely to grow more than about 1.8m (6ft) tall. Needs good growing conditions to thrive.

M106 A semi-dwarfing rootstock widely used for bush apples. The trees may eventually grow to about 4.5m (15ft). Sometimes used for fans, espaliers and cordons, which of course are pruned to a limited height.

SPUR- OR TIP-BEARER?

Most apples and pears are spur-bearing – they produce fruit buds on new shoots which develop from short woody shoots known as spurs. Some varieties are tip-bearing – they tend to produce flower buds on unpruned two-year-old shoots. If you were to prune these back to produce short spurs you would remove most of the flower buds and, therefore, the fruit. If the garden centre or nursery cannot tell you whether a variety is a tip- or spur-bearer, check in a good fruit catalogue or book. If you have an old tree and do not know the variety, observe how your tree fruits. If most of the fruit is borne towards the tips of the shoots, it is a tip-bearer; spur varieties will have lots of fruit on short spurs close to the main stems.

Most apples are spur-bearers, and only a few well-known or popular varieties, such as 'Bramley's Seedling', 'George Cave', and 'Worcester Pearmain' are tip-bearers. Just a few, such as 'Discovery' and 'Tydeman's Early Worcester', fruit on both tips and spurs.

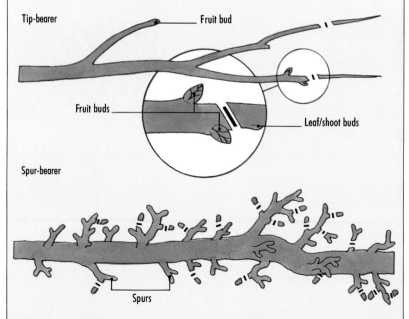

ESPALIER

ESPALIERS ARE pruned twice a year: in summer and again in winter.

Summer pruning controls the amount of growth produced each year, and maintains the espalier shape.

Winter pruning reduces the number of spurs, to ensure fewer but larger and better-spaced fruit.

Once the main branches grow too long for their allotted space, cut back the new growth at the tip to its point of origin in May.

Tip-bearing varieties (see page 192) are not used for this type of training, as it is important to have the flowers and fruit on short spurs close to the main stem.

In late July or early August, cut back the new leafy shoots produced during spring and summer. The shoots are mature enough to prune when they have dark leaves, the greenish-brown bark has started to turn brown, and they are woody at the base. The shoots are unlikely to be less than 23cm (9in) long. In colder areas, it may be early September before the growth is mature enough.

If the shoot is growing directly from the horizontal stem, cut it back to the third leaf above the basal cluster of leaves. *Remember not to count the basal cluster of leaves.*

If the shoot is growing from the stub formed by previous pruning, cut it back to just one leaf from the basal cluster.

When the tree is dormant, between leaf fall and new growth in spring, shorten any long shoots that have grown since summer pruning to about 5cm (2in). If there is a congested mass of old spurs from years of pruning, remove some of them, cutting out the weakest and any that are badly placed (on the underside or growing towards the wall, for example).

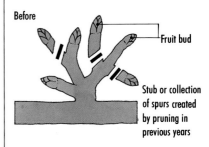

Before

Fruit bud

Stub or collection of spurs created by pruning in previous years

After

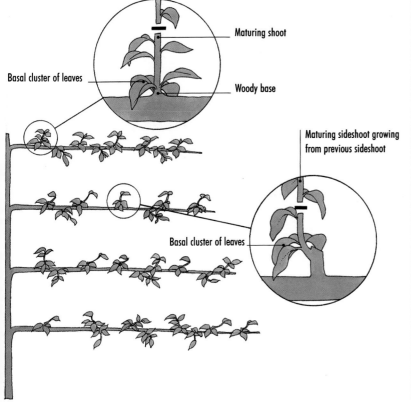

Maturing shoot

Basal cluster of leaves

Woody base

Maturing sideshoot growing from previous sideshoot

Basal cluster of leaves

STEP-OVERS

Step-overs are becoming popular for small gardens because they produce a crop of fruit in areas where it would be impractical to grow a larger tree. They can be used as a low, decorative and practical edging for a vegetable bed or kitchen garden, or even in the space in front of other fruit, such as cordon or espalier apples.

The trees are low, single-tiered espaliers trained to wires about 30cm (12in) above the ground, supported by short posts. When grown as an edging, plant the trees 3.5–4.5m (12–15ft) apart, and stop the growth when the arms meet those of the next plant.

Prune them as espaliers.

CORDON

CORDONS ARE pruned twice a year. Summer pruning controls the amount of growth produced each year and maintains the cordon shape, winter pruning reduces the number of spurs and encourages larger and better-spaced fruit.

Once the main stem grows too long, and lowering the supporting cane slightly will not give enough additional space, cut back the growth that has exceeded the height to its point of origin in May.

Tip-bearing varieties are not used for cordons as flowers and fruit should be borne on short spurs close to the main stem.

Apple 'Discovery'

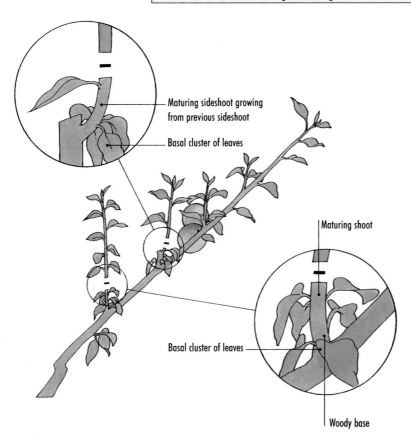

Maturing sideshoot growing from previous sideshoot

Basal cluster of leaves

Maturing shoot

Basal cluster of leaves

Woody base

In late July or early August, cut back the new leafy shoots produced during spring and summer. The shoots are mature enough to prune when they have dark leaves, the greenish-brown bark has started to turn brown, and they are woody at the base. The shoots are unlikely to be less than 23cm (9in) long. In colder areas, it may be early autumn before the growth is mature enough.

If the shoot is growing directly from the main stem, cut it back to the third leaf above the basal cluster of leaves. *Remember not to count the basal cluster of leaves.*

If the shoot is growing from the stub formed by previous pruning, cut it back to just one leaf from the basal cluster.

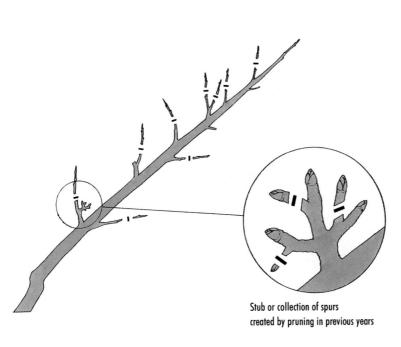

Stub or collection of spurs created by pruning in previous years

When the tree is dormant, between leaf fall and new growth in spring, shorten any long shoots that have grown since summer pruning to about 5cm (2in). If there is a congested mass of old spurs from pruning in previous years, remove some of them. Start by cutting out the weakest and any that are badly placed (on the underside or growing towards the wall, for example).

FAN

REGULAR WINTER pruning to thin out overcrowded spurs on fans will produce better quality fruit while summer pruning controls growth.

Fan-trained apple 'Cox's Orange Pippin'

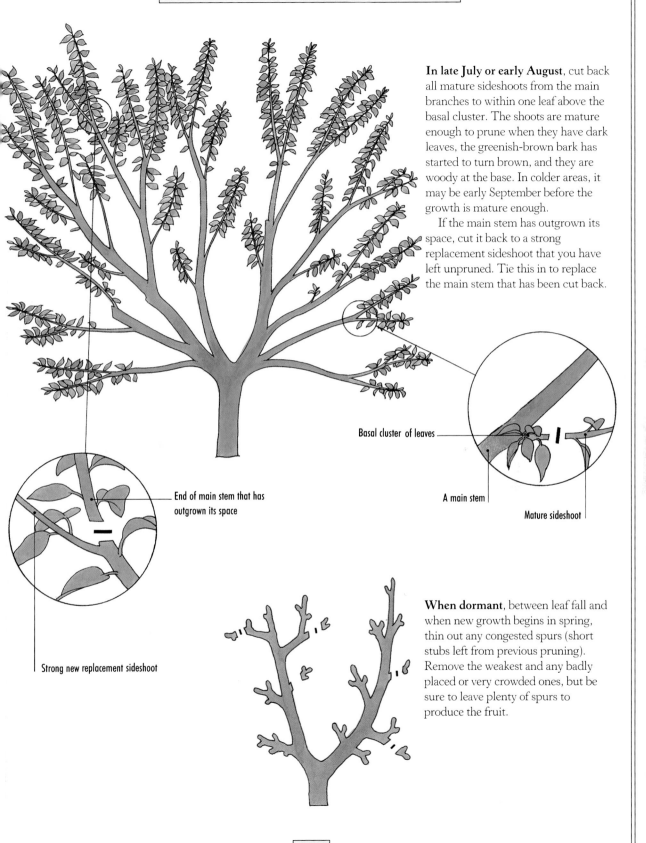

In late July or early August, cut back all mature sideshoots from the main branches to within one leaf above the basal cluster. The shoots are mature enough to prune when they have dark leaves, the greenish-brown bark has started to turn brown, and they are woody at the base. In colder areas, it may be early September before the growth is mature enough.

If the main stem has outgrown its space, cut it back to a strong replacement sideshoot that you have left unpruned. Tie this in to replace the main stem that has been cut back.

Basal cluster of leaves

A main stem

Mature sideshoot

End of main stem that has outgrown its space

Strong new replacement sideshoot

When dormant, between leaf fall and when new growth begins in spring, thin out any congested spurs (short stubs left from previous pruning). Remove the weakest and any badly placed or very crowded ones, but be sure to leave plenty of spurs to produce the fruit.

DWARF BUSH

DWARF BUSH apples have a typical rounded tree-shaped head, but they have a short trunk to make picking and pruning easier.

A dwarf bush on a very dwarfing rootstock such as M27 makes a tree about 1.2–1.8m (4–6ft) tall, but needs a permanent stake, good soil, and plenty of feeding. Other rootstocks are less demanding, but they will produce taller trees. For most small gardens, a dwarf pyramid (see page 200) may be more appropriate.

The advice given here applies to trees that have been pruned regularly and have retained a good shape. With age they tend to lose some of their early shape and it is best then to simplify pruning by using the renewal system described on page 204.

Prune in the dormant season, between leaf fall and when new growth starts in spring.

Apple 'Tydeman's Early'

For a heavily congested bush, remove any shoots or branches in the centre of the tree that are starting to cause congestion and blocking out light. Heavy pruning stimulates more growth but often reduces fruiting, so keep pruning light unless the tree is weak.

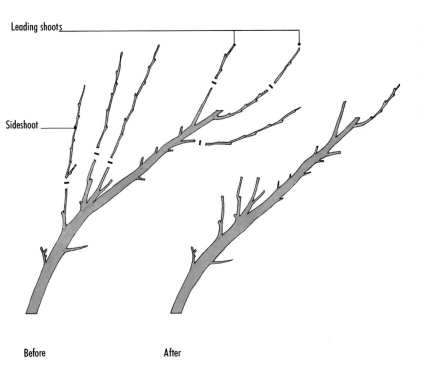

Leading shoots

Sideshoot

Before   After

For a spur-bearing variety shorten the tips of the leading shoots by one-quarter to one-third of the previous year's growth, and cut back the sideshoots on each branch that grew during the summer to four or five buds.

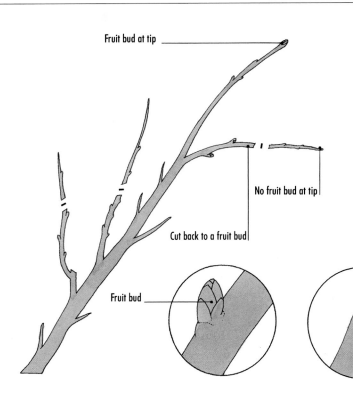

Fruit bud at tip

No fruit bud at tip

Cut back to a fruit bud

Fruit bud   Growth bud

For a tip-bearing variety shorten the tips of the leading shoots by about one-third, then prune the sideshoots. Leave unpruned any shoots that have a fruit bud at the end (these are large and round, shoot buds are smaller and flatter). If they are causing congestion, however, shorten some back to two buds from the base. If there is no fruit bud at the tip, cut back the shoot to just above the highest fruit bud (or to five or six ordinary buds if there are no fruit buds). Leave small shoots less than about 23cm (9in) unpruned unless they are too congested.

DWARF PYRAMID

DWARF PYRAMIDS were evolved by fruit growers as an effective method of growing freestanding apples intensively, and if a suitable rootstock is chosen (such as M9 or M26) this is a useful bush form for gardens.

Both summer and winter pruning is necessary.

In time the tree may lose its shape, especially if not pruned regularly. In this case you can adopt the renewal pruning method described on page 204.

Dwarf pyramid apple

In late July or August, prune any shoots growing from the main stem to three leaves above the basal cluster, and any sideshoot growing from a previously pruned shoot to one leaf above the basal cluster. The shoots are ready for pruning when they have dark leaves, the greenish-brown bark has started to turn brown, and they are woody at the base. In cold areas, they may not be mature enough until early autumn.

Do not cut the tips of the branches at this stage.

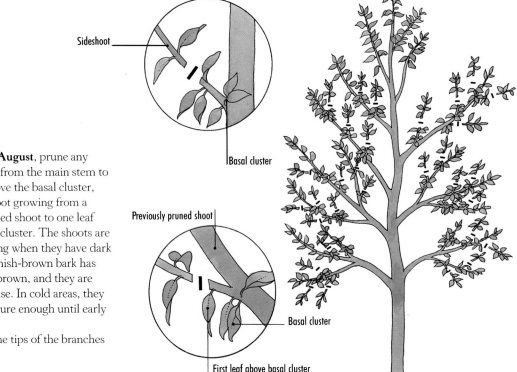

Sideshoot

Basal cluster

Previously pruned shoot

Basal cluster

First leaf above basal cluster

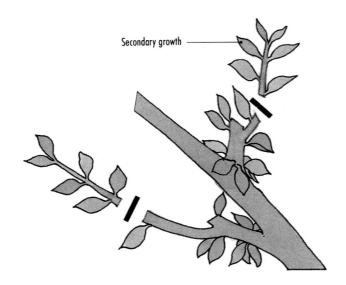

Secondary growth

In September shorten any secondary growth that has appeared after summer pruning to one bud.

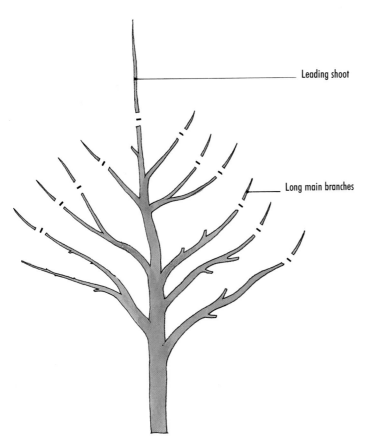

Leading shoot

Long main branches

When dormant, between leaf fall and the start of new growth in spring, if the required height has not yet been reached, shorten the leading shoot to leave about 23cm (9in) of new growth to extend the height. Once a height of about 2.1m (7ft) has been reached, cut it back to just above the point of origin.

Shorten the tips of the main branches as necessary to maintain size and shape, cutting to a downward-pointing bud to retain the horizontal growth of the branches.

BALLERINA OR FLAGPOLE TREES

Ballerina trees (there are various varieties) grow as narrow columns, like upright cordons. These naturally produce short spurs and few if any side branches, which means they require no regular pruning. Just prune the main stem once it reaches the required height and cut back any over-vigorous side branches that develop.

REJUVENATING A NEGLECTED TREE

YOU CAN encourage a neglected apple to crop well again and improve the fruit quality by pruning. If you are apprehensive about drastic pruning, phase the work over two or three seasons. Renovation work should be carried out during the dormant season.

● As a priority, cut out any diseased, split or otherwise damaged branches. Signs of canker and other diseases include badly cracked stems and sunken areas. Cut well back into healthy wood, or remove the branch completely if badly affected.

● Remove dead branches, cutting back to healthy wood or the point of origin if much of the branch is affected.

● If the tree is very congested, cut out some branches to let in more light, especially in the centre of the tree.

● Remove crossing or badly placed branches, cutting them right back to their point of origin.

● If the tree is too tall, cut back the tallest branches to strong side branches.

● Thin out the spurs drastically. It may be necessary to remove some entirely, cutting them flush with the stem. Avoid leaving clusters of spurs closer than 23cm (9in) apart. If possible, spread the spur thinning over a couple of seasons.

● If you want to spread the work over a couple of seasons, this is sufficient for the first year. Be sure to clean up any major wounds (see page 173), and use a wound paint.

Let the tree recover for a year, then prune on the renewal system as described on page 204.

Crossing branch

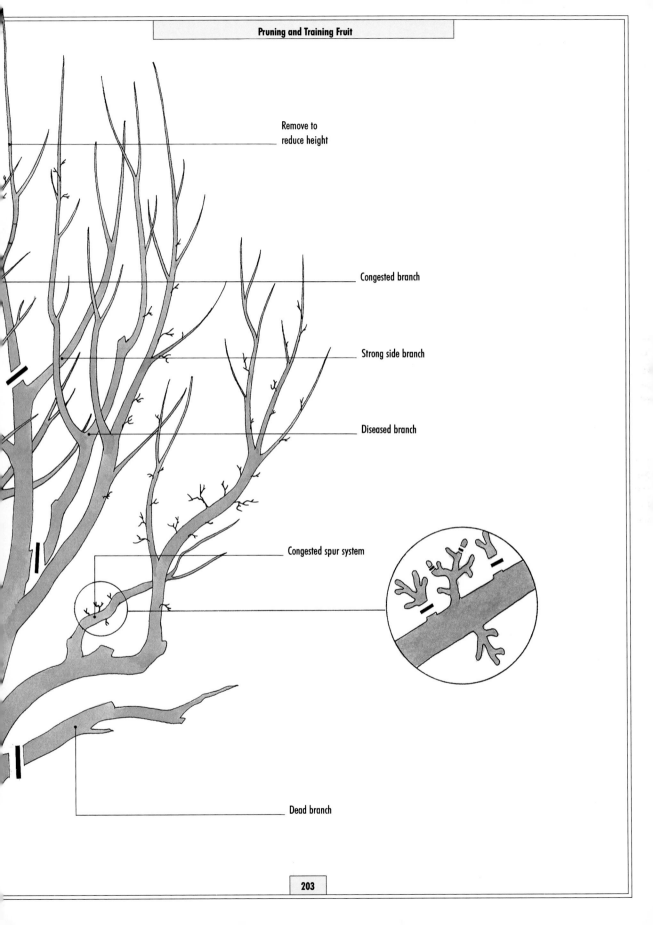

Remove to
reduce height

Congested branch

Strong side branch

Diseased branch

Congested spur system

Dead branch

RENEWAL PRUNING

RENEWAL PRUNING is a good method to use for most established apple trees, except those trained by intensive pruning such as cordons and espaliers. Renewal pruning encourages the continual replacement of old growth with new, while leaving enough old wood to bear fruit.

The method given here can be used for both spur-bearing and tip-bearing varieties of apples, but in the latter case do not remove young shoots unless they are very overcrowded – otherwise you will cut out those that will bear the fruit. By studying the position of the fruit buds you should be able to decide whether you have a spur-bearing or tip-bearing variety of apple (see Spur- or Tip-bearer?, page 192).

Always prune just above a bud pointing in the direction you want the shoot to grow. Flowering/fruiting buds are plumper than those that will produce just leaves and a new shoot.

● To begin, choose a replacement shoot on each original leading branch.

● On the replacement branch shorten the long shoots that grew during the summer. This reduces the amount of leaf and stimulates production of fruiting spurs.

● Shorten the original branch.

● Cut unwanted, over-vigorous upright growth to the base.

● Cut back excessive growth to two- or three-year old wood with plenty of fruit buds.

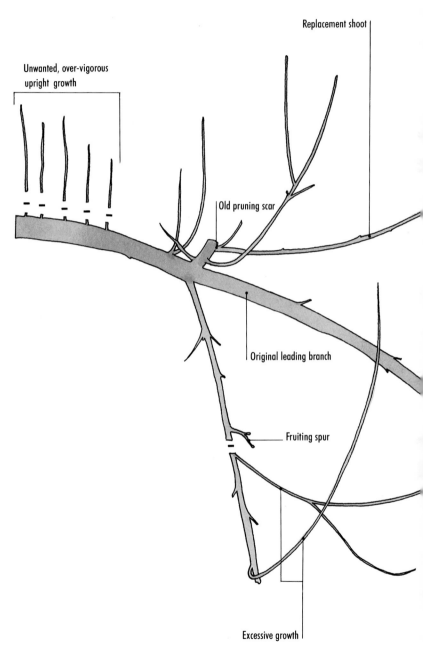

Unwanted, over-vigorous upright growth

Replacement shoot

Old pruning scar

Original leading branch

Fruiting spur

Excessive growth

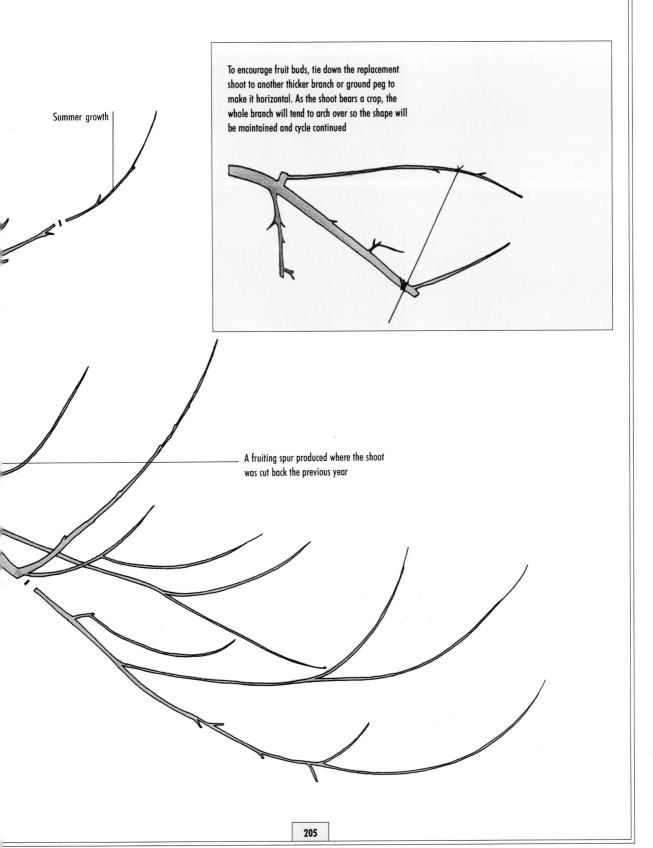

To encourage fruit buds, tie down the replacement shoot to another thicker branch or ground peg to make it horizontal. As the shoot bears a crop, the whole branch will tend to arch over so the shape will be maintained and cycle continued

Summer growth

A fruiting spur produced where the shoot was cut back the previous year

PEARS

PEAR TREES often grow large, but pears can be grown on compact plants, and even a neglected old tree can usually be improved.

Cordon pears are more successful than bush forms in cold or windy areas, as they benefit from a sheltered position.

Trees

The best way to prune pears grown as bushes or trees is on the renewal system suggested for spur-fruiting apples (see page 204). Follow that advice, but as pears fruit well on two- and three-year-old wood, do not as a rule prune back sideshoots shorter than 60cm (24in) long.

In addition to the routine pruning described, it is advisable to thin a very congested spur system on a very old tree in the winter as described on page 202.

Pear 'Conference'

Cordon pear 'Conference'

Fan pear 'Beurre Hardy'

CORDON

[I]N MAY cut the main stem back to within 12mm (½in) of the old wood if it has reached the required height.

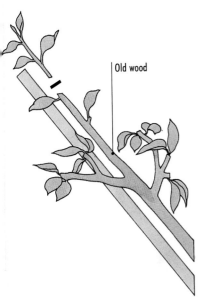

Old wood

Cordon pears

In late summer cut back all mature sideshoots over 23cm (9in) long arising from the main stem to three leaves above the basal cluster, and those arising from the spur system to one leaf.

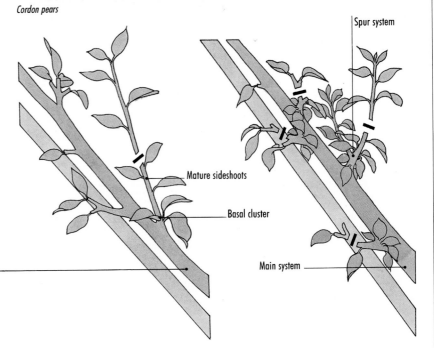

Spur system

Mature sideshoots

Basal cluster

Main stem

Main system

ESPALIER

IN MAY cut back the main stem to within 12mm (½in) of the old wood if the horizontal branches have reached the limit of their allotted space.

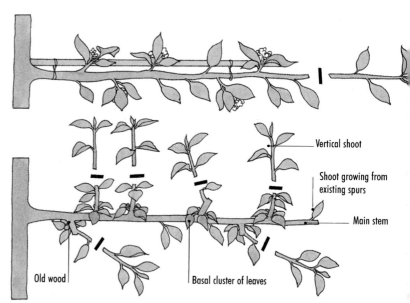

Vertical shoot

Shoot growing from existing spurs

Main stem

In late summer prune the vertical shoots that arise directly from each tiered branch back to three buds above the basal cluster of leaves, and those growing from existing spurs back to one leaf beyond the basal cluster.

Old wood

Basal cluster of leaves

Espalier-trained pear 'Merton Pride'

REJUVENATING AN OLD TREE

A VERY OLD pear tree is often best replaced with a new one, but a tree that has simply been neglected can often be rejuvenated. Do this during the dormant season.

● If the tree is large, it is a good idea to mark the branches to be removed with chalk or string, then stand back to check that you've picked the right ones. Deciding which to remove as you go along can be confusing. If the tree is large or complex, remove dead or diseased wood before continuing, so that you can assess the remaining branches more clearly.

● Next remove crossing and badly placed branches. Where there is a choice, retain the branch with the most or the fattest buds.

● Start to shape the tree, aiming for a wine-glass outline, removing branches less than 60cm (24in) apart if this will not spoil the shape. Again, where there is a choice retain the one with the most or fattest buds.

● If height is a problem, cut the central branch back to an outward-pointing side branch.

Remember, if the tree is large you must remove big branches with care (see page 172). A tree more than 4.5m (15ft) high should be tackled by a qualified tree surgeon.

● Thin the fruit spurs as described for rejuvenating neglected apples (page 202).

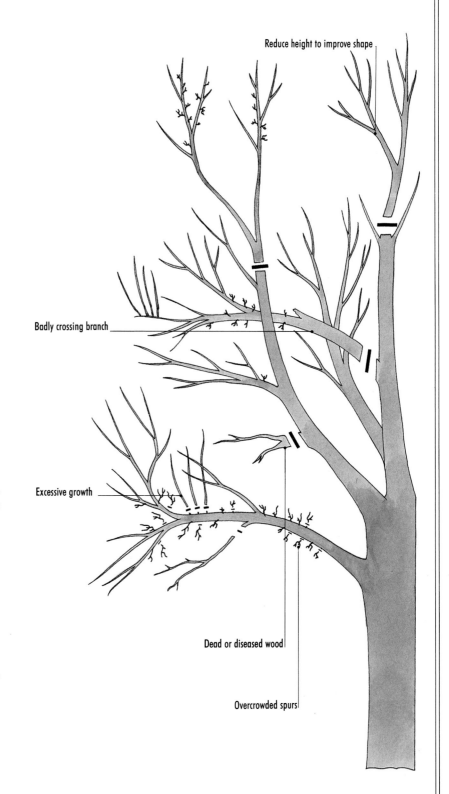

Reduce height to improve shape

Badly crossing branch

Excessive growth

Dead or diseased wood

Overcrowded spurs

PLUMS

THE FOLLOWING advice applies to gages, damsons and bullaces as well as plums. For all these the most common shapes are an open-centre bush, a half standard tree, and a pyramid tree. The trees are usually sold in garden centres as two-or three-year-old plants with the initial training done.

An open-centre bush is shaped like a wine glass on a 0.8–0.9m (2½–3ft) stem. A half standard is the same shape but has a clean stem of about 1.3m (4½ft) below the head. Standards with 1.5–1.8m (5–6ft) of clear stem are available, but grow too large for most gardens.

Pyramid trees have main branches that radiate out from the central trunk, tapering toward the top like a Christmas tree.

Plums are generally unsuitable for intensive training systems such as cordons, but to restrict size and encourage earlier cropping you can festoon them (see page 212).

OPEN-CENTRE BUSH AND HALF STANDARD TREE

MATURE TREES require no routine pruning, but as the tree becomes older and the head more crowded it is often worth thinning the branches to let in more light. This is best done in spring or early summer.

Bush plum tree

PYRAMID

IN MID- OR LATE summer, once the new growth has ceased, cut all the current season's new sideshoots back to 15cm (6in) on an established tree. Also remove any very vigorous upright shoots at the top of the tree, or any badly placed crossing or inward-pointing branches. On trees that have reached about 3m (10ft), cut back the central main stem to within 2.5cm (1in) of the previous year's growth.

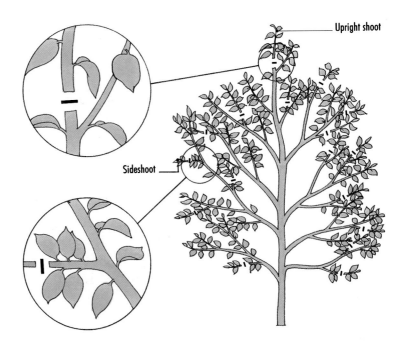

Upright shoot

Sideshoot

Pyramid plum tree

FESTOON

TRAIN A PLUM as a festoon on a very dwarfing rootstock such as 'Pixy' if space is limited. You should get a crop in as little as three years.

Festooned plum

Start with a maiden, a young tree with no side branches and let it grow for a season. The first winter after planting, bend the leading shoot right over, and tie it down to the stem with soft string.

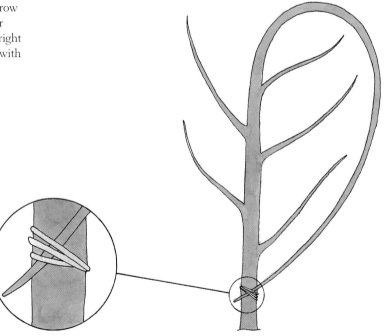

In late summer the next year, cut back the shoots that grow from the top of the arched stem to three leaves above the basal cluster of leaves. Also tie down more shoots after bending them over into hoops, and prune out any unwanted branches that are going to cause overcrowding.

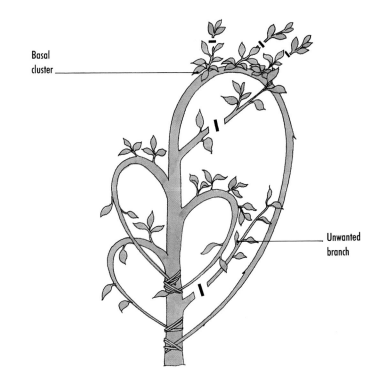

Basal cluster

Unwanted branch

Once the arched branches have 'set' and remain bent when released, cut them back by about a third to a half when dormant. Prune the shoots that grow from the top of festooned branches like a cordon. In late summer prune back shoots growing directly from the arched stems to three leaves above the basal clusters, and those that grow from spurs back to one leaf above the basal cluster (see cordon apples, page 194).

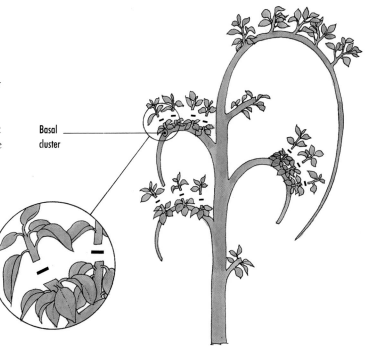

Basal cluster

CHERRIES

CHERRIES GENERALLY make large trees, and with the exception of the widely available 'Stella' all sweet cherries are self-sterile; this means you need at least two varieties in order to get fruit. Many Duke cherries, which are probably hybrids between sweet and sour cherries and are pruned as sweet cherries, are also self-sterile. Acid (sour) cherries are self-fertile, and also have the advantage of making smaller trees.

Acid cherries, such as the popular 'Morello', fruit mainly on shoots produced the previous summer, and require different treatment from sweet cherries. They are best pruned on a replacement system to ensure a good supply of year-old shoots.

Fan cherry

Morello cherry

PREVENTING INFECTION
Bacterial canker and silver-leaf disease often enter cherry trees through pruning wounds. This is less likely to happen if you prune in spring when the buds are breaking into growth, and protect all wounds larger than 12mm (½in) with a wound paint.

FAN AND BUSH

Fan

Prune established fan-trained sweet cherries in summer to restrict the amount of leafy growth and encourage the formation of fruit buds for the next year.

Very tall shoots at the top of the fan can be cut back to a weaker side branch to reduce the size. Other strong upright shoots can be reduced in vigour by tying them down towards the horizontal.

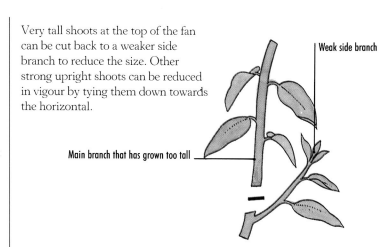

Weak side branch

Main branch that has grown too tall

Remove the growing tips of new shoots when they have made five or six leaves (cut out completely any shoots growing directly towards the wall).

Bush

If bush cherries are not pruned they quickly become tall with few branches near the ground.

Once a bush form starts to fruit, reduce the number of main branches to seven or eight, to maintain an open tree that is easy to pick. Established trees may need only the top shoots thinning or cutting back to reduce height, but prune back hard an old or neglected tree to stimulate new growth.

Shorten these same shoots to three buds in early autumn. Remove any dead wood, and thin very congested spurs (remains of old shoots) at the same time.

FAN

ACID CHERRIES make eye-catching fans which not only look decorative when in fruit, but also look very attractive when covered with blossom in spring, and they generally tolerate the shade cast by the wall or fence. 'Morello' is the variety usually grown, and this will do well even on a north-facing wall or fence, though the fruit will ripen a little later than if placed in a sunnier position.

For a compact tree that fruits early, choose a plant grafted onto 'Colt' rootstock.

In late spring or early summer thin the new shoots to 7.5–10cm (3–4in) apart along the main branches, and tie them in to retain a good fan shape. Where possible, allow a shoot to develop at the base of each sideshoot that is bearing fruit.

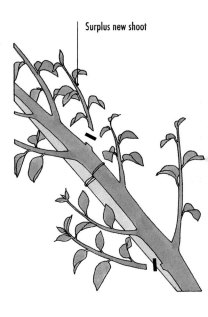

Surplus new shoot

When the crop has been gathered cut the shoots that have fruited back to the replacement that was tied in during early summer pruning.

If the fan starts to crop mainly around the edges, cut back some of the three- or four-year-old branches in early spring to stimulate new growth.

New shoot that will replace it

Old shoot that has fruited

Fan-trained morello cherry

BUSH

BUSH CHERRIES require more space than fans, but the yield is higher. It is a less popular shape for most gardens, however, as acid cherries are too sharp for most people to eat raw, and a large crop is usually needed only if you want them for cooking or jam-making.

Morello cherry

In March prune back some of the old shoots to young sideshoots produced the previous summer. This will ensure that some of the oldest wood is constantly being replaced.

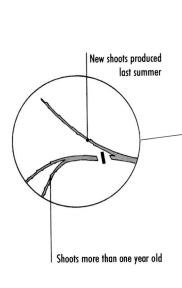

New shoots produced last summer

Shoots more than one year old

PEACHES AND NECTARINES

IN MILD areas peaches can be grown as free-standing bush trees, but otherwise they are best trained as a fan against a wall or fence. They benefit from the shelter and reflected heat, and it is easier to protect the blossom from cold.

Although peaches are discussed here, the same advice applies to nectarines.

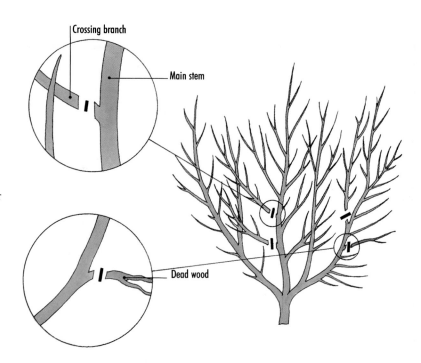

Crossing branch

Main stem

Dead wood

Bush

On mature bushes, cut back a couple of branches to the main stem in spring, soon after new growth starts. This will stimulate new shoots and prevent the centre of the tree from becoming bare. Cut back any damaged branches to just above a strong shoot. Avoid pruning in winter, otherwise dieback may be a problem.

Peach 'Duke of York'

Fan peach 'Rochester'

Fan

In spring, soon after new growth starts, take each branch in turn and remove, rub or pinch out any shoots growing towards or away from the wall. Then select two developing shoots to retain at the base of the previous year's growth to provide replacements for next year, and thin out any remaining young shoots to about 15cm (6in) apart.

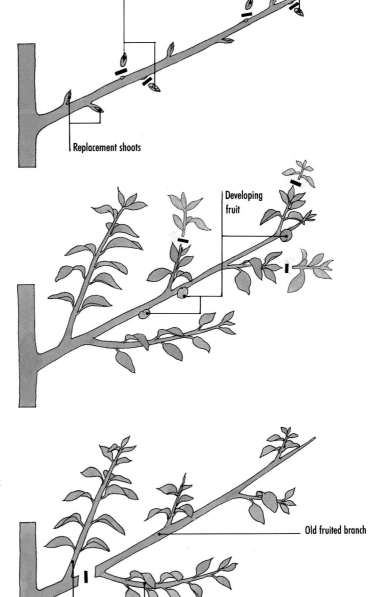

Unwanted shoots

Replacement shoots

Developing fruit

In late spring or early summer, if space is restricted and growth congested, shorten the growth to four leaves once six have been produced, except on those shoots selected as replacements for next year.

After harvesting, cut back the shoots that carried fruit to the lower sideshoot that you left as a replacement, and tie this in to the support wires. If the shoot above is in a better position, retain that one instead and cut out the lower sideshoot.

Old fruited branch

Replacement shoots

FIGS

IN WARM parts of the world figs are grown as trees, but in cooler climates they are more reliable trained as bushes or fans, and benefit from the protection of a wall.

Bush figs are a practical proposition in very mild areas, but plant them in a depression about 30cm (12in) deep and cut the young fig back about 30cm (12in) above the ground while it is dormant. This will stimulate several branches to grow from low down. Once these have grown large enough, fill in the depression and build the soil up so that the base of the stems are covered with soil.

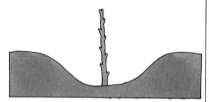

Depression

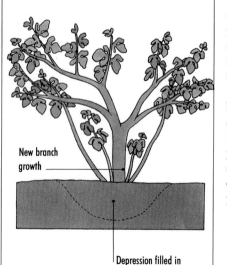

New branch growth

Depression filled in

Bush

For the first few years, cut the leading shoots back in mid-spring to allow about 60cm (24in) of extension growth from the previous season to remain. This will make a branching, bushy plant, but you will be removing the immature fruits.

 Old wood

 Two-year-old wood

 Previous summer's growth

When the bush is large enough for regular fruiting (about three or four years after planting), just thin or shorten the branches as necessary to maintain a good shape and moderate size.

If necessary thin out some of the branches and shoots if they begin to be overcrowded. If the tree becomes too large, you can restrict its vigour by root pruning (see page 172). A large, free-standing fig tree will give you a good display of foliage but few figs unless you restrain it in some way.

Shorten long branches to control height and to stimulate new fruiting shoots

Thin congested branches

Fig 'White Marseilles'

Fan

Prune in mid- to late spring rather than winter, to reduce the risk of frost damage and so that you can see winter-damaged shoots.

Cut out any damaged or diseased shoots, then thin the young shoots produced the previous summer. Cut every second shoot back to one bud from the old growth. Train those that are left unpruned parallel to the wall, and about 23–30cm (9–12in) apart.

Look for the embryo figs (see below), and if possible retain those shoots that bear the best of them. It may be necessary to cut out some further shoots if growth is becoming overcrowded.

HOW FIGS FRUIT

Figs produce two crops of fruit: an early one, which fails to grow large enough to harvest before being damaged by frost, and a later one which is so immature by autumn that it overwinters and continues growing the following year. The fruit is mature enough to eat by late summer.

The overwintering embryo figs may be damaged by a severe winter. Fan-trained trees are best protected between late autumn and mid-spring with dry bracken, straw, shoots cut from conifers, or several layers of horticultural fleece, held in position with netting.

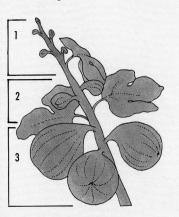

1 Next year's fruit, on new wood
2 Small vulnerable fruit on new wood
3 Ripening fruit on old wood

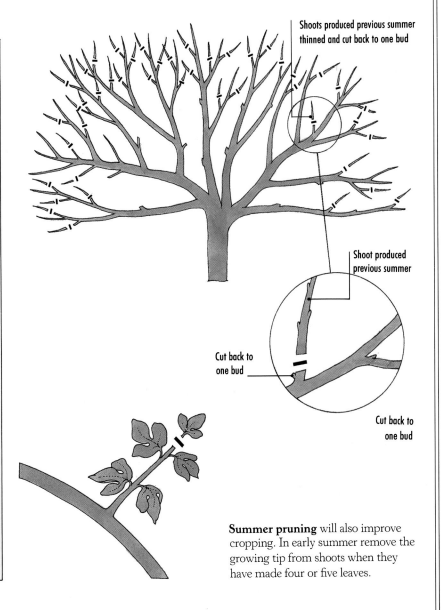

Shoots produced previous summer thinned and cut back to one bud

Shoot produced previous summer

Cut back to one bud

Cut back to one bud

Summer pruning will also improve cropping. In early summer remove the growing tip from shoots when they have made four or five leaves.

APRICOTS

APRICOTS FLOWER early so their blossom is vulnerable to frost. In cold climates they are unreliable, and even in mild areas they are best grown as a wall-trained fan.

Apricots

Apricots fruit on spurs on old wood, and on shoots produced the previous year. Encourage fruiting spurs on fans by removing the tips of new sideshoots when they are about 7.5cm (3in) long, usually in late spring. This will induce more shoots; shorten these back to one leaf.

If sideshoots are required as replacements for older branches in the framework, let them grow and tie them in while they are still supple.

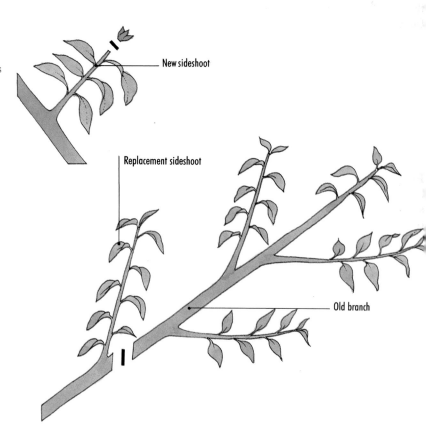

New sideshoot

Replacement sideshoot

Old branch

BLACKBERRIES AND HYBRID BERRIES

BLACKBERRIES AND hybrid berries such as boysenberries, loganberries, rayberries and tummelberries, are very easy to prune. They fruit best on one-year-old stems, so all you have to do is cut back to ground level all the old stems that have fruited, then tie in the young shoots produced the previous summer. The only exception is the blackberry 'Himalayan Giant', which produces few new canes each year but crops well on two-year-old canes. In this case just remove stems that have fruited twice.

Pruning blackberries and hybrid berries consists of cutting out the old stems in winter and tying in the new ones.

Blackberry 'Loch Ness'

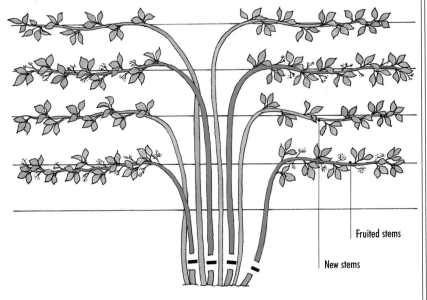

Fruited stems

New stems

RASPBERRIES

RASPBERRY PRUNING is very straightforward. You must be sure to know, however, whether the variety is summer-fruiting or autumn-fruiting.

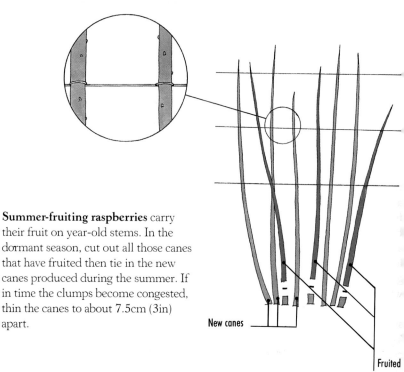

Raspberry 'Malling Jewel'

Summer-fruiting raspberries carry their fruit on year-old stems. In the dormant season, cut out all those canes that have fruited then tie in the new canes produced during the summer. If in time the clumps become congested, thin the canes to about 7.5cm (3in) apart.

Autumn-fruiting varieties carry their fruit on the current season's growth, so pruning is extremely simple. Just cut all the canes down to ground level during the dormant season.

GOOSE-BERRIES AND WORCESTER-BERRIES

GOOSEBERRIES FRUIT on shoots that are a year or more old, so they continue to fruit well even if pruning is neglected. However, harvesting becomes a prickly and difficult task and, with age, the lowest branches may be so close to the ground that the fruit becomes splashed with soil.

Gooseberries are usually grown as small bushes on a leg (length of bare stem), but they can also be grown as cordons (prune these as described for cordon red and white currants, see page 229).

Worcesterberries (*Ribes divaricatum*) make vigorous and very thorny bushes, and look similar to gooseberries in growth and leaf, but the fruit are smaller and a dull reddish-purple in colour. Grow and prune them exactly as gooseberries.

After harvest, remove any badly placed branches (those crossing, too low to the ground, or crowding the centre). Cut low branches to an upward-facing bud.

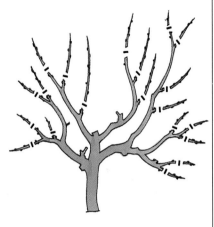

In winter, reduce the length of the summer growth from the tips of the main branches by half, and reduce the sideshoots, which produce the fruit, to two buds from the old wood.

Also, cut out any shoots showing sign of mildew (dark spots or patches), and every few years cut out one or two old shoots that are tending to die, leaving suitable replacement shoots to take over.

Gooseberry 'Leveller'

BLUEBERRIES

BLUEBERRIES, WHICH are grown as compact bushes, are slow-growing and require little pruning. Do not prune for three or four years after planting, as they fruit best on wood that is two or three years old. Once well established, prune in early spring each year to stimulate plenty of strong new growth from the base.

Blueberries require an acid soil, and they are unsuitable for neutral or alkaline soils.

Blueberry

Remove any very weak and spindly growth, then cut out the oldest and least productive shoots – aim to remove about a quarter of the bush. Prune some of the old shoots back to their point of origin, but cut others back to strong, upright sideshoots that will form replacements quickly.

BLACK-CURRANTS

BLACKCURRANTS, WHICH are usually grown as bushy plants with stems arising close to the ground, fruit best on one-year-old branches.

The plants you buy are likely to be two years old and will already have a number of shoots. No routine pruning is required until the plants start to fruit, but prune any very weak shoots to within 2.5cm (1in) of soil level to encourage stronger basal growth.

Blackcurrant 'Boskoop Giant'

Prune established plants when they are dormant, with the aim of keeping old wood to a minimum. Cut out about one shoot in three each year (Technique 5). Concentrate on removing the oldest branches and those which are badly placed, cutting them back as low as possible to stimulate more shoots at or near the base.

Rejuvenate a very old and neglected bush by cutting all the stems back to 5cm (2in) from the ground when the plant is dormant. This will stimulate the growth of new shoots which will carry a crop the second summer. Thin these to encourage a better crop of larger fruit.

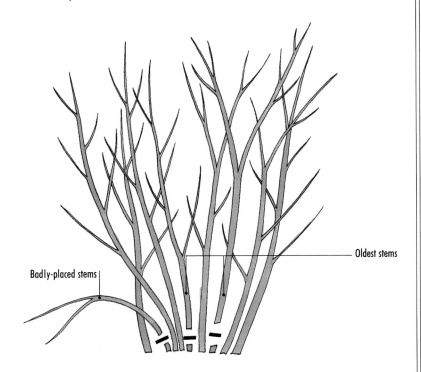

Oldest stems

Badly-placed stems

RED AND WHITE CURRANTS

RED AND WHITE currants fruit on branches that are at least two years old, and both are pruned in the same way. Most plants are sold as bushes with lots of shoots growing from the base. After planting, cut back the most vigorous shoots by about one-third of their length to encourage more sideshoots to form. To maintain a good shape, shorten any crossing shoots to within two buds of the main stem at the same time.

The following winter, shorten any crossing branches, and cut back *one* of the major branches to a bud just above ground level (this starts the cycle of regular renewal).

Red and white currants are sometimes grown on a leg (a small single stem, like the trunk of a tree) to reduce the risk of fruit being splashed by the soil, but the bushes are more difficult to train and prune.

Buy a two-year-old bush with a clear leg, and cut away completely any sideshoots appearing too low down on the main stem. Also remove any shoots that are coming from the base of the plant. Then select three or four strong and well-placed shoots and reduce the previous summer's growth on these by about half, cutting to an outward-pointing bud. Finally, prune all the other shoots produced the previous season back to within two buds of the old wood.

The following winter, prune each main branch in turn. Reduce by half new growth from the tips, and do the same to any strong sideshoots that have grown. Then cut any remaining

Red currant 'Laxton's No. 1'

White currant 'White Versailles'

sideshoots back to within one or two buds of the main stem, unless the shoot is needed to fill in a gap. It may also be necessary to cut out one or two shoots or branches if the centre of the bush is becoming too congested. If any shoots are being produced from the base of the plant, remove these too.

Red and white currants can also be grown as cordons. The yield will be less than with bush forms, but they are more decorative for a small garden.

Bush

On an established plant, cut out one main branch each winter, taking it back to a bud just above ground level. If the site is very windy, reduce the height of the bush by cutting back the longest branches to a sideshoot at an appropriate height. On established plants this can be done after harvesting or in winter.

Long branches

Sideshoot

Old shoot

Growing on a leg

In summer remove crossing or overcrowded shoots, to allow plenty of light to penetrate.

In winter work methodically on each main branch in turn.

Shorten the summer's growth from the tip of each main branch by half, then cut back sideshoots to within one or two buds of the main stems to encourage the production of fruiting spurs.

In time old and unfruitful branches will have to be cut out, but leave vigorous young sideshoots to replace them.

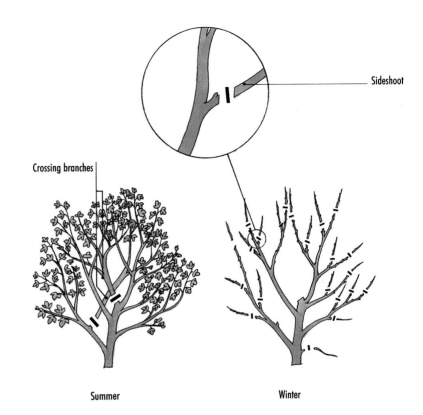

Sideshoot

Crossing branches

Summer

Winter

Cordon

In mid- or late summer, shorten all the sideshoots produced during the current season to four leaves from the old wood.

In winter, shorten the summer's growth to one or two buds, and reduce the leading shoot's new growth by half each year until it reaches about 1.5m (5ft). Once this has been reached, cut the new growth on the leading shoot back to within one bud of the old wood each winter.

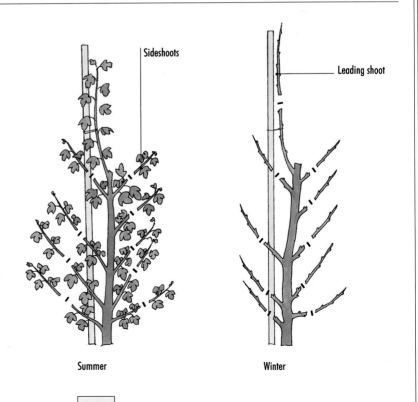

Sideshoots

Leading shoot

Summer

Winter

GRAPES

The Guyot method

Regular pruning is essential for grapes, otherwise they produce masses of growth with lots of leaf and little fruit. They require hard winter pruning, and summer pruning too. There are many methods of training, but for the garden the Guyot method is one of the best. The stems are supported by horizontal wires spaced about 30cm (12in) apart fixed securely to stout posts. Leave a gap of 15–30cm (6–12in) behind the wires if growing against a fence or wall.

Cordon training, suitable for indoor or outdoor grapes, is described on page 231. The number of horizontal branches can be adjusted to suit the space available.

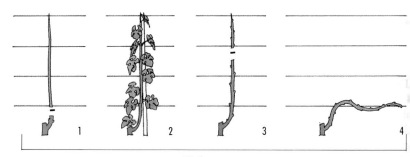

The first year

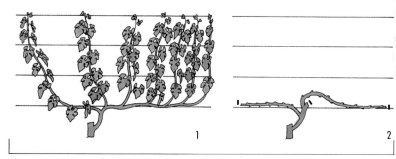

The second year

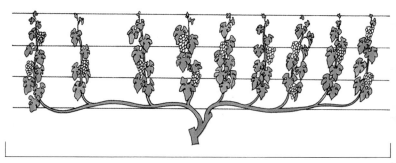

Subsequent years

The first year

1 After planting in the dormant season, cut the previous season's growth back hard to one or two buds.

2 During the first summer, train a single vigorous shoot vertically, tying it to the wires or a cane. Remove any other shoots.

3 In autumn or early winter, when growth is complete, cut back to about 75cm (30in) of the current season's growth.

4 Loosen the ties, then bend over the shoot horizontally and tie to the bottom wire.

The second year

1 During the second summer, numerous new shoots will be produced. Train these up the wires, spreading them out as shown. When the main shoots reach the top of the wires, remove the growing tips. Shorten any sideshoots to five leaves.

2 At the end of the growing season, cut out all the shoots except two that have grown from near the top of the upright part of the main stem. Shorten these two selected shoots to about 75cm (30in), then tie these down to the bottom wire.

Subsequent years

Train the new summer growth to the wires. At the end of each season, select two new shoots to shorten and tie in, then cut out the remainder.

CORDON

Grape 'Morio Muscat'

The first year

1 Cut the vine back to one or two buds above the soil after planting during the dormant season, then let a single shoot grow vertically.

2 Remove the tips from any other shoots or sideshoots when they are no more than 5cm (2in) long.

3 At the end of the growing season cut the new shoot back to 30–60cm (1–2ft), to mature (dark brown) wood.

The second year

1 Rub out any sideshoots that form below the first wire, and remove the growing tip of the main shoot when it reaches the top wire. Tie in sideshoots horizontally to the wires, cutting out any surplus ones. Remove the growing tips when these shoots are 45cm (18in) long.

2 At the end of the growing season, cut back the sideshoots to within two buds of the main stem, leaving stubs, called spurs, from which next year's fruit-bearing shoots will grow.

Subsequent years

Allow just one shoot to grow from each spur and train this along the wires. Rub out any surplus shoots as they develop. Prune back the sideshoots to within one or two buds of the main stem again at the end of each season.

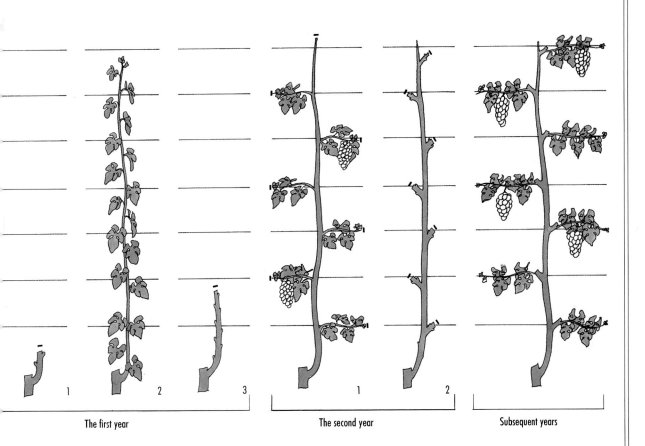

The first year

The second year

Subsequent years

GLOSSARY

Words in italics have their own entry

A

Apical bud The *bud* at the tip of a growing shoot, which extends the *leader*. Also called the terminal bud.

Apical dominance The effect of a *hormone* (*auxin*) produced by the *apical bud*, which inhibits the growth of *buds* behind it.

Auxin A *hormone* that plays an important role in plant growth, especially *apical dominance*.

B

Bark ringing The removal of a narrow band of bark to restrict growth or stimulate fruiting. See page 173.

Biennial bearing The characteristic shown by some apple varieties to bear fruit heavily one year but only lightly the next.

Bract A modified leaf that resembles a flower petal. Hydrangea 'flowers' are actually colourful bracts. Large-flowered dogwoods (*Cornus* species) also have flower-like bracts that surround the true flowers.

Branched head A tree with multiple leaders instead of one dominant *leader*. A branched head usually has a rounded appearance compared with the more triangular or conical shape of a *central-leader* tree.

Bud A small swelling where a new shoot or flower will form. Although usually very obvious on *dormant* wood, some may be undeveloped and hard to detect.

C

Callus A protective layer of corky cells that forms over a wound to protect it.

Candle The new *terminal* growth on a pine. New needles grow from these candle-like projections.

Cane A long, vigorous stem arising directly from ground level, such as raspberry or *Rubus cockburnianus*.

Canopy The spread of a tree's branches.

Central leader The main, central stem that continues the line of the trunk of a tree (see also *Branched head*).

Conifer A cone-bearing tree, mainly evergreen and with needle-like or scale-like leaves. Cypresses and pines are common examples.

Coppice Traditionally certain trees, particularly sweet chestnut and hazel grown for stakes, were coppiced: cut down to within about 30cm (12in) of the ground every five to seven years to stimulate plenty of young shoots. A similar technique can be used on many ornamental plants.

Cordon A plant (usually a fruit tree or bush) restricted to one, two or three stems by intensive pruning. Most single cordons are grown at an angle, but double and triple cordons may be grown with vertical stems.

Crotch The angle between two large branches, or between the main trunk and a large secondary branch.

Crown see *Head*.

Current growth Growth made during the current year.

D

Deadheading Removal of dead flowers.

Deciduous A tree or shrub that sheds all its leaves in winter (see also *Evergreen* and *Semi-evergreen*).

Dehorning The removal of large branches from the top of a tree or shrub. Normally only done in an attempt to rejuvenate a neglected plant.

Dieback A disease characterized by the end of the shoot turning brown or black, the dead area gradually spreading towards the base of the shoot. May result from a pruning wound or winter damage.

Disbudding The removal of surplus *buds* or shoots, to control the amount of growth and prevent overcrowding.

Dormant A plant is dormant when there is little or no growth (the leaves will have been shed on a *deciduous* plant). Most trees and shrubs are dormant during the coldest months.

E

Espalier A tree or shrub trained to grow in tiers against a support.

Evergreen A plant that retains its leaves throughout the year. The leaves are shed, but not all at the same time, so the shoots are always covered with foliage (see also *Deciduous* and *Semi-evergreen*).

F

Fan An intensively pruned tree trained with radiating, fan-like branches.

Fastigiate Upright growth with clustered branches set at a close angle to the trunk, producing a narrow, upright shape.

Feathered A young tree with *sideshoots*.

Formal In relation to hedges, clipped tightly to produce a crisp outline with a smooth surface (see also *Informal*).

G

Graft The point at which the stem or *bud* of one plant (known as the *scion*) was inserted into the *rootstock* of another. Usually the graft point is close to soil level though some weeping trees are produced by grafting a prostrate or cascading plant onto a long, upright stem of the rootstock.

H

Head The branches of a tree, above the straight, clear trunk. Also called the crown.

Hormone A chemical produced and distributed within the plant which affects the way it grows.

I

Informal As applied to a hedge, one that is not tightly clipped to a neat finish. The branches are allowed to grow more naturally, giving a looser appearance. See also *Formal*.

L

Latent bud A *bud* that fails to develop in the season it was formed.

Lateral see *Sideshoot*.

Lateral bud A *bud* that will form a *sideshoot*.

Leader, leading shoot A stem that is longer and more vigorous than the others. It is generally the topmost growth and extends the height of the plant. Leaders are responsible for forming the basic shape of a tree.

Leaf scar The point where a leaf was attached. It can usually be seen as a crescent or horseshoe shape just under a *bud*.

Loppers Long-handled pruners, sometimes called tree pruners.

M

Maiden A tree or bush in its first year after *grafting* or budding (see also *Whip*).

N

Nicking and notching Terms used to describe the removal of a small triangle or crescent of bark just above or below a *bud*, to stimulate or inhibit growth.

O

Open centre A term used to describe fruit trees where branches have been *thinned* in the centre of the tree to make spraying and harvesting easier, and to allow the fruit to receive more sun for better ripening.

P

Pinching out Removing the new growth on the tip of a shoot by 'pinching' off with the fingertips.

Pleaching A method of growing trees (usually limes) along a framework of horizontal wires and canes to produce an avenue or border of intensively trained trees with their branches in horizontal tiers.

Pollard To cut back the shoots of a tree drastically to a framework of stubs. It is tolerated by only a few trees such as sycamores and some willows.

R

Ringing see *Bark ringing*.

Root pruning The severance of some of a tree's major roots as a means of restricting growth (see page 000).

Rootstock The stems and roots to which shoots of other varieties are grafted. Varieties are grafted onto rootstocks rather than grown on their own roots for several reasons: to give dwarf characteristics to the plant, to enable the plant to be grown more easily on difficult soils, to create a small weeping standard from a prostrate species or variety, to induce early flowering or fruiting on younger plants.

S

Scion The *bud* or shoot used for grafting onto a *rootstock*.

Semi-evergreen A plant that retains its leaves in a warm climate or mild winter, but loses some or all of them in a cold winter (see also *Deciduous* and *Evergreen*).

Semi-hardy Hardy in mild winters but not in severe ones.

Self-fertile A plant which sets fruit with its own pollen.

Self-sterile A plant which needs pollen from another variety to enable it to bear fruit.

Sideshoot A shoot growing off a main stem or branch.

Split leader *Leader* that branches into two.

Spur A short stem with flower/fruit *buds*.

Spur-bearing Plant which produces flowers on short spurs rather than at the tips of shoots. Usually used to describe fruit trees. See also *Tip-bearing*.

Stool Base of the plant from which many shoots originate at ground level or just beneath. These often produce *canes*.

T

Terminal bud See *Apical bud*.

Terminal shoot The shoot at the end of a branch. Important because it contains the *apical bud*.

Thinning Reduction of the number of shoots, branches, *spurs*, or fruits on a branch. Sometimes necessary to reduce overcrowding and, with fruit, to improve size and quality.

Tie in A method of encouraging flowering and fruiting by attaching a new branch to a lower branch.

Tip-bearing Plant which produces flowers at the tips of shoots rather than on clusters of *spurs* close to the branch. Usually used to describe fruit trees. See also *Spur-bearing*.

Tip pruning Pruning the tips of shoots by cutting or *pinching out* the growth to stimulate side growths.

Topiary The shaping and clipping of a tree or shrub into a symmetrical or abstract shape, or a representation, such as a peacock.

Tree pruners See *Loppers*.

W

Whip A young tree transplanted at least once and without significant *sideshoots*.

Wind-rock Loosening of the roots through the effect of strong winds on the top growth.

Index

Page numbers in italics indicate entries with illustrations

ACKNOWLEDGEMENTS

All pictures are reproduced by courtesy of Peter McHoy except for the following:

(T = top; M = middle; B = below; L = left; R = right; FR = far right)

page 3 (M) John Glover
page 3 Peter Blackburne-Maze
page 10 Quarto Publishing plc
page 20 Quarto Publishing plc
page 16–21 Quarto Publishing plc
page 29 Harry Smith Collection
page 30–35 Quarto Publishing plc
page 34–35 Quarto Publishing plc
page 36–41 Quarto Publishing plc
page 55 (T) Harry Smith Collection
page 59 (MB) John Glover
page 60 Harry Smith Collection
page 62 (BL) Quarto Publishing plc
page 73 (MR) Harry Smith Collection
page 74 (L) Harry Smith Collection
page 75 (T) Harry Smith Collection
page 76 (M) Harry Smith Collection

page 80 (ML) Harry Smith Collection
page 82 (TR) Quarto Publishing plc
page 86 (FR) Heather Angel
page 91 (BR) Heather Angel
page 93 (R) Harry Smith Collection
page 94 Harry Smith Collection
page 96 (M) Harry Smith Collection
page 100 (R) Harry Smith Collection
page 101 Harry Smith Collection
page 102 (RB) Heather Angel
page 112 (TR) Harry Smith Collection
(BL) Harry Smith Collection
page 114 (R) Heather Angel
(B) Harry Smith Collection
page 117 (TL) Harry Smith Collection
page 118 (BR) Harry Smith Collection
page 121 (T) Harry Smith Collection
page 122 (TR) Harry Smith Collection
page 128 Harry Smith Collection
page 129 (TR) Harry Smith Collection
page 131 (BL) Harry Smith Collection
page 134 Quarto Publishing plc

page 135 Quarto Publishing plc
page 136–137 Quarto Publishing plc
page 140 (BL) Harry Smith Collection
page 141 (T) Harry Smith Collection
page 146 (BL) Heather Angel
page 149 (M) Harry Smith Collection
page 151 (M) Gardening Which? Magazine
page 161 (L) Harry Smith Collection
page 163 Harry Smith Collection
page 166 (M) Harry Smith Collection
page 190 (B) Peter Blackburne-Maze
(TR) Harry Smith Collection
page 194 (M) John Glover
page 198 (T) Harry Smith Collection
page 200 (T) Peter Blackburne-Maze
page 206 (BR) John Glover
(BL) John Glover
page 208 (B) John Glover
page 208–209 Quarto Publishing plc
page 210 (BL) Peter Blackburne- Maze
page 211 (BR) Peter Blackburne- Maze

page 212 (T) Peter Blackburne-Maze
page 214 (BL) Harry Smith Collection
page 216 (B) John Glover
page 217 (B) John Glover
page 218 (BL) Harry Smith Collection
(BR) Harry Smith Collection
page 221 (T) Harry Smith Collection
page 222 (T) Harry Smith Collection
page 223 (T) John Glover
page 224 (L) Harry Smith Collection
page 225 (R) Harry Smith Collection
page 226 (TR) Harry Smith Collection
page 227 (TR) Harry Smith Collection
page 228 (TR) Harry Smith Collection
(TL) Harry Smith Collection
page 230 (TR) Harry Smith Collection

All artwork by Rob Shone.

Special thanks to Capel Manor, Middlesex for the use of their gardens for photography.